Eric,

Thanks for attending —
hope my book adds a few

new ideas,

John Goodman

SECOND EDITION

STRATEGIC CUSTOMER SERVICE

SECOND EDITION

STRATEGIC CUSTOMER SERVICE

Managing the Customer Experience to Increase Positive
Word of Mouth, Build Loyalty, and Maximize Margins and Profits

JOHN A. GOODMAN
SCOTT M. BROETZMANN

HarperCollins
LEADERSHIP

AN IMPRINT OF HarperCollins

Published by HarperCollins Leadership, an imprint of HarperCollins.

Book design by Elyse Strongin, Neuwirth & Associates.

978-0-8144-3906-7 (eBook)

Library of Congress Control Number: 2018960958

978-0-8144-3905-0

Printed in the United States of America
18 19 20 21 22 LSC 10 9 8 7 6 5 4 3 2 1

CONTENTS

FOREWORD

by Chip R. Bell

There are times the stars align for a magical moment. John Goodman was already a giant in the field of customer service when we first shook hands. His landmark study on consumer complaint handling in America, commissioned by the United States Office of Consumer Affairs, revolutionized conventional wisdom about service. My business partner, the late Ron Zemke, wrote a best-selling ground-breaking book in 1990, *Service America*, that spotlighted Goodman's genius. I had read Ron's book about a thousand times and knew Goodman's Copernicus-like statistics and insights by heart.

We were working with a high-tech client and meeting at MIT in Boston. We had taken a break to get a bite to eat at the Marriott nearby. As we walked into the restaurant, we encountered John. He and Zemke were already mutual fans. I was expecting this Harvard MBA with a world-renowned reputation to view me as Ron's under-study or assistant. Instead, his gracious inclusion was as delightfully memorable as the content of his pioneering work. Fast-forward almost thirty years, and he has invited me to pen this foreword to his newest edition to a powerful book.

Strategic Customer Service, 2nd Edition, which John wrote with Scott Broetzmann, is the kind of wise tome I wish I had read early in my career. It provides a wake-up call about how today's customers are significantly different than they were when John and I met. In fact, they are continuing to change rapidly. Today's fad is quickly becoming tomorrow's antique. The book clearly outlines the causes and catalogues its remedies. It provides deep insight that can inform effective strategy and thoughtful execution. Unlike many books of this type, it provides a plethora of pragmatic tools with countless case examples of the very best in action. The book also provides the central link between service process and an empowered, can-do culture. It is like the great textbook you kept instead of selling it back to the bookstore at the end of the semester!

The mere existence of this book and the requirement for a new edition is itself a metaphor of the times in which we live and work. Customer service was once viewed as solely the purview of the call center or the front line in a service organization. But, times have changed. Those with a willingness to embrace service as a competitive differentiator will be the only survivors.

We have countless examples of the failure of "the way we have always done it" strategy. Borders Books outsourced their online book business to Amazon! Seen a Borders lately? Blockbuster Video could have bought Netflix for a mere fifty million dollars—but elected to stay with videotape rentals. Encyclopedia Britannica turned down an offer from Microsoft to put their encyclopedias online. And, in 1998, Kodak sold 85 percent of all photo paper worldwide. Within a few short years, they were completely bankrupt.

The graveyard of companies that refused to adapt is large—AOL, Saturn, Sharper Image, Palm, Atari, General Foods, Compaq, Digital. Their leaders' words became part of the lexicon of head-in-the-sand decision makers. "Neither Redbox nor Netflix are even on our radar screen in terms of competition," said Blockbuster CEO Jim Keyes. Ken Olsen, founder of Digital Equipment, said, "There is no reason anyone would want a computer in their home." A Twentieth Century Fox executive boasted, "Television won't be able to hold on to any market it captures after the first six months. People will soon get tired of staring at a plywood box every night."

Are you serving your customers pretty much like you did ten years ago? Better wake up and reassess your entire operation; your customers have changed and are rapidly changing!

"Whoa," you might be saying, "I am a manufacturer, law firm, or distributor of quarter-inch drill bits. My customers care about quality, expertise, and price. My customers don't expect me to be the Nordstrom of the industry." If that is your perspective, you are at risk of being left far behind. Even the concept of business to business is changing; today, it is more like P2P (people to people). And, the big differentiator is service, not product, proficiency, or price.

There are two sides to service—the outcome and the experience. If your flight lands on time, in the right city, and with your luggage in tow, those are all service outcomes. Think of them as table stakes—the givens—not loyalty-makers. If the flight attendant is super friendly and attentive to your needs, those are service experiences. Customers do not talk about the details of service outcomes; they tell stories instead about the details of their enjoyable experiences in getting those outcomes. But the standards for a service experience have also dramatically changed.

Customers today get terrific service experiences in pockets of their life and use those experiences to judge your operation . . . and everyone else. When the UPS or FedEx delivery person walks with a sense of urgency, customers expect the mail carrier to do likewise. When Disney theme park cast members treat guests extra special, they assume every other customer-facing person on the planet will do likewise. That means your customer experience competition is not your industry; it is anyone creating great experiences for those you serve.

What has elevated customers' standards for their service experiences? First, customers today have way more choices than ever. A quick trip to the grocery store for a simple loaf of bread and you are confronted with sixteen brands and twenty-three varieties packaged twelve different ways. Three decades ago, sliced bread came one way—white—produced almost exclusively by Wonder or Sunbeam! The more product choices customers have that are similar, the more they use the experience surrounding that product or outcome as their primary tool for differentiation and decision making.

Second, today's customers are much smarter buyers. The internet has not only been their source of a real-time buying education, it has become a channel for instant customer assessment. Everyone has become everyone's *Consumer Reports*. It means businesses must monitor all the details (now very transparent to customers) to get early warnings on emerging glitches, impending changes, and on-the-horizon trends. It also means customers are more empowered to make buying decisions with knowledge from a host of sources rather than relying on the reputation of a brand or the cleverness of its advertising.

And the service side is a much bigger challenge. Why? Manufacturers determine the quality of the products they put into the marketplace. But customers determine the quality of the service they receive. And riding herd on what happens in the factory is a lot more predictable than getting customers to do what they are told. You may say your service grade has improved from a C to a B. Keep in mind that yesterday's B to the customer is today's C. Poor or indifferent service has become horrible service; mediocre service has become bad service.

Even the yardstick of service has changed! "Your satisfaction is our number one goal." Sound familiar? Today, unless your organization is the only fish in the pond, using customer satisfaction as the yardstick of success will ultimately lead to disappointment, maybe even failure. Look up the definition of "satisfactory" in Webster's Really Big Dictionary. It says "good enough to fulfill a need or requirement." It also means "adequate" or "sufficient." Today's customers do not put "adequate" and "value" in the same sentence. "Sufficient" is hardly the language of loyalty. Organizations need to evoke customer feelings strong enough to make customers deaf to the siren call of competitors.

Now, if you're in the product-making business, satisfaction might be okay for object quality. Most customers want their new trash compacter to only do what they expect it to do. But, when it comes to a service experience, the customer's definition of what is adequate or sufficient quality quickly changes. Imagine coming back from a great experience—say your honeymoon—and someone asks you, "How was your honeymoon?" and you answered, "I was completely satisfied!" You'd probably land in the proverbial doghouse. Three-fourths of customers who leave an organization for a competitor say they were satisfied or completely satisfied with the one they abandoned.

One of the biggest differences between "satisfied" customers and "loyal" customers is their tolerance for error or for less-than-expected value. For satisfied customers, one strike—just one tiny hiccup—and they are ready to exit. The "loyal" customer is willing to forgive and give an organization a second chance.

However, there is one very important caveat. Loyal customers do not mean "forever and ever" customers. Disappoint a loyal customer and you just got "strike one" in the new loyalty game. What happens next will determine if you remain in the game or "strike out" and lose that loyal customer. It makes great service recovery and customer care at every point of contact a crucial organizational issue. It makes complaint handling a strategic decision, not just an interpersonal nicety.

So, what do all those "Satisfaction is Job #1" billboards get you? At best, it is a customer willing to give you a try. When that customer walks through your door or signs a contract, the marketing and sales department can score a victory. But the more meaningful measure of success is whether that customer, having taken you for a "test drive," comes back for more—and then convinces associates to do the same. When you've built that kind of loyal customer base, you have created a marketplace advantage difficult for any competitor to match.

Like all valued relationships, if you take loyal customers for granted, they soon will become yours to lose. If loyal customers were ever entrenched by the allure of your brand, they will be no more. If loyal customers were ever long-suffering and tolerant of service blemishes and experience blunders, they clearly would be no longer. Today, value in the eyes of customers must be genuine, obvious, and ever present. And loyal customers, the core of your growth, profits, and reputation, must be continually made to feel important, heard, and valued.

Finally, there is the growing proliferation of technology into the service world. In the famous ballad of John Henry, this Talcott, West Virginia, steel-driven man with a hammer was pitted against the new steam-powered jackhammer in a competition to determine who was fastest at driving a steel rod into rock for dynamite to be placed and blasted clearing the way for the railroad. John won the contest but then died of a heart attack from the stress. The man versus machine has been debated ever since.

John Henry is a metaphor for the changing role of humans in an ever-mechanized, high-tech world where friendly voices are rapidly being replaced with IVRs, chatbots, and artificial intelligence, and helpful hands with a deflection toward self-service. Leaders have to get comfortable with the alphabet of technology—CRM, KMS, ERP, IoT, etc. This book will provide those anxious about technology with more comfort; those enthusiastic about technology with more caution.

Now that you have heard the wake-up call to align around a customer-centric strategy, you might be thinking . . . what do I do next? The good news is there is a blueprint for success that begins on the next page. Customer service lends itself to heart-tugging stories and persuasive anecdotes—all great fodder for inspiration. But for strategy and practice you need solid facts, concrete research, and ironclad logic. *Strategic Customer Service, 2nd Edition* will align your stars to ensure you keep loyal customers, an enviable reputation, and a very healthy bottom line.

INTRODUCTION

Customer Service vs. Customer Experience

We love what we do. Customer service is a passion at Customer Care Measurement & Consulting (CCMC). Our careers in customer service consulting and measurement began in 1971, when Marc Grainer and I formed Technical Assistance Research Programs (TARP). Scott Broetzmann joined us in 1991. After spending several years in the early 2000s moving in different directions, we are back together at CCMC, where we continue to do what we've done for the past four decades: Help companies listen to their customers, be proactive and engaged, and respond effectively.

We have been asked, "Why haven't you gone to work for a large organization as the vice president for customer service?"

For me, getting to know different industries, seeing what works and what doesn't—and seeing what works in one industry that can be helpful to another—is a constant learning experience. We don't want to "experiment" with customers; we want to provide solid evidence and practices that work.

In a conversation with the chief operating officer and the director of customer service for a new e-commerce start-up, they stated that the company wanted to create strong customer engagement with robust education while making all interactions effortless, proactive, and inexpensive. This was a familiar formula. The customer service function handles the labor-intense customer engagement and education, and the technology folks assure effortless transactions and electronic confirmations on the web.

This formula illustrates the future challenge of the customer service field. Unfortunately, separate, parallel configurations do not work. The solution is a unified service system that integrates the human interactions in customer service with the transaction technology. You need a system where customer service can see and track transactions, and the technology side is aware of all customer service interactions related to the transaction. This gives the customer a feeling of one-stop shopping.

This book is aimed at understanding what has changed and what is the same in customer service since the 2009 publication of the first edition of *Strategic Customer Service*. Service directors must respond to the technological revolution as well as the needs of diverse customers and employees. While the first edition focused heavily on large companies serving consumers, this updated second edition adds a focus on business-to-business (B2B) customers as well as start-ups and medium-sized businesses.

The good news is that, although examples are more diverse, the basic principles are the same. For instance, we find that business customers often behave the same as individual consumers. Business customers complain at rates similar to or even lower than individual consumers because they fear damaging their long-term relationship with the business supplier and often lack expectation that complaining will improve the situation.

Another counterintuitive business customer behavior is that businesses, like consumers, often fail to read or comprehend their contracts, leading to unpleasant surprises and dissatisfaction. The bottom line is: Consumer and business behavior and expectations have remained generally constant, except for higher expectations for speed and convenience.

On the other hand, technology has evolved dramatically in the last decade. Big data, video, mobile communication (which, in 2018, began to expand from 4G to 5G), artificial intelligence, and voice recognition (e.g., Amazon's Alexa or Apple's Siri) allow companies to leverage technology to anticipate, place, and confirm transactions and capture the Voice of the Customer (VOC).

At the same time, an incident in which Alexa misunderstood a conversation and inappropriately sent messages to a third party led the online publication *Gizmodo* to ponder whether "a future of mild convenience outweighs the cost of troubling surveillance mishaps."[1]

This full range of technology is now available to all sizes of companies via software-as-a-service (SaaS) customer relationship management systems that cost-effectively provide full functionality for companies with as few as five or as many as five hundred service employees.

The buzzword *omnichannel* is very relevant. In the past, companies decided between personal versus automated service. Now companies must serve customers who want to perform tasks themselves but still desire immediate human response to their more complex questions and problems. Some customers also only want pure, fully digital service, while others want only personal service and empathy. Assigning individual customers to a particular segment based on standard demographic criteria is difficult. For instance, in an investment environment, one company assumed that high-end investors with more than $1 million on account like to be taken to lunch at least twice a year. We found that almost half of these wealthy customers did not want to have lunch and were happy with an email or phone call discussing investment results.

The challenge is to cost-effectively tailor service to the customer's current needs. Amazon pioneered the approach of delivering the product quickly, perfectly, and conveniently, eliminating the need for service. CCMC's last two *National Customer Rage* studies, in 2015 and 2017, show that severe problems are more associated with wasted time (a median of five hours) than out-of-pocket financial loss.[2] Customers value their time more than their money.

This second edition of *Strategic Customer Service* expands on five areas: customer engagement, outsourcing, VOC, technology, and staff retention. The first section of the book (Chapters 1 and 2) reviews customer expectations and behavior—what has changed, and what has not, in terms of implications for customer service delivery.

WHAT HAS CHANGED?

- *Customer expectations for speed and convenience.* As noted above, customers are more demanding and comprise more diverse segments. The book adds a focus on large and small B2B customers, especially how they can leverage word-of-mouth (WOM) to gain new customers.

- *How customers gain information.* Today, instead of reading printed instructions, customers use internet searches, review sites, and check YouTube videos.
- *Ease of doing business.* Technology must be simple and easy with little bureaucracy or excessive information. Both consumers and businesses pay a premium to companies that are easy to do business with. However, the technology must be intuitive and provide immediate access to a human if things go wrong.
- *Tight labor market.* With employment at record high levels, retaining high-quality staff requires going beyond good pay to make employees empowered and successful. They must feel appreciated and see a career progression with the company.
- *Flexibility.* Customer service must be tailored to the situation and the customer. Both technology and the frontline staff must have empowerment informed by multiple approaches to resolve issues, thereby creating a can-do, risk-taking culture.

WHAT HAS STAYED THE SAME?

- *Customer expectations of service staff.* The customer expects the service staff to be empowered, empathetic, able to explain their actions, able to ensure that the issue will not happen again, and then to follow through.
- *Processes needed for service and the VOC.* The processes recommended are similar to those in my 2009 book, but have been enhanced by technology and are available through more communication channels.
- *The payoff of great service.* The same customer complaints and market behaviors exist, leading to similar quantifiable impacts of service on loyalty, margin, share of wallet, and WOM.

The second section of the book (Chapters 3, 4, and 5) addresses basic service delivery, advanced customer engagement, creating delight, and retailer/outsourcer relationships. Basic customer service requires technology and empowered, motivated service staff to perform twenty key service processes. With a few changes, the basic customer service functions and processes are the same, although the technology has evolved dramatically in the last ten years. Advanced service, including customer engagement, has changed dramatically with online communities, video chat, artificial intelligence, and speech recognition. The second section focuses on functionality and implementation, as well as the VOC and measurement. Chapter 5 addresses best practices for delivering service through partners, which can be distribution channels, retailers, and outsourcers.

The third section (Chapter 6) covers the business case for investment in customer service and how to quantify the payoff in a manner the chief financial officer (CFO) will accept. The foundation of the business case is based on our team's research in the 1980s and 1990s, but some aspects, such as WOM, engagement, and sensitivity to price, have evolved in concept and metrics. WOM now includes review sites and online communities—and technology scrapes social media to better measure WOM (or word-of-mouse) on the internet. Analyzing the impact is more challenging because of the available mass of data that need to be integrated and reconciled. Also, CFOs are much savvier, and with the advent of big data, they expect that the payoff of investment in customer service must be "proven." Finally, there has been a proliferation of customer surveys over the past decade. Many of these surveys, which should be a critical part of quantifying the impact of improved customer service, are sometimes unprofessionally designed and executed, resulting in inapplicable and misleading results, and inaction. This undermines some business cases for service investment.

The fourth section (Chapters 7 and 8) addresses the VOC and customer experience (CE) surveys. Since 2009, the VOC is the compass for guiding the customer service ship. The VOC has changed dramatically in three areas. First, CE data sources have expanded beyond contact data and surveys to include more operational information on customer transactions. Second, the science of surveys has changed markedly due to technology and the creation of summary indices, such as the Net Promoter Score and Customer Effort Score.

These two changes are a mixed blessing. While the indices provide more data, they also encourage shortcuts and lazy thinking. Many companies are drowning in data but lack the analytical horsepower to use it effectively. A positive trend in some companies toward using this data is the alliance of customer service, customer insights, and continuous improvement departments. The third change is recognition that the most difficult problems are cross-functional; thus, the VOC will fail if it does not feed into a cross-functional, action-planning process. We devote Chapter 8 to these last two issues: conducting surveys the right way and using VOC results for impactful action planning.

The fifth section (Chapter 9) addresses the role and implementation of technology across twenty service processes. Progressive chief information officers (CIO) are now looking to customer service and marketing executives to tell them what to deliver. Therefore, the customer service executive must understand capabilities and best practices for websites, mobile apps, artificial intelligence, and video, as well as communicate and collaborate with the CIO on leveraging these tools. Customer journey maps and storytelling are critical. To assure alignment and successful application of technology, you should provide your CIO with a copy of this book.

We address people issues in Chapter 10. This is critical since the current labor market is constrained, and the global economy is in flux. We first address new research on what employees want in addition to decent pay. We leverage this intelligence to guide the creation of a can-do, risk-taking culture and how you can ensure that both supervisors and executives reinforce the empowerment of employees with recognition, appraisal, and incentives.

One key career to manage is your own. This includes you as director of customer service, director of customer experience, or IT executive. We add the tech role because CIOs have successfully leveraged support of the CE to both safeguard their position and take on more responsibility (including all of customer service and operations). We highlight a checklist of success factors seen in executives who use the customer service role to turbocharge their careers.

A last clarification is provided in answer to the question: How does customer service fit with CE? Customer service consists of all the traditional service activities plus using the VOC to directly or indirectly affect all other customer touches. In a robust CE environment, customer service makes input to CE. If no corporate CE function exists, then customer service should act as the internal CE consultant to the rest of the company. We also recommend that customer service go beyond the traditional activities of phone and email intake, response, and VOC. Customer service must include other customer interactions, such as customer onboarding (often poorly handled by sales) and response to social media (often covered by the public affairs office or marketing department). Finally, the customer service department should be a joint owner, with the marketing department, in managing the company website, especially the home page.

This book is not just the John and Scott show. We received counsel and input from many members of the CCMC staff and client base. David Beinhacker and Marc Grainer led many of the research projects we draw upon. Erik Gunther, Jennifer Johnson, and Vicky Doran helped with figure and table design and formatting. Nobu Hatanaka, our partner in Japan, contributed both data and advice on global CE strategies. We learned much from, and often quote, current and former clients. Rick DuFresne, formerly of Toyota Motor Sales USA, wrote the foreword for my previous book, *Customer Experience 3.0*, and continues to be a source of knowledge. For this book, we found inspiration from John Adamo of Moen, Jim Albert of Neptune Flood Insurance, Heather Avery and Jarmon Horton of Aflac, Lisa Dandeneau and Eliza Lavergne of Navigant Credit Union, Lynn Holmgren of Comcast, Peter North of CuriosityStream, and Vicky Soulimiotis of Chick-fil-A. Brad Cleveland added depth to my discussion of contact center operations.

We drew upon a half-dozen well-known experts to showcase the range of great ideas for engaging both staff and customers. Chip Bell honored me by providing the foreword and input to two chapters. Steve Curtin provided myriad practical examples, and Jeanne Bliss and Jeff Toister added savvy best practices.

The HarperCollins Leadership staff has been patient and easy to work with. Thanks to Tim Burgard, our senior editor, and Amanda C. Bauch, a detailed editor. Mike Snell, my agent, also provided guidance.

Most important, this book would not have been possible without the unwavering moral support of my wife, Alice, and the hundreds of hours she spent painstakingly editing multiple drafts. Scott noted that there is a special, higher place in heaven for wives who edit their husbands' books. I also received continued encouragement from my daughter, Kate ("Keep at it, Dad—it's worth it"), and from Doxie, the family dog, who never questioned my writing style or grammar.

In summary, a client asked one of our staff, decades ago, "Aren't you embarrassed to be selling common sense?" The staff's answer was spot on. She said, "There still seems to be a market for it!"

Everything in this book is common sense. All we do is organize it, so you can easily apply it in your market. Enjoy your success!

SECTION ONE

SEEING CUSTOMER SERVICE STRATEGICALLY

My wife met a friend for dinner at a high-end Italian restaurant in Washington, DC, on the Georgetown waterfront. She ordered the Dover sole, which is expensive but my wife's favorite, based on previous visits. After an inordinate wait for the entrées, the server announced that the kitchen had prepared branzino rather than the sole. With little apology, the server basically asked if she would accept the wrong dish now or wait for the correct dish to be prepared.

My wife did not accept the wrong dish but felt bad that her friend's meal may have sat around, waiting to be served while the sole was prepared. A free dessert was provided (despite my wife and her friend declining any dessert), but this attempt at a positive fix was negated when the restaurant mistakenly charged for the more expensive branzino entrée. The error and poor customer service were compounded by the added insult of the higher bill and lack of an empathetic apology for the whole mix-up.

Compare this to an experience at another Washington, DC, restaurant. When we arrived at Rasika for our reservation and a table was not ready, Santosh Bodke, the manager, seamlessly seated us in the bar area and provided complimentary drinks, appetizers, and a sincere apology. At both restaurants, the food was very good and quite pricey. In the first case, the memorably bad service guaranteed a poor rating and negative word-of-mouth (WOM). The second experience cemented loyalty and a positive recommendation.

As an executive, you cannot personally deliver excellent service to all customers. You must depend on the staff and the overall culture created by the entire service team. In some companies a customer-experience advocate looks across the whole company, but in most companies, this concern still resides with the service executive, who should view delivering consistently great service as a career opportunity. The strategic view of customer service is not to look at the function as a cost to be minimized, but as a competitive differentiator that generates revenue and positive WOM and justifies premium margins.

This view begins when you see the true role that service plays in your business and the broad impact of customer service on the company's financial performance. Furthermore, customer expectations created via technology—such as proactive communication and personalization—in companies such as Amazon, Lyft, and Intuit now make such technology critical to enabling a competitive service level. Therefore, the chief information officer (CIO) should be your new best friend.

This chapter will help you see the customer service function in strategic terms and grasp its true potential. First, we examine ways in which customer service and customer responses to service can affect an organization for better or worse. Next is a discussion of how financial decisions about customer service can be made strategically better to enhance the bottom line. After defining several key terms that arise in most customer service discussions, the chapter presents a model for a customer service function that can play a strategic role in any organization. Finally, initial steps are suggested to establish strategic customer service in your organization. At the end of each chapter, key takeaway points are summarized.

HOW CUSTOMER SERVICE AFFECTS A BUSINESS

The idea that poor customer service harms a business is intuitively correct, but the concept cannot be incorporated into decision making unless it can be quantified. Here are some of the basic, quantifiable findings from our research over the past four decades. First, the bad news, and then the good news.

The Bad News

Most customers do not complain, and noncomplaining customers hurt your business. With consumer-packaged goods and other small-ticket items, only 5 to 15 percent of dissatisfied customers complain, and usually only to the retailer. For serious problems with big-ticket items, the complaint rate rises to 20 to 50 percent of customers who report the problem to a frontline representative, but only one out of ten of these customers (2 to 5 percent of all complainants) escalate the issue to the local manager or the corporate office. This means that at the manufacturer or headquarters level, for each complaint received, about twenty to fifty other customers have problems you don't hear about. Finally, for business-to-business (B2B) customers, at least 25 percent do not complain, and often this figure can be as high as 75 percent.

Why do customers not complain, including business customers who are paying you thousands, or tens of thousands, of dollars per month?

Customers don't complain for four main reasons:

- *Customers think it will do no good.* Either they have complained in the past and nothing was done, or they believe standard industry practice causes the problem.
- *Fear of damaging a long-term relationship.* Customers are often dependent on a particular employee, or they fear conflict/retribution from the person they are complaining about. To put this in context, think of your trepidation about complaining to a

restaurant manager about your server *before* he or she brings your entrée to the table, which raises the stakes considerably.

- *The problem is aggravating but not critical.* Customers therefore feel the problem is not worth the hassle of complaining. Think of discovering a mile after you left the drive-through that the French fries are missing from your takeout order. You will likely feel it isn't worth driving back to complain or rectify the situation.

- *Customers do not know where to complain.* Many customers are at a loss to determine how to escalate a complaint beyond the staff member with whom they are dealing. Often, general requests for a manager result in an interminable wait and/or someone not empowered to fix the situation.

When dissatisfied customers do not tell the company about a problem, the problem cannot be resolved. We see the same behaviors and even worse problem-complaint ratios in nonprofit organizations (museums, health clinics, etc.) and government agencies (where expectations are lower). For example, at a major New York City museum, only 13 percent of dissatisfied major donors complained about the problems encountered. In a leading health-care system, only 15 percent of dissatisfied patients and family members complained.

Problems result in lost customers and revenue. In more than 1,000 studies of many industries in a score of countries in the Americas, Europe, Asia, and the Middle East, we found that when a customer encounters a problem, on average, loyalty drops 20 percent compared with customers who had no problem. In other words, for every five customers with problems, one will switch brands the next time he or she buys a specific product or service in your marketplace. This does not even include the effects of negative WOM, which, as you will see later, can be significant. Do the math. How many customers have some type of problem, and what does that imply about revenue left on the table?

Bad news travels far. Our landmark 1978 study for Coca-Cola revealed that, through WOM, an average of five people hear about a person's good experience, but ten hear about a bad experience.[1] Consider the impact of WOM in today's social media environment. The Customer Care Measurement & Consulting *2017 National Customer Rage Study* showed that three times as many people hear about a bad experience compared to a good experience, and the average consumer has a median of seventy friends who view the consumer's online posts.[2] In one study of consumers playing an electronic game, two of every six people who were told of a positive experience by another customer bought the product. Positive WOM can indeed be a powerful marketing tool. The Cheesecake Factory's marketing costs were reported to be only 25 percent of their direct competitors' costs, because the company "lets the customers do the marketing for them," according to David Gordon, former president of The Cheesecake Factory.[3]

Problems increase sensitivity to price. Encountering a problem causes sensitivity to price to double. If you want to charge a premium for a product, customers should not encounter problems. On the other hand, if customers have a great experience with no unpleasant surprises, you can charge a huge premium. Think of Starbucks, where customers are happy to pay more than four dollars for a specialty cup of coffee, because of the attention and experience that accompanies their purchase.

The Good News

Now, as promised, here's the good news.

Employees are not the cause of most customer dissatisfaction. Contrary to conventional wisdom, employee attitudes and errors are responsible for only about 20 percent of overall customer dissatisfaction. Our research reveals that, in most industries, employees come to work wanting to do a good job. Rather, what employees are told to do and say to customers are leading causes of dissatisfaction. About 50 to 60 percent of overall customer dissatisfaction is caused by products, broken processes, and marketing messages delivered as intended but that result in unpleasant surprises. This is good news, because redesigning your products and processes can eliminate problems. Another 20 to 30 percent of problems are caused by customers' errors, erroneous expectations, or product misuse. For example, when we ask audiences if they have read their homeowner's insurance policies, only one or two people raise a hand indicating that they have read their policy. Every homeowner's insurance policy contains significant unpleasant surprises, such as exclusions and valuables limitations, but few people read any document more than one page in length. Regardless of the cause, when customers blame the organization, it benefits the organization to prevent or fix the problem. In a later example (see Chapter 2), we highlight the three most prevalent unpleasant surprises customers may encounter.

Keeping customers is cheaper than winning new ones. We originated this widely accepted rule of thumb decades ago during an analysis of marketing costs versus customer service costs for a U.S. automaker. In the original study, we compared the expense of dealer advertising (only one part of the cost of acquiring new customers) with the average amount spent to retain a customer via effective complaint handling. The ads cost five times as much as the cost of effective complaint resolution. In a similar and more recent analysis for a construction company, we found that the cost of fixing a problem to maintain loyalty (thus leading to future projects) was one-eighth the cost of selling to and signing up a new customer. In more than two dozen other industries, depending on the specific industry and organization, the cost of winning a new customer can be two to twenty times that of retaining an unhappy customer by resolving a problem and restoring the relationship. In a B2B environment, a company can easily spend $10,000 to $100,000 to win a new client, but then undermine the relationship and future sales by skimping on installation, training, documentation, parts, or service.

Proper handling of complaints retains customers. In almost all business sectors, a customer who complains and is satisfied by the complaint's resolution is 30 percent more loyal than a noncomplainer and 50 percent more loyal than a complainer who remains dissatisfied. This means that convincing three noncomplaining customers to voice their complaints, and then resolving their complaints, produces the same revenue as winning one new customer. Clearly, it is imperative to find effective ways to resolve problems and encourage customers to complain. After seeing this data, several of our clients, ranging from motorcycle dealers to a northeastern credit union, find it appropriate to communicate on invoices or post signs with the statement, "We can only solve problems we know about!"

The economic imperative for service improvement is clear. When financial data on the value, attrition rate, and cost to win a new customer is combined with the right data on customer behavior, chief financial officers (CFOs) and chief executive officers (CEOs) can readily recognize the return on investment in customer service. Ironically, useful data (except the noncomplaint rate and WOM data) already exist in most organizations or can be developed with existing resources. Even these data elements can be quantified via a survey that asks customers if there were problems, if they complained, and how many people they told about the negative experience. As stated earlier, a critical and often missing component of the economic analysis is the average consumer's value.

In addition to data on noncomplaint rates and customer value, most companies are missing a logical methodology to model the impact of enhanced service on revenue, WOM, and sensitivity to price in a way that senior executives understand. However, to be motivated to consider such a methodology, management must understand the broad effects noted above in the "The Good News" section, and then consider the business case for customer service improvements.

Making the Business Case for
Improvements in Service

An organization can implement full-scale, strategic customer service or simply improve specific aspects of its service. Either way, the organization is improving customer service. Although some low-cost and even no-cost ways to improve service exist (such as trusting known customers, 98 percent of whom are honest and therefore need not be re-vetted each time they cash a check), most improvements will cost money. Thus, you will need to convince your organization's finance function ("Finance") or the CFO that investments in an improved customer experience (CE) will have a tangible payoff.

Unfortunately, investments in customer service improvements are rarely presented to Finance as true investments; instead, they are presented as costs on a budget line. That is why most companies just fix the problems that produce the most frequent, or the loudest, complaints. That is also why companies add service representatives and call stations when sales rise, and lay off representatives and reduce resources when sales sag. This happens when there is no real understanding of the link between service and future revenue. During a previous downturn at Toyota Motor Sales USA, the CEO protected the contact center and field service organization staff from the otherwise across-the-board cuts, saying, "We still have all those owners out there who need customer service."[4]

The usual across-the-board cost reductions during an economic downturn are shortsighted, because the reductions shortchange customers, employees, and the organization itself. Strategic customer service focuses on the long-term business case—that is, on the revenue benefits of service improvements, which are usually ten to twenty times the cost implications. This strategic customer service focus recognizes the links among customer service, customer behavior, and financial results.

These links will be a theme throughout this book because we have found that investments in customer service provide several times the return of other investments. Customer service also provides the fastest returns. When you implement a change that improves your customer service, the benefits of increased loyalty, positive WOM, and reduced risk begin accruing on that next phone call.

To bring the business case into sharper focus, let's look more closely at the revenue impact of problem prevention and resolution. In the previous section, we noted that when a customer encounters a problem, on average, loyalty drops 20 percent. Thus, for every five customers with problems, probability says you will lose one customer (5 customers × 0.2 loyalty loss = 1 customer lost, see Figure 1.1).

To make a strong business case—that is, a financial case—you must quantify the impact on revenue of preventing or fixing problems. If a customer is worth $1,000, then for every five customers with problems, the company will lose one customer worth $1,000 in revenue. You can then reverse the analysis and say that if you prevent or fix five problems, you will retain one customer who otherwise would be lost, and thus retain $1,000 in revenue that would otherwise be lost. Moreover, that $1,000 in revenue can be attributed directly to the customer service process, because that process involves identifying,

**FOR EVERY FIVE CUSTOMERS WITH A PROBLEM,
ONE IS AT RISK**

**CAN NOW LINK HANDLING AND PREVENTING
PROBLEM TO REVENUE**

Figure 1.1. Economic Model of Service Impact

preventing, and resolving the problems (discussed later when we present the model for maximizing satisfaction and loyalty). Figure 1.1 makes the basic case for this type of investment in customer service. Another financial dimension beyond revenue retention, where improved customer service contributes, is profit margin. As previously mentioned, the average problem doubles a customer's sensitivity to price. If you want to charge a premium, you must prevent problems. For example, Figure 1.2 illustrates the impact on satisfaction with prices and fees at a financial services company.

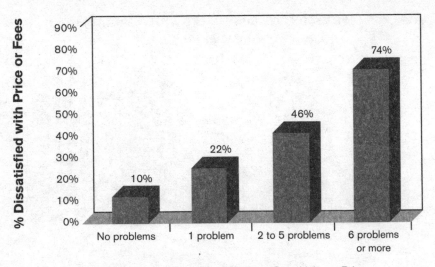

Figure 1.2. Problems Impact Customer Sensitivity to Price

Analyzing investments to improve customer service requires a company to know what a customer is worth to the organization. If you don't know how much the customer is worth, how can you decide how much to spend to keep him or her happy? This number can be calculated in various ways, such as the customer lifetime value (CLV), which is defined as the amount a typical customer will spend during his or her tenure as a customer, the average/median annual revenue per customer, or the average/median revenue for specific customer segments or product lines. I am not a fan of the CLV, because of the long time frame. Finance executives often retort, "Who knows if we're even going to be in that business five years from now?" I prefer using one to two years of revenue as a value. It is disconcerting that many senior executives, even in sales and marketing, do not know their customers' average value. Marketing should know, and if it does not, Finance must know, because loyal customers should be considered the company's most important asset. To think strategically about customer service, you *must* know the average revenue per customer for your organization.

CFOs rightly want to see the business case for customer service investments, as they would for any investment. Making that business case—the *economic imperative*, as we call it—goes to the heart of strategic customer service, which *requires* an economic rationale for every service improvement. In this way, you don't end up fixing squeaky wheels that barely warrant a drop of oil. Chapter 6 discusses the details of quantification and how to get both the CFO and chief marketing officer (CMO) on board.

CLARIFYING KEY CONCEPTS

The business case for strategic service depends on the relationship between revenue and several concepts that warrant clarification. Precisely defined terms enable you to collect, measure, compare, and track the right data and thus analyze potential investments and the resulting improvements over time. The most useful concepts relative to customer service are service, self-service, customer journey map, customer experience, problems, complaints, the multiplier (or ratio), escalation, satisfaction, loyalty, delight, and WOM. Broadly, we define these terms as follows:

- *Service* is usually viewed as handling questions and problems *after* the sale. This activity is also typically provided by customer service representatives (CSRs) or chat bots. Service may or may not include customer presale questions and customer self-service activities on the organization's website.
- *Self-service* is critical because the majority of customers with a question or problem first go to the company website, Google, or YouTube. In many companies, such web-based interaction is NOT part of service but part of the IT department's jurisdiction. We believe the customer service department must drive a significant portion of the company website's structure and content.
- *Customer journey map* is the company's process flow of all customer activities and touches, from initial customer awareness of the product through purchase and use. This journey map identifies all the areas where prospective and existing customers will have questions and problems. Ideally, either the service department will have responsibility for handling the problems, or another department will be assigned responsibility. Unfortunately, without

journey maps, responsibilities for preventing and/or handling key issues are not assigned, resulting in dissatisfaction.

- *Customer experience (CE)* is the summation of all interactions and touches between the customer and the company, its products, and services as described by the customer journey map.

- *Problems* are any unpleasant surprises or questions that arise in dealing with a product or service, whether or not the customer complains. Problems can originate in product performance, design, packaging, delivery, installation, instructions, or safety; employee performance; and customer error or expectations.

- *Complaints* are situations in which customers bring problems to the company's attention via telephone, email, tweet, letter, or in person. As you'll see, the total number of specific problems often greatly differs from the number of complaints.

- *The multiplier* is the ratio of problems encountered to complaints to service, which can range from three-to-one to two thousand-to-one. Knowing this multiplier or ratio enables you to accurately analyze investments in improvements that prevent or resolve problems.

- *Escalation* is the movement of a complaint beyond the original company recipient, either by the customer due to dissatisfaction with the first answer or by the company staff attempting to achieve a better response.

- *Satisfaction* can be tough to define because it is often mitigated by expectations. When your expectations are low, you may be satisfied, for example, if your flight is "only" sixty minutes late, or if your lunch at the local greasy spoon is edible. By the same token, a first-rate movie can seem like a dud if you were told it was the best flick ever produced. Expectations therefore represent either a potential liability or a huge opportunity, and you can affect satisfaction by setting customers' expectations precisely. An airline pilot proactively lowered expectations for a forty-five-minute flight when he announced, "We give same-day service."

- *Loyalty* is measured by expressed intention to repurchase, actual purchasing behavior, or willingness to recommend. Continued purchases are generally the most accurate and convincing loyalty measure, but we have found a high correlation between *expressed* purchase intentions (especially negative ones), as well as willingness to recommend, and *future* purchase behavior. For instance, at a major U.S. airline, we confirmed that about 60 percent of frequent flyers who said they planned to fly less often with the airline did dramatically reduce the number of miles flown. However, organizations must not confuse loyal customers with captive customers. The latter are merely doing what is convenient at the moment. Therefore, one of the best ways to measure loyalty is to use intended WOM as a surrogate: Would the customer recommend the product or service? This is the basis of the Net Promoter Score, which has its own challenges.

- *Delight* occurs when an organization surprises a customer by exceeding high or reasonable (as opposed to low or unreasonable) expectations. But not all delight leads to increased loyalty, so always exceeding expectations may be a major waste of money.
- *WOM*, either positive or negative, is almost always the most important factor in a customer's purchase of a new product. WOM occurs because people have a social and psychological need to tell one another about good and bad experiences. WOM and its cousin, word-of-mouse, which includes comments about your organization on social media (e.g., Facebook posts, tweets, review sites, and blogs), are increasingly important to customers. Certain product areas, such as consumer electronics, autos, home services, and travel, are so sophisticated that consumers rely heavily on friends and other consumers who have researched, purchased, and experienced the product or acquired expertise. CCMC's *2017 National Customer Rage Study* found that 9 percent of consumers post about problems on review sites, and 23 percent post on social media about serious problems.[5] While more consumers see such posts, the majority of WOM is still spread the old-fashioned way, talking to friends and neighbors. WOM is critical to gaining new customers. Sophisticated companies now develop programs aimed at generating positive WOM as part of marketing and service strategies and include actions that delight customers. For example, Carl's Jr. engaged influencers when they opened their first restaurant in Australia. A member of their influencer panel, who had

tens of thousands of followers, bought the entire menu and posted a YouTube video in which he tasted and evaluated each menu item.

The above concepts enable organizations to think about customer attitudes and behavior in ways that can be quantified. Knowing that a customer is happy or did not come back will not, by itself, help you improve the CE in the future. By managing customer service using the quantified basis of the customer journey map, problems, complaints, escalations, satisfaction, loyalty, delight, and WOM, you can build a business case and create the economic imperative to know your customers and their needs better, and to meet those needs more effectively with tools like self-service.

We'll now examine the operational model for the strategic service approach to managing your customers' experience.

A MODEL FOR MAXIMIZING CUSTOMER SATISFACTION AND LOYALTY

Our model for strategically managing the CE and maximizing customer satisfaction and loyalty, and thus revenue, boils down to a simple acronym: DIRFT, or "Do It Right the First Time." DIRFT is usually the stated goal of every organization. But despite the best intentions, training, and resources, organizations often fail to do it right the first time. Thereon hangs the role of tactical service in the CE, which consists of two parts: *setting expectations and preparing the customer to use the product* and, if the customer's experience isn't perfect, *orchestrating the customer's interactions with the service process.* Setting expectations and helping customers get the most from the product are intrinsic to strategic customer service.

As the findings presented earlier (in the section "Making the Business Case for Improvements in Service") indicate, customers' interactions with the service department represent opportunities to solve problems and prevent future problems, increase loyalty, and generate positive WOM—or to do the opposite and create damage. Figure 1.3 illustrates the dynamics of DIRFT and thus presents a framework for customer experience and service systems.

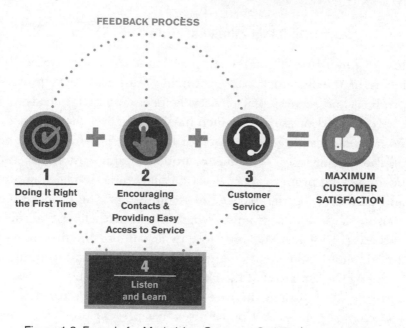

Figure 1.3. Formula for Maximizing Customer Satisfaction and Loyalty

Figure 1.3 illustrates the four things an organization must do to cost-effectively maximize customer satisfaction:

- Do it right the first time—minimize the number of problems encountered.
- Provide easy access to service—which includes encouraging customers to complain and providing convenient communication channels tailored to the customers' preferences.
- Provide great service by responding to questions and problems in a manner tailored to the customers' expectations. Also, when appropriate, sell customers other useful products and services.
- Listen and learn from all three aspects of the customer journey by feeding data about questions and problems to the right company functions and partners so that problems can be prevented or proactively dealt with.

The next section provides greater detail about each of these steps.

Do It Right the First Time (DIRFT)

Joseph Juran stressed that a company must commit to doing the job right the first time.[6] The company must *consistently* provide products and services that *consistently* meet customers' needs and expectations. Consistency is much harder to deliver than the occasional "wow" experience, but one of the greatest delighters is "no unpleasant surprises." This means understanding customers' true needs, setting proper expectations via marketing, selling honestly, and then meeting the expectations completely. The expectations constitute the brand promise, whether you are selling Starbucks or a Mercedes-Benz. Meeting those expectations—the first time or quickly after a failure to do so the first time—builds brand equity, as defined by Roland Rust of the University of Maryland.[7]

To do the job right the first time, the company must develop and employ policies and procedures that prevent problems while concurrently generating customer satisfaction. Responsibility for no unpleasant surprises lies with everyone: product developers and production line workers, dispatchers and delivery people, marketing and sales professionals, installers and service technicians, billing and collection personnel—everyone who directly or indirectly touches the customer. This prevention effort is continuously improved, based on the listen and learn feedback loop depicted in Figure 1.3 and described here. A key factor in DIRFT and setting expectations is to proactively educate customers about product uses, quirks, and requirements. Customer onboarding presents one of the largest opportunities in most companies.[8]

Encourage Contacts and Provide Easy Access

This activity has two discrete parts. The first part is breaking down barriers to complaining. These barriers can be operational, like where to complain during off hours, but most are motivation based—the customer feels that complaining is too much hassle, will not do any good, or will sour the relationship. The second part is providing all available communication channels whenever the customer is using the product or service. Digital and mobile channels are now critical, particularly since customers are always carrying, and often sleep with, their smartphones.

Effectively Respond and Possibly Cross-Sell

The third component of Figure 1.3 is the customer service system. Problems and questions will inevitably occur, and customers may become frustrated and/or dissatisfied. Therefore, the company needs an effective system for handling questions and resolving problems, and for alerting customers to ways of accessing the customer service system. The customer service system itself must also be easy for customers to use, as explained in Part 2 of this book. Websites and search results are critical because up to 90 percent of customers go to the company website or search on the internet before calling. The website should also offer chat in addition to frequently asked questions (FAQs), with the five most prevalent issues highlighted on the home page.

Many consumers conduct an internet search for "how to fix X problem with Y product." Therefore, a search optimization function should ensure that your company's website and YouTube guidance are the first sources accessed. Being a primary search result is critical, because the company can provide its customers with the best and most correct guidance. In addition, the customers' use of the company's website provides data on what issues customers are encountering.

If the consumer cannot self-service, then the CSRs must have the knowledge, skill, and authority to address most issues on the first call. If not, the CSRs must assume ownership of the issue by finding a resolution and halting or mitigating any frustration or loss to the customer. If those solutions are impossible, the CSR must route/escalate the customer *directly* to someone who can assume that responsibility.

Many managers assume that if a customer complains, the employee who had contact with the customer is responsible for causing the dissatisfaction and should be punished. However, as mentioned earlier, frontline employees are not the primary cause of dissatisfaction. The third item in Figure 1.3, customer service, used to be labeled "managing complaints," but we found that the word *complaint* often had a negative connotation that implied a customer or employee was to blame. Therefore, this label was eliminated. Several of our telecom clients adopted the useful term *request for assistance*, which shifts the focus away from blame and toward the customer's need for a solution and a resolution process. It was a smart move.

It is important to note that, in the customer service function, customers with questions or complaints often present sales opportunities to CSRs. While sales is conceptually different than service, the same capability and skills must be included in both. A complaint about a failed faucet can turn into the sale of a new, more advanced faucet or a maintenance agreement. Some customers, particularly price-sensitive ones, tend to buy a grade of product or level of service that fails to meet their needs but is the least cost. The customer actually needs more capacity, speed, power, durability, maintenance services, expertise, premium channels, or financial flexibility than they signed up for. When the customer realizes this, they call the company to find out how to get what they want. This creates an upselling opportunity. A well-trained CSR, armed with the right customer data and a few targeted questions, can recognize potential customers in these situations. Moreover, many customers will take advice about future purchases from a CSR more readily than from a salesperson.

Our experience at three different copier companies revealed that if the service technician attributes a breakdown to an overtaxed machine, customers will believe the technician when he or she says, "You need a bigger machine to handle this volume" more often than they will believe a sales representative, who is typically viewed as "just trying to make a sale." In fact, our research shows that cross-selling a product that a customer can use is a delighter. Of course, not every customer with a question or problem is a sales prospect.

Listen and Learn—Feed Data About Issues to the Right Parties

The fourth component of Figure 1.3 is "listen and learn." The first three service system components—DIRFT, access, and customer service—must collect and compile customer contact data and other data describing the CE, so the right internal people in the company and its partners can identify and remedy the root causes of customer problems. As the DIRFT formula shows, this feedback loop supports doing it right the first time, which includes doing the *right* job right. For instance, to better meet customer needs, the company may need to modify the product usage instructions or the product itself. You need to know which step is the right one. Failure to address the root cause allows a problem to continue, which increases customer dissatisfaction and service costs, decreases loyalty, and reduces future revenue. Remember that many customers do not complain—they just take their business elsewhere. In addition, some customers will spread negative WOM, further decreasing your future revenue.

In many companies, the customer service department is the focal point for the entire corporate VOC. In other companies, customer service feeds contact data into a customer insights department, which also includes and analyzes customer surveys, operational data, and employee input. If your company does not have an insights function, the creation and performance of this function can be a huge opportunity for customer service. For the VOC to be effective, it is essential that clear descriptions of problems—such as incorrect expectations set by sales messages, misfires in product design or performance, snafus in delivery or installation, unclear directions for assembly or use, or systemic failure to resolve problems—must be routed to people who can act on the information received. For instance, at Carl's Jr., the customer insights department receives reports on who is using the data and who is not, and highlights those not using the data to senior management.

So far, we've examined some positive and negative effects of customer service, noted the importance of the economic imperative for investments to improve customer service, and defined our terms. We've also introduced a strategic customer service model that addresses situations where the organization has failed to do it right the first time, listens and learns from those situations, and suggests adjustments to DIRFT, access, and customer service. We now conclude this discussion by turning to the first steps you can take toward establishing strategic customer service in your organization.

FIRST STEPS TO STRATEGIC CUSTOMER SERVICE: ECONOMIC IMPERATIVE AND VOC

Most organizations have the resources required to boost the performance of their tactical customer service functions and to move toward a strategic customer service process. Key components include customer service functions, customer relationship management (CRM) systems, and, most important, VOC capabilities. An additional useful resource is a continuous improvement department. This staff is adept at pilot-testing concepts and assembling fragmentary data to make a business case.

The VOC is the mechanism that describes the overall CE using all inputs, not just market research surveys, but also customer data sources, such as warranty claims, customer complaints, and employee input. A true VOC extends beyond the traditional issues of product features and price to include gathering data on all dimensions of the CE, such as sales tactics and messaging, warranty provisions, dealer service, and preferred selling and financing methods. In most organizations, the VOC tends to be fragmented. In one auto company, when asked, "Who owns the VOC process?" the head of service replied that about seven different people owned various parts of it. That's unfortunate, since a fragmented VOC effort is more damaging than none at all, because it generates erroneous findings, contradictions, confusion, and paralysis.

The first step toward establishing strategic customer service in your organization is to start viewing customer service strategically. That means thinking about the end-to-end customer journey. It also means thinking in terms of the financial impact of problems (especially the ones you're not hearing about) and complaints, and of the way customer service handles them. And it means thinking about how to get your resources organized and focused at the action level, as well as at the strategic level. In all these areas, better a small success than a big disaster.

Although we'll discuss how to organize the customer service function in detail later, here are seven basic design guidelines for you to consider, and perhaps start implementing, in the meantime:

- Identify two problems you can empower the service staff to fix right now. Ultimately, you want to empower CSRs to succeed at least 90 percent of the time. If CSRs are not empowered to fix issues on first contact, you increase customer service costs by 50 percent and reduce loyalty by 10 to 30 percent.

- Make information easy to find. Have clear links to the website map and FAQs prominently displayed at the top of the home page, and display the phone tree menu wherever you post the toll-free number.

- Map the customer journey. Until you have at least a rough map of the whole journey, you will not know the true cause of problems and which problems are the most prevalent.

- Make it easy for customers to complain. You can only solve problems that you know about. Post an invitation to complain on invoices and the website home page.

- Use customer service to tap each customer's full potential value. Position your CSRs to capitalize on cross-selling and upselling opportunities. Recognize gold, silver, and lead customers (even if only internally); treat all customers with respect, but expend resources based on their profitability.

- View the customer service function as a WOM management function. Every transaction has potential positive or negative WOM impact, and you must measure both. Then you can design explicit tactics and incentives for intelligently delighting customers and generating positive WOM.

- Make the economic imperative the basis for customer service decisions. When you identify the links between the customers' problems, complaints, points of pain, service, WOM, delight, company margins, customer acquisition, and financial performance, you can manage the CE for maximum revenue and profitability.

These guidelines all point toward a customer service system that achieves strategic goals. Such a system does not just deliver the right level of service quickly, efficiently, and cost-effectively—it also plays an explicit role in revenue retention and generation. The economic imperative for strategic customer service emerges when you quantify the benefits of preventing, fixing, and resolving problems; of creating delight and positive WOM; and of cross-selling and upselling.

☞ Customers with problems often do not complain, and their loyalty is 20 to 40 percent lower than that of customers without problems. This is especially true among B2B customers, who are afraid that complaining will sour the relationship.

☞ On average, problems will damage loyalty by 20 percent; that is, for every five customers who experience a problem, one will stop buying the product or service.

☞ Encountering a problem usually doubles a customer's sensitivity to price.

☞ While customer service is primarily responsible for contact handling, it must also focus on providing customers with easy access and substantive input into the listen-and-learn activities. The input to listen and learn is critical to improving DIRFT and moving from firefighting into a preventive customer service mode.

☞ Understanding the customer journey is critical because marketing and sales usually set customer expectations long before customer service becomes involved. Customer service must either provide input to customer onboarding or take responsibility for that function.

☞ Customers delighted by proactive education or superior problem resolution are usually 10 to 30 percent more loyal than customers without problems.

☞ Failure to invest in the VOC allows problems to continue, increasing service costs and decreasing future revenue.

WHAT DO CUSTOMERS WANT?

After landing at the Nashville, Tennessee, airport, I hoped to send a few emails before heading to my client's location. The airport advertised free Wi-Fi everywhere. When I tried to connect online, the classic "no internet connection available" message appeared, even though the airport website was reachable. I complained to the airport administration, whose website and general phone number were accessible. The airport administrator's receptionist said, "No one from IT is available," and "Our system does get overwhelmed at busy periods." These days, business travelers expect free Wi-Fi in airports, and the excuse given was unhelpful and revealed cluelessness. The lesson is: *You must deliver what you promise, and never promise what you cannot consistently deliver.*

This chapter explores customer expectations and how organizations can set strategic and tactical goals that will meet those expectations. The chapter concludes by looking at ways an organization can set service goals that meet customer expectations at both the strategic and tactical levels.

UNEXPECTED REASONS
FOR UNMET CUSTOMER EXPECTATIONS

Most executives assume that if you have an unhappy customer, a frontline employee is the probable cause. *This is usually not true!* The hapless airline employee did not cause the mechanical delay. The CSR on the phone did not reject your health insurance claim. In most cases the front line is the messenger bearing the bad news. The cause goes much deeper than the frontline employee.

Customers approach each purchase or transaction with the expectation that they will receive exactly what they intended to buy, with no unpleasant surprises. Expectations are set by your company's image, brand promise, reputation, pricing, advertising, and marketing messages. If a customer is unfamiliar with your product (e.g., never used a ride-sharing service before), the customer also brings preconceived notions, based on what he or she has heard about your industry. Your brand promise of what will be delivered combines with your customer's previous experiences and results in a set of expectations that the company is expected to fulfill.

The basic formula for meeting customer expectations is the DIRFT model introduced in Chapter 1. The organization must recognize that customer expectations should be properly set at the beginning of the customer journey. The initial intake function needs the resources (e.g., educational materials) and the process to ensure that all customers are onboarded in a manner that confirms or resets their expectations and then delivers on the promise. Further, customer service must be positioned to identify and address situations in which the organization fails in this endeavor. When customers' expectations are not met or when customers are disappointed, one or more of three factors—listed below in order of importance—are almost always at work:

- *Company (unwittingly) causes dissatisfaction* via defective products, misleading marketing messages, ineffective policies, or broken internal processes. Most marketing executives will cringe at this suggestion, while most service executives will nod in agreement.

However, an honest review will show that this factor causes the majority of problems—50 to 60 percent in most organizations. Companies design the best products and processes they can, but they can still have inherent problems. As mentioned in Chapter 1, this is actually good news, because the problem causes can be discovered and, usually, eliminated. In cases where it is impossible or impractical to eliminate problems, warning customers in advance can mitigate the effects. For example, an Alabama insurance company sends customers a welcome letter with a copy of the homeowner's insurance policy, pointing out the provision limiting coverage of valuables to $5,000 unless the customer buys a supplemental rider at extra cost. This reduces the number of denied claims for losses the consumer thought were covered.

- *Customer errors or unreasonable expectations.* Customers misuse or abuse products, fail to read directions, or develop unrealistic expectations, either on their own or through erroneous WOM. This factor causes 20 to 30 percent of problems. Note, however, that the general consensus of service professionals is that dishonest customers represent less than two percent of all complaints.

- *Employee mistakes or bad attitudes.* As mentioned in Chapter 1, this factor causes a maximum of 20 percent of problems. Although almost all bad service is blamed on employees, few people come to work intending to disappoint customers. Often the employees, along with customers, are victims of unmet expectations, in that the employees are given defective products, tools, processes, and response rules, as well as limited authority. How many times have you heard the reason, "Because it's company policy"?

These three factors account for virtually all the problems that lead to customers' unmet expectations and disappointments. Customer service should be instrumental in preventing or solving the problems, even though the problem causes are typically found outside the customer service department. As indicated by the feedback loop portrayed in Figure 1.3 (the DIRFT model), customer service feeds information on problems and their causes back to the rest of the organization. Such data, combined with satisfaction surveys and operational data on quality, create the VOC.

TRENDS IN CUSTOMER EXPECTATIONS ABOUT SERVICE

Over the past two decades, research from CCMC, including the *2017 National Customer Rage Study*,[1] identified a number of trends in customer expectations, in addition to several operational expectations for tactical customer service.

The following are seven broad, sometimes contradictory, trends in overall expectations that customers bring to interactions with organizations, particularly with the service function:

- Clear brand promise
- Transparency
- Consistency in delivery
- Easy access and convenience via all communication channels
- Immediate resolution of problems at the first point of contact
- Genuine empathy when things go wrong
- Recognition and knowledge of the customer

Clear Brand Promise

Starbucks, Southwest Airlines, and 1-800-Got-Junk have all capitalized on a clear product statement to properly set their expectations. We are delivering X product at Y price. Starbucks delivers a cup of coffee at a high price, but tailored to your desires in a comfortable environment. Southwest Airlines delivers a reliable, budget product with obvious limitations, like standing in line to board. 1-800-Got-Junk stresses convenience and flexibility: "Just point— we'll make your junk disappear," and "We work until midnight, so you never have to take off from work." The company is more expensive than the competition, but that facet isn't stressed; convenience is the key differentiator. The cheese expert at Whole Foods Market, the shipping associate at the Amazon warehouse, and the mechanic at the Ryder Truck Leasing maintenance center all contribute to, or detract from, the experience. Thus, everyone in an organization must understand the customers' expectations and the employees' roles in delivering the customer experience.

Transparency

The difference between brand promise and transparency is in the details. Many customers do not accept the requirement to read detailed contracts or directions. While this may seem absurd to legal and compliance officers, regulators generally now agree with consumers that contract provisions should be simple and transparent. The onus is on the company to be clear concerning what is promised and expected. If the product has limitations beyond the industry norm, the limitations must be explicitly communicated. Transparency in customer service includes an honest explanation of what caused the issue and assurance of input into the VOC and continuous improvement process.

Consistency in Delivery

Customers expect promises to be fulfilled consistently across transactions and locations. This concept originated with locations. Holiday Inn and McDonald's first pioneered the idea of the same product and service across the country and then the world. Now, companies like Amazon, eBay, and Tesla are requiring their vendors and supporting suppliers to provide the same product and delivery quality across the marketplace. Amazon and eBay encourage customer ratings and will drop vendors with excessive dissatisfaction and complaint ratings. Tesla requires energy suppliers that create car-charging stations to place the stations near coffee shops or entertainment, so the car owners won't be bored during the forty-five-minute charging period.

Easy Access and Convenience

Many companies define easy access as a company answering the phone quickly. More important than answering the phone is convincing customers to tell you when they are dissatisfied. CCMC's *2017 National Customer Rage Study*[2] shows that a primary reason for consumers *not* complaining is the belief that it will do no good or, especially in B2B relationships, may cause uncomfortable conflict in the business relationship.

In industries such as air travel, insurance, utility, and government organizations, customers have developed "trained hopelessness." Customers learn that complaining fixes nothing and may have negative consequences or lead to retribution (as when Elaine, in a *Seinfeld* episode, was labeled "difficult" in her medical charts at multiple doctors' offices). Low complaint rates in some industries create the myth that, "Complaints are down, so things are improving." Not true!

Customers expect that the first person they speak with will be empowered and have the necessary information to resolve the problem. Involving a second person, who then provides an answer that the front line should have been able to convey, decreases satisfaction by 10 to 20 percent, even if exactly the same answer is provided. The solution is to empower the front line to provide the same answer a supervisor would give. The ease of searching the internet and the availability of mobile communications have contributed to customers expecting instant gratification from every service activity. Customers now want mobile and chat options. Companies like Intuit and Liberty Mutual Insurance are introducing video chat and real-time video streaming for insurance claims, which will soon be routinely expected. For customers, sending an email and waiting twenty-four hours for a response is now unacceptable.

Our analysis of the key drivers of satisfaction in tactical service transactions at call centers and retail outlets consistently supports the adage, "Be efficient first, friendly second." Not all customers expect or want "warm fuzzies" in service interactions. Nor do many want "a relationship" or canned cordiality of the have-a-nice-day variety, especially when it's 9:00 p.m. in the customer's time zone. Also unwelcome is repeated use of the customer's name. However, respectful onetime use of a surname may make a good impression. Most of all, customers do not want to hear an answer that on its face is absurd or nonsensical.

My favorite example comes from my personal bank, when I was on my way to Tokyo and my wife called the "Gold" customer line to notify the bank that I would be using my ATM card at 2:00 a.m. EST at Narita Airport. The bank representative said that my wife, even though she was a joint account holder, was not authorized to report my travel and that my ATM card probably would not work at an out-of-country ATM. When asked why a joint account holder, who jumped through all the security question hoops, could not authorize an international travel flag on the account, she was told, "That is company policy." The damage of a reply that did not provide a clear, believable explanation is huge. Such an answer was also demoralizing for staff members to give, because they knew it would evoke both anger and challenges to which they didn't have a more convincing explanation.

Immediate Resolution of Problems

Customers now expect frontline employees to resolve problems on the spot. This requires much more empowerment than companies are typically willing to impart. However, if you look at the cost of supervisor involvement to make a decision that will be the same 92 percent of the time, tripling the cost, it is cheaper to trust the frontline employee. Further, if you add the 10 to 20 percent drop in loyalty by forcing the customer to wait, and otherwise gumming up the works, the case for immediate resolution and trusting the frontline staff becomes compelling.

Genuine Empathy When Things Go Wrong

Recently, my Amtrak train from New York City to Washington, DC, was delayed. There was an automated announcement of the delay and an Amtrak apology for the inconvenience. This announcement was repeated seven times over a fifteen-minute period. The apology was not satisfying. First, it was automated and second, it mentioned inconvenience, a term that almost always trivializes the problem. In an even worse example, I was on an airline flight to Washington, DC, that was diverted at midnight to Pittsburgh. As soon as we got off the plane, the ground staff said: "Welcome to Pittsburgh. We are not responsible for hotels or anything else." Not a great welcome.

A customer's desire for empathy, sympathy, or at least concern when an unpleasant surprise occurs has little to do with who caused the problem. When your flight is cancelled as a result of bad weather, you *know* the airline isn't responsible, but you're still stuck, perhaps until the next day. You want the employee to acknowledge your pain and validate your anger and frustration. We call this response "apologizing without accepting blame" (for example, "I'm sorry you're stuck here. I'd be *really* upset if it were me"). An apology costs nothing and goes a long way toward validating and soothing the upset customer. When people are upset and emotional, the blood drains from their head, and they often are not thinking clearly. The apology calms down customers and helps them think more rationally.

While an apology is necessary, Janelle Barlow and Claus Moller advise in their book, *A Complaint Is a Gift*, to never refer to the situation as an "inconvenience" when apologizing.[3] A cancelled flight is not an inconvenience; it is a potential major personal or business hassle, such as a missed day of vacation or a missed critical business presentation. Eliminate the word *inconvenience* from your vocabulary.

Recognition and Knowledge of the Customer

Over the past ten years or so, the definition of "good service" has evolved from personalized service delivered by someone who knows the customer to service from someone who simply knows the customer's value to, and history with, the organization. In most cases, the long-term personal relationship is nice but not necessary, except for B2B account management. Customers simply want someone who can answer questions and act immediately, based on knowledge of the customer's world. Customers are annoyed if they must reestablish their value as a customer and recount their previous interactions. Most customers value efficiency and effectiveness even more than they value warmth and consolation.

OPERATIONAL EXPECTATIONS FOR TACTICAL CUSTOMER SERVICE

The above trends provide a context for customers' expectations of tactical level service. There are six operational expectations for tactical customer service:

- Customer education and effective onboarding
- Convenient and genuine accessibility
- Accurate, clear, complete responses
- Reliable follow-through
- Cross-selling
- Creating delight

Customer Education and Effective Onboarding

It is challenging to effectively educate and onboard customers with complex products because these activities are often delegated to the sales department ("Sales"), without customer service's involvement. Once a contract has been signed, Sales wants to move on to the next customer. Education and onboarding are given short shrift.

Customers expect to be proactively apprised of product quirks, common difficulties, and potential glitches. The word many companies are applying to this activity is *transparency*. Customer education also increases safety and reduces risk to the organization. When customers find an initiative confusing, as often occurs with a new product or promotion, customer service can clarify matters for those who call. Also, customer service should work with Sales to create accountability for proactive customer education for customers who don't have a reason to call. An approach is to send a welcome package via mail, email, or post a website alert.

Alternatively, customer education through CSRs boosts revenue by informing customers about the availability of products, add-ons, and higher levels of service that can solve problems or enhance the CE. Even customers who are not ready to buy at that moment will frequently return in the future. Customer service can also educate customers about other, less costly methods of accessing the service system, such as the company's website. The company website, in conjunction with search engine optimization (SEO), is among the most economical and effective tools for customer education. SEO is also needed and should be supported by customer service, because many consumers immediately Google a question—such as, "How do I change the cartridge in a Moen faucet?"—and expect to find a YouTube video on the topic. Moen, for example, creates instructional videos and then works to have these as the first results for a general web search on such topics.

Convenient and Genuine Accessibility

Decades ago, nine-to-five business hours were the accepted norm, and postal mail was the usual contact medium. In the early 1980s, our research, as highlighted in *BusinessWeek*, helped companies recognize that easy, free, instantaneous, anytime contact from customers was worth providing because it allowed customers to get problems solved. The result was the massive expansion in the use of toll-free numbers.[4] With the addition of websites, email, social media, and chat, customers now hold five general expectations regarding accessibility:

- *Open hours.* Customers want accessibility to your customer service system, in some form, whenever they are using your product or service, reviewing your invoices, or considering a purchase. This includes daytime, evenings, weekends, and perhaps even the dead of night on a holiday. Christmas Eve and Christmas Day are among the busiest periods for customer service at toy and consumer electronics companies (e.g., "I'm having trouble assembling this toy!").

  One mitigating factor to this immediate availability requirement is that, for basic questions and problems, 80 to 90 percent of customers will go to the company's website or conduct an internet search to find an answer, prior to calling. If your website provides easy access to answers to prevalent questions (e.g., highlighted on the home page, not three clicks into the FAQs), customers are often willing to self-service.

- *Human contact.* Consumers' acceptance of mobile, internet, and telephone access to purchases, bank balances, flight boarding passes and updates, and similar information doesn't eliminate the need for competent CSRs. CCMC's *2017 National Customer Rage Study* indicates that when problems get serious, customers still want to talk to a human by a seven-to-one ratio.[5] For serious problems, the emotional component, CSR expertise, flexibility, and empowerment become critical.

- *User friendly.* While customers using an automated phone system will tolerate up to three choices (for example, "Press one if [this]; press two if [that]," and so on), more menu choices or a second menu tier will cause frustration *unless* the customer has been educated in advance about what he or she will encounter when calling the toll-free number. Customers don't want more than fifteen seconds of introductory statements, such as: "Welcome to the XYZ Company automated service center. If you're calling from a touch-tone phone, please press one," and so on. For systems that customers use often, it is also critical to have a "break in" capability, so the customer can say "representative" or "operator" at any time without having to listen to the entire instruction. Finally, while voice recognition systems that say, "How can I help you?" can work in simple situations, applying them to complex environments almost always fails. These systems are generally limited to key words and are unhelpful for anything even slightly unusual.

- *Minimal transfers.* Our research reveals that a customer will tolerate *one* warm transfer during an initial call to customer service *if* he or she then reaches someone who can solve the problem. This should not be confused with a transfer to another phone queue or to a department where the customer's whole story must be recounted from the beginning. On average, such transfers result in 20 percent lower satisfaction than if resolution is achieved on first contact.

- *Tolerable waiting period.* CCMC's analyses of a wide range of companies on key satisfaction drivers for phone service have found that phone queue waiting time, if not excessive, is less important than the service delivered once customers are connected. A sixty-second wait is usually acceptable if callers then reach someone who can resolve the issue on that first contact. For high-tech and insurance products, wait times of up to two minutes are usually acceptable because customers have traditionally encountered longer wait times in these industries.

CCMC's research implies that, in most cases, spending the resources needed to answer all incoming calls within thirty seconds is not cost-effective. Even a target of answering 80 percent of incoming calls in twenty seconds is unnecessary. What's more important is the "tail"—that is, how many calls are *not* answered within sixty or ninety seconds. Once ninety seconds elapse, significant damage can be done. Incidentally, perceived waiting time decreases if the customer is reading something useful on the screen or hearing useful information while on hold (not an ad for flights when you're calling the lost baggage hotline).

For situations where longer wait periods may occur during peak periods, the application of "virtual queue" technology is strongly advised. This technology announces the current wait time (e.g., five minutes), and then provides the customer an option to receive a call back in five minutes. The customer's phone number is usually captured by automated number identification (ANI) technology. Wait time dissatisfaction significantly dissipates because the customer can engage in another activity for a few minutes and then be prepared for the call back. One potential glitch is that if the customer calls from a business, the ANI may not properly capture the incoming phone number's extension details.

Today, customers want instant access to answers and solutions. This has important implications for organizations that use voice mail, email, chat, or social media contact in their service delivery systems. Voice mail, which is often used in account representative and B2B environments, automatically delays access to service and erodes satisfaction 15 to 20 percent if a customer has an issue that requires an immediate response. Based on this information, many companies require sales representatives' voice mails to allow callers to dial "0," which connects them to a "must answer" phone with a live person.

Customers have also come to think of the internet as they do the telephone: They expect an immediate, automatic acknowledgement and a substantive answer within two to eight hours, depending upon the industry. When a CSR offers to chat with a customer on a website page and provides immediate assistance, this action can raise first-contact resolution 30 percent. It is critical that customer requests for a chat be accepted within thirty seconds. As an illustration of longer delays' potential damage, go to a website, request a chat, and sit there staring at the screen for thirty seconds to see how long the time span feels like.

Accurate, Clear, Complete Responses

Ideally, the service system should resolve the issue during the customer's initial contact. As noted above, failing to do so decreases satisfaction 10 to 20 percent. For example, at a beverage company, we conducted research using matched sets of calls, where half the requests for service were completely resolved on the first contact, and the other half were resolved with callbacks within twenty-four hours. All callers were given the same answers to each issue, whether on first or second contact. The set that achieved complete resolution on the first call received a 10 percent higher satisfaction rating. Three contacts to resolve an issue can cost a company about 30 percent in satisfaction and loyalty ratings.

Resolution on the first contact satisfies customers and precludes their having to call customer service again, and/or customer service having to return customers' calls. By definition, a return call is not first-contact resolution (FCR). FCR typically cuts costs up to 50 percent, by eliminating the need for callbacks. The cost of customer callbacks becomes significant when you consider that only 30 to 40 percent of callbacks reach the customer on first attempt, which means that one callback commitment can require your employees to make two to four, or more, calls.

FCR does, however, require the following four components:

- *Competence and empowerment.* CSRs must have the requisite knowledge, authority, skill, experience, and temperament to confidently address customers' problems.
- *Support.* In addition to having the information required to resolve problems, CSRs must have confidence that the organization will deliver as promised. Further, CSRs should have access to a continuous improvement process to report issues. Their ability to convey such access assures customers that the same issue will probably not recur.

- *Empathy.* CSRs must listen well, thank the customer for presenting the opportunity to address the problem, and when necessary, apologize, even if the company isn't at fault. Empathy defuses the customer's anger and generates a more efficient resolution.
- *Clarity and fair treatment.* CSRs must clearly explain what happened, present the rationale for company policies, acknowledge customers' logical arguments, explain what action will be taken regarding their issue, and leave customers feeling they have been treated fairly. Fairness is a key goal in all problem resolution, especially when the answer isn't the one the customer prefers. For instance, health insurance companies can maintain customer satisfaction and loyalty levels even if a claim is denied, as long as customers feel the explanation regarding the reason for the claim's denial is clear and fair.

Reliable Follow-Through

When CSRs cannot resolve a customer's issue on the spot, the CSR or someone else must follow through to deliver the promised next step or resolution. That promise, even if the word *promise* is never used, sets an expectation that must be met, or dissatisfaction will ensue. Thus, CSR promises must be realistic, convincing, and satisfying. Customers particularly dislike situations where the CSR treats them well but makes unkept promises (e.g., "the service tech will arrive tomorrow between 10:00 a.m. and 12:00 noon"). In such cases, the immediate post-call survey says the CSR was great, but then the broken promise destroys long-term loyalty. This is a common problem with post-call surveys fielded immediately after the call; they do not detect whether the organization follows through.

CSRs who know that follow-through will occur project confidence to the customer, rather than vague hopes or, worse yet, cynicism. CSRs who can rely on the back-end system will assure customers of a resolution. That, in turn, translates into fewer follow-up calls from the customer and lower costs for the organization. A mutual fund company where the CSRs protected themselves with weasel words (e.g., "It usually happens") received 100,000 confirmation calls per month from customers making sure that transactions had occurred as specified. One popular tactic, which can create delight, is proactive confirmation, as when Amazon communicates the progress of your purchase moving through the company's system.

Cross-Selling

Many companies have increased revenue and profit per customer, as well as satisfaction and loyalty, through well-designed cross-selling and upselling programs. Companies like Southern California Edison (SCE) and Cisco Systems work with customers to identify new opportunities to link their products to the internet of things (IoT). For example, in exchange for a rate reduction, SCE will turn on your dishwasher via the dishwasher's wireless connection portal at 2:00 a.m., when electricity loads are low, and turn off your air-conditioning for fifteen minutes every hour during peak periods. Other examples include a bank selling overdraft protection when fielding complaints about bounced check fees, and a cable company converting complaints about download times into sales of greater bandwidth.

The CSRs must focus primarily on solving the customer's actual problem rather than on making a sale. However, if the problem can be solved or prevented or the customer experience improved with an enhanced product, add-on, or higher level of service, the CSR can delight the customer while also making a sale. This finding, which will be covered in the "Creating Delight" section that follows, should make service-oriented CSRs more comfortable executing appropriate cross-sells.

Creating Delight

Many companies have created a goal to continuously delight customers, which is neither feasible nor desirable. Our research, shown in Table 2.1, indicates that service far above and beyond expectations is often not cost-effective and results in only moderate improvement in loyalty and satisfaction. A recent example was a Japanese hotel club floor lounge, where staff insisted on making customers a fresh cup of coffee each time they needed a refill, even going in the back room to individually brew it. Instead, however, many customers wanted to simply refill a cup at a coffee urn, without having to flag down a server, ask for a cup, and wait four minutes for the server to return. While this service mode might be culturally based, it lacks recognition that a large segment of the lounge customers wanted faster service, even though it was less personal. In this case, the extraordinary service became an irritant.

Delight Experience	Average Lift to Recommend (Top Box Score)
Service beyond expectation (heroics)	12%–14%
Friendly 90-second staff interaction	25%
Personal relationship over months	26%
Tell me of new product or service I can really use	30%
Proactively provide information on how to avoid problems or get more out of your product	32%

Table 2.1. Impact of Delight Experience on Top Box Recommend Scores

On the other hand, as shown in Table 2.1, our research indicates that *appropriately targeted actions*, such as friendly interactions, cross-selling a relevant new product, or educating a customer about how to avoid problems, can both create greater delight and benefit the company via additional revenue or prevention of future customer problems.

Our conclusion is that the objective for delightful service interactions should direct CSRs to deliver education and "cheap delighters" like friendly interactions. But as previously noted in the club lounge example, not everyone wants hyper-personal interaction. The CSRs must be able to read customers and/or ask what they want.

Other ways to create delight include the occasional free service or extra product, but this approach has a liability. For years, the local Starbucks gave me a free cup of coffee when I purchased a one-pound bag of ground coffee. One time I wasn't offered the free cup and was disappointed when the previous delighter was not delivered. When I asked about it the next time I bought a one-pound bag, I was told,

"We have discontinued that practice." The lesson here is: *A consistently delivered delighter soon becomes an expected part of the basic product.*

The six operational expectations discussed above are the basic expectations for service. However, another factor complicates things: Customers also derive expectations of your service function from the previous good experience they had with another organization. Customers tend to compare their service experiences across industries. For example, if a customer receives exceptional service while interacting with an overnight delivery company, such as flexibility scheduling a delivery time, that customer will expect a similar performance level from the home repair or appliance delivery service they interact with next.

SETTING SERVICE GOALS STRATEGICALLY

Strategic customer service demands that you set customer experience goals and then work down to tactical objectives. Although many companies work hard to deliver superior service, senior executives typically haven't thought through the fit between customer service and the business, marketing, and overall customer experience strategies. Thus, companies set only process-level goals along tactical dimensions, such as time spent in the queue and calls handled per CSR. To set goals strategically, management must first define the service function's overall strategic and tactical role and goals, then translate these roles and goals into targets the CFO and Finance can buy into and fund.

The role of customer service can be anything from a complaint department and cleanup crew to a value enhancer and competitive differentiator. Companies committed to customer service as a value enhancer and competitive differentiator must consider the entire customer journey and, therefore, must staff, manage, and fund the service function as such. Additionally, in the company's marketing and sales messages, as well as front-end customer onboarding, the company must communicate the role that customer service plays in ensuring a great experience. Further, the company must ensure that traditional service operations can deliver at the back end.

In general, strategic customer service and experience goals should include the following:

- *Loyalty,* fostered by problem prevention, positive WOM, and cross-selling that is measured with surveys and, ultimately, sales revenue
- *Value,* driven by a reputation for premium service and quality, ascertained by customer surveys that measure value for price paid and satisfaction with price
- *WOM,* represented by the percentage of new customers resulting from positive WOM
- *Effective VOC,* by identifying points of pain and revenue damage per month, the largest opportunities to add value, and tangible action on those opportunities (no action means no payoff)
- *Reduced risk and associated costs,* driven by DIRFT, providing customer education and preventing problems, as measured by the level of insurance and product liability claims, and regulatory complaints and interventions
- *High employee satisfaction* that reduces turnover costs, as represented by at least 80 percent of employees feeling successful at their jobs and proud of the brand

While these goals are logical, the second goal, value, may seem counterintuitive, given the success of Walmart, Southwest Airlines, and other companies that successfully compete mainly on price. Even as an evangelist for superb customer service, I understand that some companies pursue a low-cost provider strategy and deemphasize the role of service in the CE. Yet customers have value expectations for price paid, even for companies that are low-cost providers. Those companies communicate a specific value proposition—a mix of selection, location, quality, pricing, and, yes, service—on which they must deliver.

Thus, in any market segment, management must translate customer expectations into specific, measurable, and realistic experience goals. These goals must be firmly linked to one another and to operational performance measures according to the dimensions of access, response content, follow-through, and data capture.

Management must then define target levels for these measures and identify the most economical, highest-return ways to raise performance to the target levels. The final step is to translate the customer experience goals related to satisfaction, loyalty, reduced risk, and positive WOM into goals for revenue, margins, market share, and profitability, which also takes into account cost and cost reduction (bottom-line profit goal).

The overall metric framework should include process, outcome, and financial measures. *Process* measures include the average and range for the amount of time customers spend in the phone queue; *outcome* measures include customer satisfaction and loyalty and service employee satisfaction; and *financial* measures include revenue attributable to service in the form of problems prevented or money saved through improved service efficiency, not to mention enhanced margins and market share. Table 2.2 shows how process, outcome, and financial goals are linked.

Process Goals	→	Outcome Goals	→	Financial Goals
1. Accessibility		• Increased loyalty		• Increased revenue
2. Response		• Increased value for price paid		• Increased market share
				• Increased margin
3. Follow-Through		• Increased delight		• Lower service costs
4. Delight Actions		• Enhanced WOM		• Reduced employee turnover costs
		• Reduced problems		
5. Education		• Increased complaint rate		
6. Problem Prevention and Innovation		• Reduced risk/warranty		
		• Increased VOC impact		
7. Cross-Selling		• Greater employee satisfaction		
8. Empowerment				

Table 2.2. Metrics for Linking Customer Service to Financial Goals

Other useful measures include the percentage of customers who encounter problems (problem rate), the complaint rate per one hundred problems encountered, the number of problems resolved, and the time frame for resolution.

Here is how the linkage among the goals occurs:

- Process goals measure accessibility and response, and targets for problem prevention, education, and cross-selling.
- Outcome goals are the performance results derived from the process goals, which determines customer attitudes and behavior, such as complaint rates, loyalty, WOM, as well as employee satisfaction and, broadly, customer service efficiency.
- Financial goals result from performance on the outcome goals and measure the contribution to increased revenue, increased market share, increased margins, and lower service costs.

The following sections will show how service can set specific performance goals within the process and financial categories. We show how achievement of the outcome goals are translated into financial impacts in Chapter 6.

Process Goals

The most common process goals are the easiest to quantify, which may be why they also foster so many customer service problems. You may be familiar with a Scott Adams *Dilbert* cartoon, in which Dogbert's average talk time improves only because he is hanging up on customers. Certain process measures, particularly those that measure CSRs' performance, can twist behavior in ways that reduce customer satisfaction. For instance, a call-center manager established a standard of eighty calls per shift and a limit of three minutes per call. This prompted CSRs to increase their call counts by rushing customers through calls and even hanging up on callers. The result was decreased customer satisfaction and no self-service education of customers.

Keeping in mind the need to carefully set and implement process goals, examples of useful goals might include the following:

Accessibility

- Provide website access 24/7, with at least 99.5 percent uptime.
- Provide the option of being able to speak with a live CSR from 6:00 a.m. to midnight, perhaps with shorter Saturday and Sunday hours. Think about when the customer is primarily using your product, and be available at those times. If you have retail outlets, travel operations, or ATMs open broad hours or 24/7, your support system must be available then as well.
- Maintain an average forty-second call queue waiting time, with a ninety-second maximum, and an abandoned call rate of 3 percent or less.
- Supply clear guidance on the company's website (via home page banner, chat button, "contact us" page, and site map) and in literature and invoices regarding who to contact for which needs, including a satisfaction advocate or escalated complaint contact.

Response

- CSRs handling ongoing customer accounts should be able to answer 95 percent of questions and inquiries on first contact.
- CSRs in durable-goods markets should be able to resolve at least 85 percent of problems on the first call and assure the customer that the issue will be handled without a callback.

Follow-Through

- Assure a resolution time of twenty-four hours or less, for at least 80 percent of referred problems. In many environments, this standard may be as short as four hours.
- Maintain a system that enables CSRs to communicate in real time with problem solvers in the field.
- Operate a problem-logging system that updates the CSRs (and customers by email) at least twice daily, if not in real time, on

the status of the problem's resolution (e.g., when a technician is assigned, an order is confirmed, or a refund is credited).

■ Assure no callbacks from 98 percent of customers regarding solutions in process, because the customers are satisfied or were contacted proactively about any change.

Delight Actions

■ Track the number of CSR attempts to create customer delight when the CSRs create rapport with the customer.

■ Track the number of CSR actions that provide the customer with extra value resulting in delight.

Education

■ The percentage of customers who are effectively onboarded should be tracked via monitoring and/or surveys.

■ Track the number and quality of CSR actions taken to educate customers on preventable problems.

Problem Prevention and Innovation

■ Track the decreases in the number of routine inquiries on specific issues.

■ Track the increases or decreases in the number of inquiries that can be handled via automatic response mechanisms.

■ Quantify the number of inquiries regarding specific product or service enhancements (a significant volume implies the message was unclear).

■ Track the reduction in customer problems requiring warranty expense as a result of reduced customer misuse, fewer incorrect expectations, and improved product performance.

■ Track the number of product innovations created based on input from the VOC.

Cross-Selling

- Quantify CSR cross-selling offers as a percentage of total calls handled (including transfers to sales staff), as well as the percentage of offers appropriate to the customer circumstances. Inappropriate cross-selling creates significant dissatisfaction and many expensive subsequent cancellations.
- Quantify the value of sales as a percentage of CSR-presented offers.
- Quantify the number of sales cancelled because the sale was inappropriate for the customer.

Empowerment

- Quantify the percent of customers indicating dissatisfaction with action taken on different issues.
- Quantify the percentage of issues escalated to a supervisor.

Measures of CSR performance on process goals should balance efficiency (speed of call handling and number of calls handled) and effectiveness (satisfactory problem resolution, effective education about self-service, and successful cross-selling). In all performance measurements, anticipating unintended consequences is as important as designing useful goals and incentives. Part of the challenge involves establishing the right culture. For instance, when CSRs use a hard-sell approach to upsell, it may work in the short term, but this strategy rarely maximizes long-term customer value. Thus, CSRs must be trained in soft-sell techniques and be given incentives to build relationships rather than sell aggressively.

In light of the importance of problem resolution to customer satisfaction, service must measure customers' actual satisfaction with the solutions provided. Brief follow-up surveys can establish that measure, in addition to future purchase intentions and the potential for positive or negative WOM. Inevitably, some portion of customers with problems will be dissatisfied or mollified rather than satisfied. Measuring the lost revenue caused by problems—thus establishing the economic imperative for fixing or preventing them—requires accurate measures of customers' satisfaction level and loyalty when they encounter these problems and receive a solution.

As we saw in Chapter 1, not all customers who experience problems complain. This makes the customers who contact the company incredibly valuable, and so satisfying them is important. When you satisfy a complaining customer, you retain a customer who might otherwise be lost. Similarly, when you prevent a problem from recurring—by fixing the design, performance, or product flaw or by educating customers—you retain not only those who would have encountered the problem and complained, but also the much larger number of customers who would have encountered the same problem and not complained.

Setting Financial Goals

Lower service costs may be a counterintuitive concept to many customer service executives. The overall payoff, including revenue and margin, of fixing or preventing a specific problem must be considered as well. We grant that this isn't a new concept. Short-term cost is the reason organizations don't fix most problems they know about. Continuous improvement teams have prioritized and selected process improvement projects for decades, based on which project will most reduce costs. A new and more strategic approach is quantifying the potential revenue lost each month that a specific problem goes unaddressed, and quantifying the impact of enhanced employee success on reducing employee turnover.

We strongly recommend understanding the revenue impact of strategic customer service. Specific revenue goals should initially consider incremental revenue from reducing customer attrition, rather than revenue from cross-selling and upselling. Once good resolution capabilities are in place, customer service can then adopt what we call "aggressive customer service." Aggressive customer service includes cross-selling, upselling, and actively delighting customers, all of which increase revenue.

In addition to receiving credit for increases in revenue from selling, customer service should get recognition for revenue saved from problems fixed or prevented as a result of its efforts that led to the retention of a percentage of customers. This is both fair and the correct way to calculate the return on investments (ROI) for improving service and fixing or preventing problems. This calculation of potential revenue enhancement will transform management's view of customer service from a cost center to a revenue source.

Revenue and margin goals should include customer service's contributions toward lowering risk, heightening innovation, increasing brand equity, and maintaining and increasing employee satisfaction. Customer service's impact on these areas is real and, in many cases, measurable, and thus constitutes valid strategic objectives.

When the right roles and goals are strategically defined, you can meet customer expectations in ways that mesh with the organization's business, marketing, pricing, and other strategies. Most importantly, you can link process goals to outcome goals and link outcome goals to financial goals. A strategic approach also calls for setting and pursuing goals in a logical order. For instance, you must link process goals to outcome goals (see Table 2.2), or you may warp CSRs' behaviors in ways that hurt customer satisfaction and loyalty. Similarly, you must develop a service process that effectively handles customer contacts and captures useful customer data before you attempt to cross-sell and create delight.

Unfortunately, even in companies that go beyond process measures to establish outcome goals, few executives broaden the focus beyond satisfaction and loyalty to include WOM measures, let alone the impact on revenue and risk. Fewer still employ customer service to its full potential in the VOC. The VOC element enhances revenue and margin by increasing innovation, reducing risk, and lowering service costs and employee turnover. At Procter & Gamble, one aspect of its VOC process is a file of digitally recorded customer calls titled "Listen to the Boss"—"Boss" meaning the customer. Product managers routinely listen to what customers think of the company's products.

All of the process and outcome goals can be logically rolled up into the financial goals of increased revenue, through greater loyalty and increased margins via higher value for price paid and lower costs.

KEY TAKEAWAYS

☞ Executing DIRFT means properly setting and consistently meeting expectations, and eliminating unpleasant surprises. Quality marketing and sales, including customer onboarding, are just as important as traditional manufacturing and operational quality.

☞ Poor product design, misleading marketing messages, and broken business processes cause more customer dissatisfaction than employees with bad attitudes.

☞ What CSRs say after they answer the phone—providing clear, believable answers and fair customer treatment—is more important than how fast the phone is answered.

☞ WOM and reduced risk are two major contributors to great customer service and the bottom line, but few companies set goals for and then measure these outcomes.

☞ Achieving the proper mix and linkage of process, outcome, and financial goals increases the effectiveness and the efficiency of customer service and assures buy-in from Finance.

SECTION TWO

3

CREATING A CUSTOMER SERVICE SYSTEM WITH TACTICAL RESPONSES AND STRATEGIC PROBLEM PREVENTION

The building of the tactical customer service system is described in four stages and illustrated in Table 3.1. First, the three objectives are outlined: access, response, and input to the VOC. Second, the functions that facilitate achievement of the objectives are described. These seven functions are critical for any service system in any environment, small or large, for-profit or nonprofit. The operational processes underlying each of the seven functions are provided within the context of each objective and function. How the processes are performed will vary dramatically depending on the environment, the product or service, and the organization size. Many of these processes can be executed by technology that is appropriate even for small companies. Next, we'll address the nine metrics that measure the effectiveness of the customer service system in meeting its objectives. Finally, the chapter concludes with a discussion of key drivers for how to be "easy to do business with" (ETDBW) and how this relates to other service parameters.

Strategic Service System Objectives, Functions, and Supporting Processes			
Objectives	Access	Response	Input to VOC
Functions	Awareness	Reply	Customer Insights
	Intake	Staff Support	Reporting
		Evaluation	
Processes	1. Motivation	5. Assessment	16. Storage and Retrieval
	2. Facilitation	6. Investigation	17. Statistical Generation
	3. Routing	7. Classification	18. Analysis
	4. Logging	8. Resolution	19. Input to Organization
		9. Confirm and Coordinate	20. Proactive Communication
		10. Tracking	
		11. Knowledge Management	
		12. Hiring and Training	
		13. Development	
		14. Incentives	
		15. Appraisal	
Metrics	Complaint Rate	First Contact Resolution	Problem Rate
	Percent Issues Logged	Customer Effort	Use of VOC by Executives
		Satisfaction	VOC Issues Resolved
		Staff Turnover	
Global Metric	Easy to Do Business With		

Table 3.1. Strategic Customer Service Framework

OBJECTIVES OF TACTICAL CUSTOMER SERVICE

The three objectives of tactical customer service are to encourage and facilitate access, provide a complete response, and deliver input to the VOC system.

Access Objective

When DIRFT fails and the customer is unhappy or confused, you must encourage that customer to contact the company. Remember, customers often feel complaints are unwelcome or unproductive. Access also includes providing a convenient channel for the customer to communicate with the company and reach a person or process that can respond on first contact. A key output of this objective is to increase the percentage of disgruntled customers who will voice a complaint. Another key output is to decrease the effort it takes for the customer to find the right response location.

Response Objective

To provide an effective response to customers at the front line means a company must evaluate the issue(s) and provide a reply with explanations, replacements, coupons, and/or immediate solutions. The response process also includes an evaluation of the response's effectiveness. In addition, the staff, processes, and knowledge base must be available to support the response.

The response objective will consume at least 75 percent of your resources. The challenge is not just training and empowering the staff to respond, but assuring that the website allows effective self-service. In addition, a mechanism must be in place to ensure the company is receiving feedback on responses, so the response knowledge management system (KMS) can be continually improved. The KMS is the repository for information and response guidance on company processes and policies, which provides the explanations given to customers. Because other departments create much of the information in the KMS, customer service must liaise with the rest of the company to keep the KMS up to date.

Finally, you must hire, train, evaluate, develop, and retain the staff. In many companies, most aspects of the human resources (HR) function lie outside the customer service department. This can be an advantage because HR may have more resources and expertise that can enhance the quality of hiring, training, and development. The potential disadvantage is that HR may not fully appreciate the stresses and requirements of customer service positions, unless educated by customer service.

Input to the VOC Objective

The information derived from the customer contact input to the VOC should be used internally to enhance the customer service process, as well as the entire organization and its partners. The first impact area is the CSRs' contact-handling performance and the effectiveness of the tools being used, such as response guidance, systems, and processes. We find that, in most companies, 90 percent of the effort is devoted to evaluating CSRs' individual performance. However, the greater opportunity for impact exists in improving the marketing message, operating process, and/or the product design.

A broader and more strategic use of the customer service input is to make it part of the listen-and-learn activity described in the DIRFT model in Chapter 1. We have found that, in most companies, the service input constitutes the primary VOC source. In the balance of companies, the customer service input is melded with survey data and analysis by a customer insights department. As discussed in the listen-and-learn section in Chapter 1, where a customer insights department does not exist, performance of this broader VOC customer insights function can be a major opportunity for the customer service director.

An additional benefit of the customer insights function is the enhancement of customer service staff morale; when the CSRs see corporate activities or problems fixed, customers no longer complain about them. Conversely, when CSRs see the same problems, despite repeated reports and absent an explanation, they conclude that management does not care about the customer, or perhaps about CSR input.

SEVEN SERVICE FUNCTIONS
AND THEIR SUPPORTING PROCESSES

The achievement of the three strategic service objectives—access, response, and input to the VOC—requires seven broad functions. The functions define what must be done. In turn, the twenty processes define how the seven functions are performed.

Performing the functions and processes at the tactical level is a challenge, partly due to the nature of the business and the distribution system. For instance, a commercial bank dealing with electronic transfers and accounts faces a different set of challenges than a tire manufacturer that depends on a dealer network to both sell and fix tires, while explaining the exclusions in the road-hazard warranty. The bank has far more control over front line, tactical-level resolution (e.g., adjusting an account) than the tire manufacturer. Essentially, the bank's customers will complain to the branch manager or call the bank's service function, both of whom directly work for the bank and have access to, and the ability to fix, the account. Most of the tire manufacturer's customers will complain to the salesperson or dealership service manager. Thus, the manufacturer may not even become aware of problems. We worked with a tire manufacturer that logged fewer than 4 percent tire failures per month, yet our survey showed that 20 percent of customers experienced problems.

Fortunately, the functions for achieving the access, response, and input to the VOC are the same seven functions for all organizations, though customization is warranted. The seven functions are: awareness, intake, reply, staff support, evaluation, customer insights, and reporting.

FUNCTIONS AND PROCESSES
FOR ACHIEVING THE ACCESS OBJECTIVE

Awareness Function

We are entering a new era of customer behavior characterized by ever-more cynical customers who will not use a ponderous complaint process. Therefore, customers must first be motivated to take the time and effort to contact a company. The methods customers can use to communicate with companies are multiplying. To maximize the percentage of customers who complain to a company, the customer must be convinced to use the service system before deciding not to complain or turning to social media. If customers who contact the company are not quickly conveyed to the correct person, the customer will most likely give up, switch brands, and/or complain on social media.

Once customers decide to contact your company, you must provide the full range of effortless channels that take the customer to an effective response process. This process, depending on the customer's preference and the issue encountered, may be self-service or human operated, and might be transmitted by email, text, Facebook Messenger (a form of instant messaging), other IMs, Twitter, chat, voice telephone, or streaming video. Internationally, WhatsApp, WeChat, and Line are popular. CCMC's *2017 National Customer Rage Study* suggests that other channels, like Instagram and Snapchat, are still very minor in customer service.[1] Further, the study also indicates that few U.S. customers want to complain on social media as the first step of customer service. Only about 3 percent of consumers immediately go to social media because most prefer to complain directly to the company in private and only go public if they are rebuffed and subsequently become angry. The latest buzzword for this accessibility is *omnichannel.*

The awareness function has two parts: motivating customers to contact, and facilitating contact by providing the customer's preferred channel at the exact time the customer wants to use it.

The process of *motivation* entails encouraging every customer with a question or problem to contact the company. Contact will allow the company to either win/retain the customer or enhance the customer's loyalty and foster positive WOM. As stated throughout this book, it is more profitable to resolve contacts from customers needing assistance than to not hear from customers about their issues.

For the motivation process to be effective, the message "we can only solve problems we know about" must be communicated before a customer has a problem. More important, it must be communicated exactly when the customer experiences a problem or has a question. This message will raise the probability the customer will contact the company. The message should be placed prominently on invoices, contracts, product labels, and websites. Dyson places its website address and 800 number on its vacuum-cleaner handles, so the information is visible when the customer uses the appliance. In Japan, Dell Computer puts the complaint solicitation message on the keyboard. In retail settings, eye contact with the customer and asking if everything is OK encourages the raising of questions and problems. Customers are also encouraged if you communicate actions the company took based on previous feedback. For example, one restaurant chain said, "We brought back BBQ sauce, based on your input!"

Soliciting complaints and contacts is more effective if they are genuinely welcomed. The CSR should thank the customer for going to the trouble of pointing out the problem and giving the company an opportunity to make things right. Of course, CSRs must also be trained to deal with irritated or angry customers. Do not make the mistake of believing that hiring people with "the right personality" can substitute for rigorous training and role-playing in skillful listening, demonstrating empathy, and acknowledging the customer's viewpoint.

Facilitation means making customer contact with the company as effortless as possible. Customer expectations for easy access were described in Chapter 2. The following section operationalizes the expectations for the range of communication channels. All of the appropriate communication channels a customer might want to use must be provided at each stage of the customer journey. For example, a company can provide a mobile app and a phone number for the store location, because a consumer might not want to complain in person or has had difficulty getting a staff person's attention.

Some companies prefer that customers self-service on the company's website because it is cheaper, and thus do not want the 800 number or "call us" button placed on each webpage. The company's theory is that if customers really want to call, they will look further on the website. This is usually wrong—the customer will simply not contact and remain dissatisfied.

For the basic communication channels mentioned above, the accessibility expectations mentioned in Chapter 2 apply: hours of operation, ability to reach a human, user friendliness, minimal transfers, and a tolerable wait period. We give one or two principles for each of these accessibility dimensions below. Remember, your company must be easy to do business with. For a detailed discussion of managing contact center operational accessibility, see Brad Cleveland's book *Call Center Management on Fast Forward.*[2] We highly recommend Cleveland's book, which focuses on electronic customer service communication channels and interaction. Since customer service continues to be provided face-to-face and by field sales reps in B2B environments, we also provide some suggestions in those areas:

- *Hours of operation.* The customer service system should be available whenever the customer is using or thinking about the product. For instance, we found that investors read their statements in the evenings and on the weekends and therefore would like to ask questions during those times. Likewise, physicians read medical journals and have questions on pharmaceuticals during the evenings and weekends rather than during business hours, when they are seeing patients.
- *Ability to reach a human.* During a call to a company, a customer should always be able to press 0 to get to a human. Likewise, on a website, a phone number or "call us" button and/or chat button is now expected. In B2B environments, sales reps often hand out their business card and say, "If you have any issues, call me." The only problem is that the sales reps are often traveling or attending meetings, and the customer reaches voice mail. Therefore, B2B sales reps should always provide the phone number of an inside support person or team that is readily available. In one medical sales environment. this specific action led to a 20 percent increase in customer satisfaction.
- *User friendliness.* Complexity should be low. Top issues should be visible on the website home page with the next level of detail visible via "rollover." Site maps and FAQs should be highlighted at the top of the website, not at the bottom in small print. With calls

answered by an automated interactive voice response (IVR), there should be no more than three choices and three menu levels, unless the IVR menu is included everywhere the 800 number is published. An additional dimension of user friendliness is the amount of information required to submit a contact. While account number and mailing address is helpful, name and either email address or cell phone number should be the only required fields. Remember, you are facilitating easy access and the ease of doing business with your company. Labeling optional fields with how the information will be used (e.g., "to help us route your call to your personal account representative") will motivate the customer to take extra time to find his or her account number. Another critical, and expected, requirement for phone centers is computer telephony integration (CTI), which captures the inbound phone number and matches it to records, to identify the customer at that number.

- *Minimal transfers.* Customers will tolerate one warm phone transfer. Customers now assume that if they provide an account number, via the IVR or personally, anyone they are transferred to should have that information as well as the key details of their issue. As mentioned above, CTI facilitates this information transfer and is now expected.

- *Tolerable wait period.* Customers tolerate up to sixty seconds of holding in queue for a live phone representative. More than sixty seconds does damage and should be supplanted with virtual queue technology that calls the customer back when the customer's contact reaches the front of the queue. For chat, more than sixty seconds creates dissatisfaction, unless you reset expectations with a message that says, for example, "We'll get to you in four minutes." For email, the traditional twenty-four-hour time frame has now been reduced to two to four hours, unless you reset and communicate expectations.

Intake Function

Once one of the above-noted channels has received a contact, the intake function executes two critical processes, routing and logging.

Routing is critical to the FCR because both efficiency and satisfaction can be damaged if the customer must tell their whole story to multiple CSRs. Optimal routing depends on the type of information the customer has provided. This could be the website "contact us" form completed for an email, the criteria and terminology the customer used to search the company's website, or the phone number or account number the customer punched in (or spoke) on his phone.

Many companies route everyone to the first-level support, hoping that most calls will be handled at that point. The problem is, if the customer must be transferred to second-level support, he or she often must wait in a second queue or be called back. In many cases, a combination of customer history and customer indication of the problem type can allow more important or savvy customers to be transferred to second-level support, thereby eliminating the unnecessary first-level interaction. Customers should never have to wait for a callback from level two because, unless a virtual queue is being used, the chances of a level-two CSR reaching the customer on a callback is no more than 30 percent, creating both customer frustration and wasted CSR effort at level two.

As noted above, B2B sales representatives are often not immediately available and often do not have all the tools and information that customer service can access. This causes the sales representative to say, "I'll check and call you back." The company has now lost FCR, and many times the promise is forgotten, causing more dissatisfaction and inefficiency.

Sales representatives must encourage customers to contact customer service if they have any issues after the sale is complete. There are strong reasons to cast customer service as the problem solver. One reason is to free up salespeople for more remunerative activities. Most salespeople readily understand this rationale. However, because sales reps want to maintain the relationships, they must be kept in the loop on all contacts, via an automated notification process.

Logging records the contact's information, such as customer name, time of receipt, email address, account or phone number, and routes the contact to the best area for response. This ensures that the contact cannot become permanently lost. The additional purpose of creating a record is to initiate a case and provide the response function with initial information to start an investigation, if needed. A good example is a CTI system: If the customer is calling about an insurance claim, their inbound phone number, possibly accompanied by an account or claim number, will allow the phone system to route the call to the right unit or claims CSR, as well as populate the CSR's screen *and* start the claim file retrieval process. Unfortunately, many companies still lack a CTI system.

In many contact centers, simple calls are not logged or recorded because of the perception that the time expended in logging is wasted. This is incorrect for two reasons. First, if the contact is not logged, the type of and the reason for the contact cannot be analyzed, and, therefore, future problems cannot be prevented. Second, if the same customer calls back, there is no record of the call, which can lead to both CSR and customer frustration. All contacts should be logged!

FUNCTIONS AND PROCESSES FOR ACHIEVING THE RESPONSE OBJECTIVE

The response objective depends on three functions that, as mentioned earlier, will consume 75 percent of the customer service department's resources. The first function is the reply function, which includes all the processes to understand the customer's issue and assemble and dispatch a complete answer. The second function is staffing and support, which covers hiring, developing, and maintaining all critical customer service human resources. The final function is evaluation, which appraises individual CSR success, as well as the service processes' ratio of cost to effectiveness.

Reply Function

The reply function includes the seven processes that assess the contact, construct a credible response, and dispatch the response to the customer. The following is a short description of the seven parts of the reply function.

Assessment of the customer issue allows the CSR to understand what the customer wants, to know where the responsibility lies, and to place the issue within the context of the customer's history with, and value to, the company. The greeting both confirms that the customer has reached the right company and sets the tone for the rest of the call. It can even create an emotional connection. For instance, at Frontier Communications, the CSR says, "Welcome to Frontier Communications. This is John Doe in Dallas. How may I help you?" Using both the first and last name and naming a nearby location (ideally) helps personalize the greeting and creates a genuine emotional connection.

Customer authentication usually follows the greeting. But if the customer has a simple question that does not involve account information, authentication may be an unnecessary aggravation. The website and phone center should have as much information outside the computer security firewall as possible, to allow customers to obtain basic answers without going through authentication.

While a call to customer service may begin with, or move quickly to, the substance of a complaint, identifying a customer's issues will often require getting beyond their feelings and to the facts of the situation. This step may involve letting the customer talk—or vent— for a bit, while the CSR clarifies what has been said and, if appropriate, expresses empathy. If the customer is angry, he or she must be calmed down before the conversation progresses to gathering facts. An angry customer cannot think clearly and may omit critical information. In this step, the CSR aims to learn the problem's overall nature.

Open-ended questions such as "What can I do to help you?" should be used to get the customer started. This can be followed by "What can I do to make this right?" These questions will help the customer move from using the emotional part of the brain to using the cognitive part. Such questions also allow the CSR to identify the customer's short-term issues, such as having been told that the technician is running late and will not be at the house by noon, when the customer has to leave. Once the customer is assured that the service call can be moved to the early evening or the next morning, he or she will calm down, and the issue of rescheduling can be addressed.

An innovation in this area (phone and email) is for the CSR to ask, "How soon do you need this?" While most CSRs fear the answer will be "now," most customers give reasonable time frames and some show great flexibility (e.g., "sometime in the next week"). This approach also allows resetting expectations if the customer appears to be unreasonable, as well as load-leveling by spreading out workload to match capacity.

Finally, the CSR should assume the customer is honest. The overwhelming majority of customers are honest (estimates range from about 96 to 98 percent in most companies), and nothing will anger an honest customer faster than insinuating that they are otherwise. Jim Blann, former senior vice president at American Express, said, "Why run the 98 percent through the gauntlet to catch the 2 percent?"

The CSR must manage the tension that may arise between the goals of resolving the customer's problem in the initial contact and finding the problem's root cause. The company needs to learn enough from the customer to understand the problem's nature, origin, and potential ramifications, yet the customer mainly wants the problem solved. The customer may therefore perceive questions regarding usage, storage, maintenance, and expectations as irrelevant or even as attempts to shift blame onto him or her.

The goal is to satisfy the customer while gathering requisite data, such as model number, place and date of purchase, and salesperson's name (if applicable), and then ask questions designed to detect the problem's root cause. Thus, it is essential to phrase questions designed to identify causes in a nonaccusatory manner and to pose questions with sensitivity and proper timing. The more information the system can deliver to the CSR's workstation, based on the serial number or phone number, the better.

Investigation consists of gathering additional information needed to establish the customer's history and value to the organization and map a path to resolution. While many customers willingly, and sometimes even aggressively, inform the CSR about their tenure as customers or their monthly volume, not all will do so, and some customers will inflate their value. A sophisticated information system will enable the CSR to know whom he or she is dealing with and the next step to more effectively negotiate a win-win for both the customer and the company.

Here is where technology becomes critical. If a CSR must look for the information to either identify the customer or understand his or her current situation (e.g., search for the claim file), then the CSR's attention will be divided, with much of it focused on retrieving the needed data. This reduced attention to the customer is often conveyed through the CSR's more distant tone of voice and decreased responsiveness. These pitfalls can be reduced if the computer automatically retrieves the information the CSR needs. For instance, many CRM systems will use the ANI to identify the customer and automatically populate the screen with customer identification data, as well as information about the three most recent interactions the customer had with the company.

Classification is one of the most critical processes because it is both the bridge to customer insights and can drive the provision of appropriate response guidance to the CSR. At the same time, most customer service managers dislike the classification process because they believe it slows down the reply function.

Classification usually takes place when the CSR gathers additional information from the customer. Information that should be collected includes details about the problem or question, the underlying cause (e.g., defect, incorrect customer expectations, confusing marketing message), the problem severity, and a code describing the remedy the CSR is implementing. Locating a problem's root cause may not be a customer service responsibility. However, it is important to gather data on the general cause (e.g., customer education vs. product dead upon opening the box) to guide subsequent root cause analysis. Whether customer service or another unit is responsible for root cause analysis will depend on the problem. The apparent problem or problem symptom may not be the root cause. For that reason, the analysis may begin in customer service and then move to the department best positioned to discover the cause.

To facilitate efficient root cause identification, the IT system must support easy data entry with a significant amount of granularity. In the analysis function, the contact data is integrated with information from all sources (including warranty claims, operations information, survey data, and returns from various channels) and compiled into concise, readable reports for management. Data classification schemes are discussed further in Chapter 7. Methods of structuring an IT system to facilitate efficient CSR use of classification schemes are discussed in Chapter 9. This classification provides a guide to resolution as well as feeding the analysis and the storage and retrieval processes. At a high level, classification involves four best practices:

- *Detailed, granular coding.* The problem codes should number between 100 and 300 categories and subcategories.
- *Inclusion of coding in CSR job description and evaluation.* Coding quality is crucial to root cause analysis and must be a critical part of CSR evaluation.
- *Periodic update and coordination with other VOC data sources.* As marketing and products evolve, new codes must be added and unused codes retired.
- *Flagging preventable calls.* The CSR can place a flag (yes or no) on the customer's record to indicate when, in their opinion, a call was preventable—for example, if there had been better up-front communication.

The adage "garbage in, garbage out" is absolutely correct. If data is not effectively coded, effective analysis is impossible.

Resolution takes the information gathered in the assessment and investigation processes and proposes an answer to the customer's issue. This answer might be as basic as a specific list of spices contained in a product (where the label simply says "spices") or as complex as a suggested strategy to resolve a difficult out-of-warranty car repair. The latter situation may be a back-and-forth negotiation that involves multiple parts of the company and distribution channels, such as a car dealership.

Given the cost of replacing a good customer, it is *always* better to err on the side of giving the customer what he or she feels is fair to retain his or her business. In most organizations, a manager or CSR will never be penalized for taking whatever steps are necessary to save a customer. In most cases, the customer can be saved for less than $100, which is usually less than it costs to acquire a new customer. Service-oriented retailers have commonsense policies for full refunds if a customer is not completely satisfied, because such polices make economic sense for these companies.

That said, no organization can afford to give away the store, and full, unconditional refunds are not practical in every industry or situation. As a result, it is often necessary to negotiate a resolution. A negotiated settlement occurs when what the company offers over-laps with what the customer considers a fair remedy. The remedy often has two parts: what the customer needs to resolve the basic problem and what he or she wants as compensation for the incon-venience. The best way to facilitate negotiated settlements is to give CSRs what is known as a flexible solution space. This "space" is bounded by parameters that give latitude to negotiate resolutions in a high percentage of cases (the organization's targeted percentage for frontline, full-resolution interactions). In addition, the CSR is directed to refer the case to a second-level subject matter expert (SME) in the 2 to 5 percent of cases that might exceed the param-eters. This flexibility enables the CSR to successfully negotiate and solve problems when a single set of solutions will not work for all customers, which is the situation in most organizations.

Ideally, solutions—and the parameters considered within the flexible solution space—should include the problem cause (com-pany, customer, distributor, weather, and fate), the customer's trans-action history with the company, and the situation's economics (the customer's value, the damage to the customer, the cost to the com-pany, and the revenue at risk due to negative WOM). For a partic-ular issue, there should be between two and four standard solutions that CSRs can choose from using common sense, a sense of fair-ness, and experience combined with general guidance. Also, CSRs should be empowered to add a little mercy, as described in Chip Bell's book *Kaleidoscope*, which notes that customers in crisis only value your competence after they have witnessed your compassion.[3]

As an example, I recently arrived at an airport for the final leg of a four-city trip to find that my flight was running at least three hours late. The employee noted my long week and my high-level elite status and offered, without my even asking, to book me on a competitor's flight leaving within the next hour. While the airline lost a little revenue on that one flight, I felt valued as a customer, and the airline received four times the revenue on my next trip to a more costly destination.

Solutions should also be consistent for similar problems and customers, while recognizing the unique characteristics of certain situations. The best way to train staff on the range of flexibility is via storytelling. Describe a problem area, with three acceptable approaches to the issue depending upon the circumstances, and tell the story about how each was handled. This puts stakes in the ground for guidance. The key is to let staff use their judgment. The policy should also recognize that sometimes the answer to the customer must be "no," and it is better to deliver that negative answer—and the reasons for it—than to string the customer along. However, the "no" has to be delivered with both empathy and a clear, believable explanation as to why such an answer constitutes fair and reasonable treatment. In many cases, rather than throwing money at the issue, a clear explanation for the rationale behind the policy will move a customer from dissatisfied to at least mollified.

A final consideration in managing a resolution is that the CRM system can provide the CSR with a flexible solution framework and talking points if a granular classification of the customer's problem was initially noted in the system by the CSR. This approach can enhance consistency across the contact center and significantly reduce training time. CSRs need not memorize all the possible solutions and talking points.

Confirmation and coordination ensures that what has been promised takes place, and all other company functions that need to know are made aware of the promise made to the customer. The key to effective follow-through and coordination is automation. Automation is less expensive and reduces human error.

The first step after the resolution negotiation is to create a written confirmation of the action to be taken (for instance, on an invoice or in an email). Next, specify any steps the customer must take as well as a time frame for the resolution. CSRs and other responsible parties should provide their names and contact information, and be sure that the customer's current contact data is noted. In emotional situations, customers often fail to take down a name. If the CSR proactively provides contact information, it shows confidence and goodwill. It is also good form to thank the customer again for bringing the problem to the organization's attention. Proactive confirmations reduce customer follow-up calls by over 50 percent.

It is essential that information about a problem be captured and routed to the right parties in the organization. For example, the accounts payable department needs to be notified to issue a refund check. Further, the continuous improvement department should be automatically notified of the issue via the CRM. This links the resolution process to the VOC analysis and prevention process. The continuous improvement department may be called "process excellence" or "project management." About half of companies have this centralized function. If this activity does not exist in your company, the customer service department can create the continuous improvement function in-house, and thereby raise the department's impact and stature.

Tracking of contact handling ensures that customer issues do not fall through the cracks. Tracking is needed in two situations. First, if a CSR must conduct an investigation outside his or her unit (e.g., asking a car dealer for details of the customer's repair), a message is sent to the dealer, and the CSR must await the reply. This creates the possibility that the case will be forgotten. The second situation is when the case is fully transferred to another unit for resolution. A referral tracking process assures that the other unit receives, handles, and closes out the case, with the results being transferred back to customer service and placed in the customer history as part of the storage and retrieval system.

The *KMS* should ideally be administered by the customer service department. The KMS should be a catalog, at minimum, of key marketing, sales, and warranty policies; responses to FAQs; and product information that is critical for responding to customer inquiries and complaints. The response to each FAQ should be accompanied by a rationale supporting the explanation of the response, purpose, or company policy to the consumer in a clear, believable manner. A best practice is for the response guidance to have four parts: a short answer; a longer, more detailed answer; responses to the two or three most prevalent objections the customer may raise; and reference material.

The KMS can also provide guidance to distribution channels on the diagnosis of customer and product problems. A complication in establishing and maintaining a KMS is that, while customer service is the primary user of the KMS, other departments may be the information source. For example, in the case of a food manufacturer, the marketing department formulates product promotions, the product development department formulates the ingredient list for food products, and the supply chain provides information on the ingredient source. Obtaining this detailed and ever-changing information in a timely manner can be difficult. In the ideal world, the same KMS also drives the website content, to allow customers to self-service, which enhances the need for all information to be clear and up-to-date.

This need for up-to-date, detailed information from all parts of the organization to support an accurate customer response creates three customer service challenges. First, a governance process must exist to ensure that all KMS information is accurate and updated frequently. Second, the KMS must be linked to the website content management system (CMS), possibly also driving the self-service email response/FAQ process. The website, with its heavy marketing content, will often be counter to the transparency needed for customer service. Therefore, the KMS will usually be partitioned with much of the basic information and FAQs available to both the consumer and customer service staff, while the full detail of underlying rationales, email templates, and procedural guidance is only available to internal company employees. Third, customer service needs the basic operational information (e.g., the requirements of a sales promotion) and clear, believable guidance on how to explain the sales promotion's mechanics to a consumer.

Campbell Soup and Harley-Davidson have each developed effective best practices for KMS creation and operation. Campbell Soup created a governance process that requires all departments to identify when an action will affect the KMS domain, such as a change in sales promotion or product ingredients. Departments provide the necessary information in a specified format within a time frame. A performance metric is the number of incidents where customer service receives consumer contacts for which the KMS is not up-to-date or has no information. Harley-Davidson created a process where the CSRs are empowered to research a new issue, such as a problem with a motorcycle electrical system, until it is understood and resolved. Upon resolution, the CSR submits an issue summary, and accompanying diagnostic and resolution information, to the KMS maintenance staff. The KMS process also assures that the incident is input to the VOC process. The KMS maintenance staff member will properly format the guidance and create the appropriate index/search labels, so any future CSR can immediately access the information about the issue. In this manner, each new issue is only researched once, leading to high efficiency and rapid input to the VOC process.

The KMS should be linked to the website, because most customers visit the website prior to calling the company. Finding the answer on the website eliminates the need for a call to the company. In a perfect world, the customer service system will own most of the website content, since the majority of site visitors are existing customers needing service.

Staff Support Function

The staff support function includes hiring, training, development, and incentives. As you will see, the appraisal process overlaps the staff support and evaluation functions. These processes will be discussed in great detail in Chapter 10. Along with a basic description of each of the five processes, the discussion here is limited to a few best practices for each process.

The staff *hiring and training* process is often managed by an HR department that does not report to customer service. The customer service executive must strongly advocate for three principles when hiring and training staff.

First, companies with successful customer service usually pay 10 to 20 percent above the average wages for CSRs in their region. They attract much higher-quality staff, and turnover is dramatically lower because employees do not leave for a dollar-an-hour higher wage. Second, preliminary interviews should be conducted via telephone, since this will be one of the key channels for which the CSR is hired. Third, a nesting period must be provided, where CSRs are answering calls in a sheltered environment from real customers, assisted by mentors with whom they continue to work with over the long term. This allows the CSR trainee to ask questions and develop good habits and self-confidence before being exposed to the workload's complete challenge.

The *development* process recognizes that while employees are motivated by money, they are even more motivated by success, progress, and recognition. Therefore, employees should be provided with individual development plans (IDP) early in their career, so a career ladder and job growth are evident. For example, good CSRs can develop into subject matter experts. The development process requires input from the appraisal process, discussed in the evaluation function below.

Incentives should be frequent and positive. An undervalued but potent incentive is regular recognition for a job well done. This should be at least weekly rather than only during biannual reviews. This positive recognition is a strong indicator of a service-oriented culture. Stress positive outcomes over routine processes. For example, the company Blinds.com encourages supervisors to provide positive feedback to every CSR each day, based on a short period of call monitoring. Finally, gamification should be applied to allow recognition and motivation for all CSR levels, especially the bottom two-thirds.

Evaluation Function

The evaluation function consists of the *appraisal* process of the other six major customer service functions. The focus of the appraisal is threefold: Are CSRs meeting their job requirements? Is the reply process working effectively to respond to customer contacts? Are the insights and reporting functions achieving improvement in the rest of the company functions, such as marketing and operations? The CSR appraisal process supports individual skill building and will bring customer service process improvements that will make the CSRs' jobs easier.

If the CSRs are provided with appropriate empowerment and tools, the appraisal results will be so positive that employees will look forward to receiving the appraisal. If employees fear appraisals, something is wrong.

In addition to individual CSR appraisal, the contact center customer service process and the corporate-level functions that impact the CE should be evaluated. Evaluating whether the reply, customer insights, and reporting functions are effective is probably the most important opportunity area. If customers are unhappy when receiving a particular response to a problem, it is because the response guidance is ineffective, and a new response must be formulated. The third level of appraisal addresses whether the customer insights and reporting functions highlight the problems caused by other parts of the company and effectively feed this information back to management.

FUNCTIONS AND PROCESSES
FOR ACHIEVING THE INPUT TO THE VOC OBJECTIVE

Two functions fall under the VOC objective: customer insights and reporting. The customer insights function consists of the storage/retrieval, statistical generation, and analysis processes. The reporting function consists of the input and proactive communication processes.

Customer Insights Function

Storage and retrieval, statistical generation, and analysis processes take the data collected by customer service and integrate it with other sources such as surveys and operational data. Findings and recommendations are produced based on the data.

Storage and retrieval feed the statistical generation and analysis processes. It is critical for the storage and retrieval process that all data elements are entered using the same classification scheme and that all data elements be machine-readable. This even includes emails from customers, CSR text descriptions of calls, and wave files of calls (remember that most analysis units now have access to text and speech analytic tools).

Statistical generation produces the raw data reports that are analyzed to produce value. A key mistake made by most customer service and customer insights departments is to produce massive data dumps that are then sent to many different departments. Such a data dump mainly communicates two items: see how many contacts we have handled, and see how busy we are. Few, if any, other departments care about either of those facts. The other departments want to know what customer service has learned that will help the departments succeed. Therefore, the data must be analyzed and tailored.

Analysis consists of taking the raw data from the customer service department and combining it with customer survey and focus group data, operational failure data (e.g., missed appointments, returned products, or invoice adjustments), and employee input information. After analysis, the result is a unified picture of the end-to-end customer journey. With a fully integrated complaint system, issues are clustered and reported to the proper corporate area, via the customer insights team. Issues that appear to be cross-functional or have murky causes can be researched either by the continuous improvement or customer experience departments. These departments set priorities and, if appropriate, take action or suggest that another corporate department take action. Not everything gets analyzed, and not all items analyzed will result in action. The customer issues with less financial and revenue impact may get rectified at the individual complainant level with no further investigation and no attempt at systematic prevention.

Reporting Function

The reporting function consists of two processes: VOC input to the rest of the organization and feeding the proactive communication process.

The *input* process consists of taking the previously discussed VOC analysis and tailoring it to each audience in the organization. In many companies, data are tabulated and distributed to the entire organization in one format. As noted earlier, these reports are seldom read, analyzed, or acted upon. The best approach to organizational input is a short report tailored to each major function, such as supply chain, manufacturing, and marketing. Each tailored report should highlight the top serious issues relevant to that function and the top quick fixes, which meet a minimum level of economic impact. In many organizations, this report is followed up with a short meeting to assure the report is understood and to assist in developing an action plan based on the opportunities identified. The VOC input unit can also assist in mobilizing efforts when the issue is cross-functional. For example, if there are questions about the life of consumer electronics and laptop batteries, product development of longer-lasting batteries can become part of the long-term DIRFT enhancement. Customer education, changes to marketing, sales messages, and product labels can become part of the short-term response.

The *proactive communication* process prevents problems and questions throughout the customer journey via just-in-time communication. This can consist of enhancing the marketing website to set proper expectations. For instance, many cable companies have certain areas where faster optic fiber is installed and other areas where only slower configurations exist. A map or index by zip code can educate customers about which products are offered in their area. Likewise, a Latin American cellular company publishes maps that show weak coverage areas, so customers know in advance not to start an important call when driving into these areas. This action has significantly reduced complaints and customer anger. We believe that the best defense is a good offense. If customers are warned before encountering a problem, trust is increased, and dissatisfaction is decreased.

Further, it is wise to notify customers and distributors when problems are fixed. A manufacturer of a leading detergent sent letters with coupons to the roughly 2,000 customers who complained about the scent. The letter described how the scent had been modified and included a coupon and a request to give the product another try. Some 60 percent of the coupons were redeemed, and the company received dozens of letters saying something to the effect of, "I am amazed that a big company like you actually listened to a few consumers and acted to change the product."[4]

PROCESS SYSTEMS FLOW

Figure 3.1 illustrates the relationship of the twenty processes that the customer service staff and technology must perform to deliver on all the service objectives. This figure helps the technology department to understand how each process requires information feeds from other processes. Further, it emphasizes how critical the classification process is—it is the linkage between the reply and the insights functions.

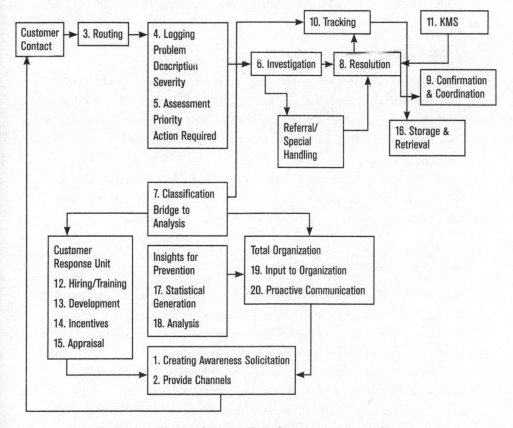

Figure 3.1. Process Systems Flow Showing Linkage of Twenty Customer Service Processes

When a customer presents a CSR with a problem or question, the CSR must collect enough information on the factors relating to the problem. The resolution process must produce enough data in the VOC system to facilitate future analysis. The detailed components and design of such a system are examined in Chapter 7.

METRICS FOR MEASURING THE ACHIEVEMENT OF THE THREE OBJECTIVES

While myriad metrics can be used, most organizations only focus on a small number. Therefore, we suggest nine metrics that can be applied across the three objectives—access, response, and input to the VOC—and a global objective, "Easy to Do Business With" (ETDBW).

Measuring the Access Objective

The *complaint rate* is the percentage of customers with problems or questions who contact the company via any channel for assistance, including self-service. If the motivation and facilitation processes become more effective, a higher percentage of customers will contact the company.

The *percent of issues logged* is an important metric because, if issues are not logged, the issues cannot be analyzed for prevention or included in the customer history to enhance the response.

Measuring the Response Objective

First contact resolution is the traditional service metric. It should address both self-service as well as phone/email/chat channels and must be measured from the customer's perspective. Customer effort aims at the same objective but is less precise.

Customer effort is a recently introduced metric that quantifies the amount of "hassle" a customer encounters in resolving a problem. The challenge is that customers will include website difficulties in their evaluation, when the contact center usually lacks authority over website content.

Satisfaction with the reply is the most critical metric. Complete satisfaction should be the metric focused on. Customers who are only somewhat satisfied are more price sensitive.

Staff turnover measures the health of the support system that drives both customer satisfaction and service cost/effectiveness.

Measuring the Input to the VOC Objective

The *problem rate* is the percentage of customers that encounter problems per month. This identifies the size of the opportunity for enhancing service and preventing problems. This metric can be derived from operational data, surveys, or from an extrapolation of complaint data. However, the metric is measured, the objective is to use input to the VOC to reduce the problem rate over time, ideally focusing on the problems doing the most damage.

Use of the VOC by executives measures the degree to which each function embraces the report and creates actions based on it.

The VOC issues resolved are the number of issues raised and reported by the VOC that are assigned to an executive and are eliminated or significantly mitigated—for example, the number of customers who report the targeted issue declines by at least 50 percent.

Where Does Being Easy to Do Business With (ETDBW) Fit In?

Being ETDBW is a major goal of most companies, and many have survey questions measuring it. However, confusion abounds as to what ETDBW means. CCMC's research suggests that ETDBW has five components, many of which logically overlap other service objectives, but some of which go further, such as ease of finding information and reducing bureaucracy.[5] The key drivers of ETDBW are:

- *Ease of finding information and assistance.* Most customers go to a company's website or the welcome literature before contacting customer service. These resources often fail to provide adequate information and can be a major source of customer frustration. Many negative ratings in metrics, such as the customer effort score, result from customer frustration with the inability to find service or information.[6] It is ironic that this score results in the traditional service system being blamed for a problem with the website, which often is not in customer service's jurisdiction.

- *Ease of access of the service system.* This dimension, including hours, speed of answer, etc., is addressed in the "Access Objective" section above as a key service expectation and objective.
- *Minimum of bureaucracy.* This dimension is one of the most insidious and hardest to fix. It requires minimizing the amount of information that a customer is required to provide and the number of people or steps involved in decision making. Both of these requirements are anathema to risk-adverse organizations and their accompanying compliance and legal staffs.
- *Complete FCR.* Ideally, the resolution will include emotional connection and effective input to prevention. Jeanne Bliss, in *I Love You More Than My Dog*, suggests that CSRs must imagine their customers' lives and deliver a solution within that context and the company culture ("be there" and "be real").[7]
- *Follow-through.* Reliability is a critical prerequisite. The tracking and coordination processes are responsible for keeping promises.

ETDBW is an overarching metric highly correlated to satisfaction with value for price paid and high loyalty levels. It is useful as a metric for diagnosing process problems outside of the service area and as a broad metric to be viewed by executives in gauging progress in improving the CE.

In this chapter, we've looked at an overview of how the customer service system achieves the three key objectives: access, response, and input to the VOC. The next two chapters will address two special aspects of response: creating delight and engagement, and working with partners. Each of these aspects builds on the framework of strategic service functions and processes.

KEY TAKEAWAYS

☞ Focus first on enhancing performance of the response objective for existing contacts and easily prevented issues. Only after improving responses to an acceptable level should you focus on motivating more customers to complain.

☞ Assume customers are honest, ask them what they want, and give it to them. Going for a rapid fix almost always reduces risk expense. As an alternative, a clear, believable explanation for a less-than-satisfying outcome is often better than throwing money at an issue.

☞ Focus on barriers to FCR—usually a lack of CSR tools, training, and empowerment. Analyze why cases are escalated to a supervisor or sent to another department and provide CSRs what is needed to avoid escalation.

☞ CSR turnover is due more to lack of success, progress, and recognition than to pay rate, although a best practice is to pay 10 to 15 percent above regional averages. Supervisors are critical to achieving CSR success and progress through positive recognition, celebration of CSR performance, and encouraging CSR use of empowerment.

☞ Effectiveness of input to the VOC depends upon the granularity of customer problem classification as well as tailoring reports to each corporate function. Tell your customer base and employees what you have learned from your feedback loop—"feedback the feedback!"

GOING BEYOND BASIC SERVICE: ENGAGEMENT AND DELIGHT

An auto manufacturer had the goal of "continuously exceeding all customer expectations." The company further expanded on this concept by explaining that they wanted employees to continuously engage and create customer delight. This goal was problematic for three reasons. First, it was impossible to *continuously* exceed all customers' expectations. Second, it was not cost effective because, in many cases, creating delight on top of already high customer expectations could be expensive and often impossible. Finally, the company never defined what they meant by engagement and delight.

Engagement is often used interchangeably with the word delight, but they are different concepts. Engagement means charming a customer to help build trust and enhance a relationship with them. Engagement can be aimed at individual customers or communities of customers. Delight means to surprise and give pleasure to a customer and is always directed toward an individual. In many cases these terms are incorrectly viewed both as identical and as critical to every interaction.

This chapter first clarifies the definitions and objectives of engagement and delight. Then, best practices for each activity are presented, adapted to a range of face-to-face, telephonic, and electronic interactions. Finally, we provide metrics for measuring success.

CLARIFYING DEFINITIONS

Engagement can be a noun or a verb. We define engagement as the extent of the relationship a company has with a customer. This can range from a single, plain vanilla transaction to an ongoing emotional relationship where the customer is highly engaged, and completely trusts and advocates for the company. The verb of engaging a customer describes interactions and customer touches, which attempt to increase the extent of customers' involvement along the continuum described above, and strengthen the relationship.

Delight consists of a positive surprise or unanticipated pleasant experience. Delighters may be minor or major events. A positive, funny comment during a boring or negative airline experience or an unanticipated to-go cup of coffee after a restaurant breakfast can cause delight. Likewise, an unexpected upgrade to a hotel suite can also cause joy and pleasure.

Engagement and delight actions have four objectives:

- *Strengthening relationship.* Effective engagement moves customers farther up the relationship/trust continuum. Highly engaged customers are three times as likely to say they "will definitely repurchase" a product than those who are not highly engaged.[1]
- *Fostering WOM.* By causing/providing pleasure and joy, the company makes the interaction remarkable and thereby fosters WOM and word-of-mouse. Also, 90 percent of highly engaged customers make positive recommendations of the company's brand versus 60 percent for less-engaged customers.[2]
- *Cross-selling.* When the customer is highly engaged and delighted, trust is high, and the customer will be more willing to buy other products and services from the company.

- *Providing value to the customer community.* By providing value in the form of entertainment and knowledge to the customer community, the company creates a self-reinforcing process where customers confirm the special value of the company to other customers.

BEST PRACTICES FOR CUSTOMER ENGAGEMENT

Engagement can be achieved via a single one-on-one interaction or by a series of interactions that provide value and fulfill the customer's expectations. It also includes trusting customers and showing you value them. A company can also create engagement by supporting a community that the customer belongs to, such as an online community or professional association. Such communities can provide value in a manner that entertains or provides valuable information to the customer, while giving the company some of the credit for sponsoring the activity or community.

Customer engagement has two parts: *knowing* the customer and then taking *engagement actions*. If there is no information at the beginning of the transaction, the CSR must devote the first few seconds of the interaction to try to "read" the customer and then pick the best engagement approach. We first describe a few approaches to knowing the customer and then provide some examples of best practices for engagement.

Knowing the customer in a retail face-to-face environment is a good model for what can also happen in a contact center environment or B2B environment. For example, when a customer walks into a restaurant or coffee shop, the server may recognize the customer and immediately acknowledge him or her, rekindling the previous bonds.

The challenge is when the serviceperson does not recognize the customer. The server (or CSR) should introduce himself or herself, welcome the customer, ask how he or she can help, then listen intently. Chip Bell recounts in *Sprinkles* that when he walked into a coffee shop, he heard from the back, "Good morning, how would you like your coffee? Take any table you like, and I'll have your coffee there before you can sit down!"[3] On the other hand, Jeff Toister recounts in *Service Failure* a situation where a hotel desk clerk told an arriving customer that he had no reservation, and the hotel was fully booked.[4] The customer had a meltdown and caused a scene that required calling the security guard. In the first example, the server anticipated the customer's need and made a positive emotional connection, and in the second, there was no anticipation of the negative reaction and no attempt at empathy.

Tom Peters, in his most recent book, *The Excellence Dividend*, places listening as the number one employee attribute and curiosity (in this venue, wanting to know about the customer) as another "must have." He quotes former New York mayor Michael Bloomberg as telling *Vanity Fair* magazine that curiosity was one of his most significant traits for success.[5]

A middle ground of recognition is when a customer comes in sporadically, but the retail staff does not recognize them. At some Harley-Davidson dealers, the staff takes pictures of the customer on his or her new bike and sends the pictures to the customer in celebration of the event. The staff also keeps a copy of the picture in the customer's file. Each morning, the service staff reviews the files of the day's appointments, including the pictures, so they can recognize the customers as they walk in and greet them by name.[6] At PetSmart, if a staff member recognizes a customer walking in, the staff whispers the name into their wireless intercom, often with the pet's name, so the rest of the staff can also recognize the customer.[7] Likewise, we personally observed at some Ritz-Carlton Hotels, the bellman unloading the car whispers the name electronically to the front desk. Several companies are now experimenting with facial recognition software to perform this recognition and notification function.

The foundation of knowing the customer in a contact center environment is the CTI function that captures the inbound phone number, and any account information input by the customer, to the IVR and pulls up the basic account information and previous three transactions.

While authentication of the customer's identity is paramount in the current heavily hacked environment, it should be deferred until after the customer has stated a reason for the call. CCMC finds that, for our clients, 30 percent of calls are on general policy or procedures rather than the customer's specific account. In these cases, the authentication process creates unnecessary burden and wasted time.

Once the CSR "knows" the customer, either from previous records or from the interaction's initial fifteen seconds, the CSR can build rapport and engage with the customer to understand his or her needs and current mindset. If a file is retrieved, the last transaction can be acknowledged—for example, "How have you enjoyed the running shoes you bought last month?" If no file is retrieved, then the representative is in the same boat as the restaurant server who does not recognize the repeat customer. The employee should identify himself or herself, ask an open-ended question, then listen intently for not only the operational request but also, according to Jeff Toister, for clues to "how the customer is thinking and feeling in a given situation."[8]

Dozens of books exist about best practices to create engagement and delight. Here is a summary, based on several well-known experts and my observations:

- Demonstrate knowing the customer by asking about a previous purchase, transaction, or product the customer bought or used.
- Proactively deliver a service or product the customer most likely will desire—for example, offer coffee in the morning.
- Publicly recognize a customer's loyalty by acknowledging the customer in front of others, sharing that you are providing a complimentary upgrade, or giving a coupon for a free breakfast.
- Treat the highly engaged customer like a family friend. Jack Mitchell, CEO of the high-end clothing stores Mitchells/Richards/ Marshs/Wilkes Bashford, suggests in his book *Hug Your Customer* that successful retail and B2B service staff know, for example, the name of their regular customers' dog or their golf handicap. In his book, Mitchell defines "hugs" as personal touches that make customers feel important and valued, trust you, and enjoy your company.[9]
- Provide education and knowledge to assist the customer, so he or she receives more value from your product. In addition, communicating information makes the customer's life easier by avoiding frustration and hassles. On a recent train trip, the Amtrak

conductor told passengers as they boarded at an intermediate stop that the train was sold out, and "there will not be two seats together, so this is a chance for you to make a new friend." Warning people in advance with a touch of added humor mitigates dissatisfaction and, as shown in Chapter 2, is a strong delighter.

- Trusting the customer is a good investment, even when he or she is not exactly "following the rules." Chip Bell quotes Stanley Marcus describing a Dallas debutant who returned a gown in 1935 after it had obviously been worn. But the customer spent lots of money over the next thirty years and brought in all her wealthy friends. Marcus's wise comment was that "trusting her turned out to be a great investment."[10] Likewise, in Jeanne Bliss's new book, *Would You Do That To Your Mother?*, she argues that you should trust customers (it should be reciprocal trust) and treat them like your mother.[11]

- Help the customer feel good by doing good. Chip Bell tells of Rosa's Pizza in Philadelphia, where customers are invited to buy a slice of pizza for a dollar and give a dollar for a slice of pizza for a homeless person along with a written message on a sticky note for the person. The homeless recipient can take down one of the sticky notes and redeem it for a slice.[12]

- Know the customer in advance via assigning them a persona. A persona is a short personality description that identifies aspects of the customer relationship that are most important to that type of customer. CSRs should assign a persona to a customer after the first transaction, so future CSRs can start from that basis. Further, some companies, such as Avis, ask customers to self-categorize themselves using an online set of six personas, such as type of car and options preferred. Why do costly research to identify the customer's segment when you can ask them directly?

- Show caring (Tom Peters's second most important service trait) by asking the customer an open-ended question about his or her situation.[13] For example, Neiman Marcus Direct's management suggested that CSRs ask the customer about something other than the transaction (e.g., "How is your day going," or "What kind of dog is that barking in the background?") to personalize the conversation and not make it just about the sale.

- Greeting the customer by name is engaging and satisfying to customers. However, if the name is used multiple times and in inappropriate situations (e.g., too formal), it becomes transparent that the communication is a structured process. Also, in a phone situation, it is appropriate for the CSR, after noting the CTI identification, to ask, "Am I speaking with Mr. Jones?"
- Provide entertainment for customers. Old Spice created funny advertisement videos that have become YouTube sensations promoting the brand, some with over two million views.
- Provide public recognition and "fifteen seconds of fame" via recognizing customers on your website. Chick-fil-A runs an annual Cow Appreciation Day where families and their pets arrive at the store dressed up as cows. The corporate Facebook page posts videos of their costumed customers. Customers are also cheered by the store staff and receive free sandwiches. Until May 2017, Starbucks had hosted MyStarbucksIdea.com for nine years. Customers who suggested ideas that received positive votes from many other customers received recognition (including their pictures posted) for ideas implemented. This site has been simplified in the last year but was a key source of innovation at Starbucks for nine years.
- Do social good as a corporate purpose and/or in the customer's name. Starbucks stresses that its coffee is ethically sourced coffee and that customers who buy a bottle of Ethos® Water are contributing five cents toward clean water systems in water-stressed nations (according to the website).
- Provide useful, novel ideas to customers. Customers, especially B2B customers, always look for new ideas. An analytics firm, Unmetric, recently published an infographic that provided twenty-three universal ideas that marketers could post on Instagram. For example, the content can be linked to holidays, national sports events, and seasons.[14] In many ways, the list was common, but the examples in the infographic showed how the mundane can be made engaging.

Engagement is often aimed at individual customers, but similar activities can be directed to online and physical customer communities. For example, Intuit sponsors a community of accountants and

CPAs who discuss accounting and tax issues. It also relieves Intuit of the liability of trying to answer messy tax questions. An example for face-to-face communities is the Starbucks locations that provide a bowl of dog treats for pet owners. A West Coast utility manager told me she specifically stops at her local Starbucks when walking her dog because of the treat bowl—a five-cent investment that produces at least a dollar of profit each time.

Online communities work surprisingly well in connecting customers with other customers in the same situation. Health-care institutions, such as the Mayo Clinic, MD Anderson Cancer Center, and Inova Health System, all have forums for patients and families grappling with specific medical conditions. The American Association for Clinical Chemistry sponsors a community of lab directors. This community has a robust online element where questions about lab test procedures and equipment maintenance receive dozens of answers and advice. In addition, the community has monthly meetings in eight cities to allow peers to meet and socialize. The forum has become a major source of value to association members.

BEST PRACTICES FOR DELIGHT

Delight entails surprise and joy. Chip Bell suggests that delighters can be purely whimsical and ingenious. Because it is the unexpected that leads to delight, delight is often contingent on creativity and innovation. Here are some tried-and-true practices for delight from experts and our own observations:

- Encourage innovation and cheap delighters by providing examples. Southwest Airlines provides employees with a booklet of in-flight and gate-area games to play, such as offering a $25 gift certificate for the ugliest driver's license picture or the biggest hole in a sock. The airline honors employees who can add to the list of successful diversions and silliness.[15]
- Encourage employees to take risks. Tom Peters notes, "Whoever tries the most stuff wins." Innovation comes from "try it fast." He also notes that General Motors's strategy from 1950 to 1980 was

"Ready. Aim. Firc." while Microsoft's strategy from 1981 to 2000 was "Ready. Fire. Aim." and Google, which he says is most successful, uses "Fire. Fire. Fire."[16] Peters argues that rapid experimentation is the best approach.

- Do many well-measured experiments for process improvement and customer response such as A/B testing.[17] Amazon does over 10,000 A/B online tests each year, measuring impact carefully and learning from each experiment.[18] Companies should encourage CSRs to try innovative responses and then measure the customers' reactions via surveys. Many ideas will fail, but your company will learn many innovative, remarkable delighters.

- Humor can make a plain transaction engaging and memorable. Steve Curtin, in *Delight Your Customers*, devotes a chapter to intentional, appropriate humor, the best analysis I've seen. His discussion is savvy because, while he recognizes that service providers must read the customers and avoid inappropriate application of humor, he suggests some innovative approaches that can be systematically applied to make a lasting impression that fosters positive WOM. He advises tourism bureaus to work with local police departments to modify their approach to parking violations by out-of-state visitors. For example, in Cheyenne, Wyoming, parking violation notices given to cars with out-of-state licenses say, in part, "Howdy, Pardner! Welcome to Cheyenne. The Patrol Officer has noticed that you have violated one of our parking ordinances . . . but seeing as how you are a visitor to Cheyenne, we want to make your stay here as enjoyable as possible . . . the offense will be overlooked this time." The visitor is also reassured that a posse will not pursue him or her.[19]

Pitfalls—Too Much of a Good Thing

Trying to deliver continuous engagement and delight presents three difficulties. First, not every transaction can be made delightful, and the attempt can become awkward. Second, engagement and delight often require significant investment but produce little payoff in terms of loyalty and positive WOM. Third, in some situations, trying for delight will damage both the relationship with the customer and with other customers. Some customers may be embarrassed by the attention; other customers may be annoyed by what they perceive as the company wasting their personal, valuable time on another customer. Therefore, as noted in the Amazon A/B testing example above, impact measurement is a critical requirement for experimentation.

Watch out for four pitfalls in trying to create engagement and delight:

- Do not try creating an emotional connection with or delighting someone who does not want to connect. New Yorkers in a hurry usually match their stereotype. They want what they asked for with minimal chitchat.
- The company should not try to become the customer's friend. While Jack Mitchell noted that an individual retail employee could be seen as a caring friend, the same does not apply to companies as a whole, especially in online environments. The conclusion of an analysis by the Keller Fay Group in the *Journal of Marketing Research* found that customers on a website or online community are looking for what I call "golden nuggets of information" and entertainment, but do not want the sponsoring company to be their friend.[20]
- Going significantly beyond customer expectations risks unnecessarily wasting money, unless the CSR has an indication a specific opportunity exists to WOW the customer. Zappos's training program guides the CSRs in determining where WOW is appropriate. If the shoes cannot be delivered by Sunday, and they are for the bride in a wedding, the CSR will try to find the shoes locally and have them delivered, since 200 guests will hear about it. If the woman just wants to wear the shoes to a party, the shoes will arrive on Monday.
- Delighter actions can become the expectation. If the local coffee shop always has doggy treats, the pet owners expect them. If the shop runs out of treats one day, the customers with pets will be disappointed because an expectation is not fulfilled.

Metrics to Measure Engagement and Delight

Two types of metrics apply to both engagement and delight. The first type of metric counts the attempts and perceived successes of engagement and delight. The second type of metric measures the impact of the events.

CSR attempts to engage or delight should be noted in the contact record, at a minimum with a yes/no flag or with a code noting what action was taken—for example, special shipping, replaced multiple products, complimentary unexpected upgrade. Ideally, a second metric should note the degree to which the CSR believes he or she was successful, again with a successful/unsuccessful flag. The output is customer records with flags noting those customers who were engaged and whether the CSR felt the engagement succeeded.

These metrics support two important actions. First, in future customer contacts, the CSRs will be aware of the special treatment afforded these customers. A full history is helpful for future service. More importantly, surveys should be conducted with these customers to determine the impact of the engagement and delight action on customer loyalty and WOM. These surveys should be conducted with a significant sample, if not a census (100 percent sample), of customers who have been engaged.

The surveys provide the second set of metrics critical to managing engagement and delight—the impact of the engagement and delight activities. The impact is calculated by comparing the level of satisfaction, loyalty, and WOM for those customers who were engaged versus customers who did not receive any conscious engagement actions. In many cases, the rise in loyalty and satisfaction with price paid will be 10 to 20 percent.

Metrics for online and face-to-face communities again consist of customers exposed to the actions as well as the impact metrics of loyalty, WOM, return community visitors, pages read, and social media shares.

KEY TAKEAWAYS

☞ Engagement consists of actions to enhance the customer's relationship, thereby improving trust, loyalty, and WOM. Delight is a positive surprise.

☞ Successful engagement requires knowing the customer either from history or from an assessment at the beginning of the interaction.

☞ Proactive education and warning the customer of possible problems is almost always a cost-effective engagement and delight strategy because it also reduces problems and service expense.

☞ Frontline employees are the best source for innovation in engagement and delight.

☞ The loyalty and WOM impact of engagement and delight actions should be measured to support ongoing innovation.

☞ A possible downside is that systematically delivered delight becomes an expected standard of the product or service.

WORKING WITH PARTNERS:
RETAILERS AND OUTSOURCERS

Whether selling to consumers or businesses, most companies now sell through a distribution channel or network, e-commerce hub, retailer, and/or franchise (hereafter "retailer"). Additionally, many companies outsource some or all of the contact center and logistics processes. The advantage of using retailers and outsourcers is that a company can focus on its strengths and sell to more customers. The disadvantage is that the company delegates much of the customer relationship and care to a third party. This disconnect can damage customer loyalty and insulate you from your company's customers, losing both feedback and engagement. This chapter discusses objectives for working with retailers and outsourcers, best practices for effective retailer relationships, the pros and cons of outsourcing service functions, best practices for outsourcing, and metrics for measurement of success for both retail and outsourcing.

OBJECTIVES FOR USING RETAILERS AND OUTSOURCERS

The use of retailers and outsourcers has two objectives. First, by leveraging partners, the company can sell to and serve more customers and gain market share in a cost-effective manner. Selling through retailers reduces marketing and sales costs. Care must be taken to ensure that the customer's experience with the partner does not damage the customer's satisfaction and thus loyalty to your company. Second, the company can focus more on its core competency by outsourcing technology and labor-intensive secondary functions, such as customer service.

The challenge of these two objectives is maintaining a quality CE, ensuring that your company's values and image are maintained while delegating control to a third party. The key to successful partnerships is a combination of structures, measurements, and incentives. The partnership must be an overt win-win-win for your company, your partner, and the customer.

Best Practices for Effective Retailer Relationships

Formalize the Customer Journey Map

With any retailer, there must be an agreed-upon customer journey map that defines the end-to-end customer experience relative to the company and the retailer. This map must identify the expectations that will be set and key points of pain (POP) that will be encountered at each phase of the journey. For illustration purposes, Table 5.1 shows two POPs, for example, 1 & 2, for each of the eight major phases of the customer journey. The expectation for each phase of the customer journey is included with the POP. After identifying who is responsible for each phase and POP, the map should provide detailed guidance on how the customer will be serviced.

The head of service and CE then work with the retailer to develop three responsibility flows: 1) highlighting your company's responsibilities, 2) highlighting the retailer's responsibilities, and 3) a small set of situations where responsibility is shared.

Customer Journey	Product Design	Marketing	Sales	Delivery/ Onboarding	Product Use	Billing	Provide Service	Obtain Feedback
Expectation & Key POP	1 & 2	3 & 4	5 & 6	7 & 8	9 & 10	11 & 12	13 & 14	15 & 16
Guidance for POPs								
Company Responsibility								
Retailer Responsibility								
Shared Responsibility								

Table 5.1. Division of Service Responsibilities Across Eight Phases
of the Customer Journey

The boundaries for who handles what and who is responsible for dealing with each POP must be clearly defined at a granular level. The division of labor for setting customer expectations during sales and delivery/onboarding is probably the most difficult. If the division of labor is murky, the retailer's staff will not take ownership or will blame the manufacturer. For instance, at one insurance company, the agents and their staff blamed all mistakes on "those people at the home office." However, our client assessment found that the insurance agents' staff made two-thirds of the mistakes.

Setting expectations is always a challenge, and the more complex the product, the more difficult the task. For a simple food product, the label bears the brunt of expectation setting. This might focus on a range of expectations such as heating instructions, ingredients, refrigerating after opening, and expiration date. On the other hand, a cell phone or appliance retailer will have a great deal of responsibility for educating and onboarding customers. The manufacturer should supplement the retailer-provided education with references to the website. For instance, Dyson and Whirlpool both have stickers on their products that refer the consumer to the website, where videos can enhance customer learning.

A company has primary responsibility for servicing the customer unless a formal contract states the contrary. Even when relationships are formally defined, things can get messy. For example, when a yard tractor manufacturer first started selling through big-box discounters, retail dealers carrying the manufacturer's brand often resisted servicing products not purchased through their store. The retailers were unhappy because their dealership lost the full retail selling margin but were still expected to provide service to the discount buyer.

Ideally, the company provides guidance to partners on how to answer all prevalent questions and POPs. The guidance should indicate who handles which POP and questions. For example, in the auto industry, product failure issues in warranty are handled by the dealer (retailer), and those out of warranty usually are paid for by the manufacturer. Even for out-of-warranty issues, the manufacturer authorizes many auto dealers to spend up to $2,000 of the manufacturer's money for goodwill adjustments. If, in your division of responsibilities and guidance, you create provision for the top sixteen POPs (top two for each of the eight customer journey phases), you will be ahead of most companies in your marketplace.

Encourage Retailers to Solicit and Handle Complaints on the Spot

The minute customers must contact someone other than the retailer where they made the purchase, many will not complain. Therefore, the company should endeavor to empower the retailer to solicit complaints and handle almost every question and POP on the spot, but to always feel comfortable passing complaints on to the company. This should be part of the guidance and training. A major tire manufacturer provided signs to retailers that said: "Questions or problems about your X-Brand tire? Talk to the store manager OR call us at 1-800-XXX-XXXX." If the store was uncomfortable handling the issue, the employee could point to the sign.

Ensure the Company Has Access to the End-User Customer

In many cases, retailers will say that the customer is *their* customer. While this is true, the company has a critical interest in understanding the end-user's experience and satisfaction. Therefore, you must have customer access to safeguard your company's brand.

The company can maintain contact with the front line with three simple approaches. First, the company's 800 number should be on everything, providing broad hours. Second, the company's website and Facebook page are where most millennials go before calling an 800 number. Website chat and Facebook Messenger are both increasing in popularity, since they are almost instantaneous. In many cases, if the company obtains feedback directly from the customer and provides the information to the retailer in a positive manner, the retailer will view your intervention as a positive. Finally, providing an incentive to the customer to take an online survey will obtain a strong response. Several companies have obtained a 20 to 35 percent response rate. For example, Carl's Jr. and Chick-fil-A directly survey the end-user through invitations printed on the receipt that communicate an incentive for a response. We find that a coupon good for a free item is more effective than a drawing for a potential $1,000.

For companies with more sophisticated or technology-based products, the IoT provides a direct channel to the end-user. The Coca-Cola Company installed RFID (radio-frequency identification) chips in their fountain dispensers that use the IoT to communicate when the dispensers are running low on product or having mechanical failures. Several auto companies now monitor the use of the dashboard navigation/entertainment systems to see which functionalities are not being used. The companies then send helpful emails to customers with links to short educational videos on the use of the underused functionality.

Trust but Verify

When working with retailers, use visible communication channels between the end-user and your company, to receive customer feedback on problems and resolutions at the retailer—such as a survey link on the product, receipt, or your website, and your company 800 number. For major products and B2B contracts, proactively reach out to the customer with a welcome letter and/or a "first impression" satisfaction survey. Several communications and technology firms interview every new customer after the first thirty days about the effectiveness of the onboarding process.

Create Incentives for the Retailer to Do What Is Best for the End-User

Use customer feedback channels to the company to identify retailers and their staff that have delighted customers. Celebrating retailer employees and their managers is one of the best ways to foster a customer-focused culture. Toyota honors not only dealership principals for great satisfaction scores but also honors the service managers with events and trips. General Motors and AAA provide recognition and reward trips for the road-service crews with the highest ratings.

Build in a Quick-Start/Onboarding Package

A short, attention-grabbing onboarding package will increase the likelihood that the employee will make use of it, and the customer will see it and ask questions. One company used a headline—"We know you don't like unpleasant surprises!"—that resulted in high readership. Both telecommunication and auto companies use printed and DVD-based welcome packages to educate consumers, with mixed results. Many customers perceived the material, especially the DVD, as requiring too much time, resulting in, "I'll do it later," which never happens. Panasonic and Whirlpool provide delivery packages for electronic/appliance retailers to hand to the customer with a request that the quick-start pages be pointed out—also with mixed results. It is important to separate the critical quick-start guidance from the main manual and warranty. Most consumers will only look at one page prior to product use.

Provide Job Aids, Videos, Education, and Technical Support

This type of support for retailers will allow them to service the customer on the spot. Charles Schwab provides education and consulting to about 2,000 independent financial advisors (FA), who sell a wide range of investments, including Schwab products. These FAs usually have a staff of five to twenty. The Schwab consultants and inside service staff educate the FA's staff on operational best practices, including the benefits of adopting the latest technology Schwab provides. Schwab created an index of technology adoption that monitors and communicates how much of the available functionality each FA and his or her team are using. Laggards are flagged and reeducated.[1] In another example, PetSmart monitors the retail-level employees' use of the training materials. When 90 percent of a store's employees have finished the training for the month, the whole store is entered into a contest.[2]

Give Employee Discounts

We strongly recommend that company employees be given discounts so they can use and appreciate the products they are selling or servicing. Our research shows that when service employees do not own cars, they cannot appreciate the difficulty of breakdowns or repairs. Likewise, PetSmart consciously recruits staff who own pets and offers large discounts, so employees can use the merchandise.

Identify Retailers That Use the Customer Feedback

Most companies collect customer feedback on problems including those caused by or encountered at the retailer. A company then electronically distributes the feedback to the retailers in simple diagnostic formats that highlight the biggest improvement opportunities. Carl's Jr. distributes customer feedback survey results online, notes which field managers and retailers download the feedback and realize improvement, and those who do not. Retailers who fail to achieve satisfaction improvements using the feedback receive visits and retraining.

Get Input from Partners and Retailers

Moen created a formal process to capture input from more than a half-dozen channels, from new home builders to distributors and big-box stores and master plumbers. The input from all channels is collected and coded into the same VOC process, to allow rapid detection of product issues and innovation opportunities.

TO OUTSOURCE OR NOT TO OUTSOURCE?
THAT IS THE QUESTION

If you are considering outsourcing part or all of the customer service function, you must consider the basic objectives of any service system. First, all customer contacts must receive low-effort resolution to preserve loyalty and create positive WOM. "Customer effort" is one of the operational metrics that is now being used to measure effectiveness of the reply function, as noted in Chapter 3. Second, customers whose basic needs are satisfactorily resolved should be cross-sold, when appropriate. This means the CSR needs to know enough about the customer to make an appropriate offer and avoid inappropriate cross-selling. Third, the CSR should gather market intelligence and information on how to prevent unnecessary calls.

In an outsource environment, there is a risk that parochial incentives can corrupt the second and third objectives. Management may pressure CSRs to sell inappropriate products or not take the time to set proper expectations. Further, it is possible that CSRs will not collect data on preventable calls. If information is collected, it is useless if not analyzed and passed back to the company to identify problems and calls that can be prevented. As one outsourcer told me, "The cash register rings each time the phone rings." Thus, the outsourcer needs incentives for quality data collection and analysis. This three-part objective statement presents the first challenge to outsourcing. If all you want is to have the phone answered and contacts resolved, outsourcing is a simple proposition. If you want to achieve the two other objectives, the challenge is far more complicated. The following is a review of the major benefits and pitfalls of outsourcing service functions.

The Benefits of Outsourcing

- Lower capital investment is required because the outsourcer buys the physical plant where the contact center is located. However, if you use home-based contact center CSRs, this argument becomes less compelling.

- It is easier to upgrade contact-handling technology by letting the outsourcer make the purchase and spread the cost across all clients. However, if your CRM is cloud based, updating is less expensive.
- The outsource firm can be more responsive to demand fluctuations because it can either hire more temporary staff or shift existing staff to your call project. Hiring and firing staff every six months is a formula for more expensive and mediocre service. However, one large outsourcer adeptly matched a soup company with a winter peak, and a vacation company with a summer peak, thereby achieving relative stability.
- In companies located in high-wage and high-rent areas, outsourcing can free up physical space and achieve lower hourly costs by shifting the call center to a much less expensive location. When the location is outside the United States, the payoff of lower hourly CSR costs is more problematic because quality can suffer unless strong safeguards are built in. If the company has millions of customers, all of whom have a limited number of relatively simple problems, it may make sense to outsource because a large staff is required. In some foreign countries, outsourcers can retain staff for long periods, even if there is little prospect of viable career ladders over the long term.
- Outsourcing allows smaller companies to provide twenty-four-hour service without the HR management hassles of scheduling and staffing three shifts. In many companies, the overnight shift is outsourced, and the morning and evening shifts are handled in-house. The problem is that the overnight shift is often isolated and poorly managed, and more expensive, than maintaining two or three CSRs at the facility.
- Outsourcing can enable a smaller company to achieve professional call center management when the size of its workload may not justify paying enough to get a top-notch in-house manager. While this can be true for a purely contact-handling function, if the manager is also responsible for the VOC analysis and input process, he or she will still be cost effective in managing the contact handling as well as the VOC process.

The Downsides of Outsourcing

- The company is disconnected from customers, and immediate marketing intelligence is reduced, due to the separation of the outsourced call center staff from the marketing and operations units. Data in a month-end report are no substitute for daily interaction of phone representatives with marketing and operations staff. This issue has been mitigated in some companies by having the outsourced call center co-located in the company's facility, although the company then incurs the real-estate cost.

- Many outsourcers are located in countries where English is not the CSRs' native language. Further, in many less-developed nations, the CSR does not have an adequate product and cultural context. CCMC's *2017 National Customer Rage Study* found that strong accents are a major POP with American consumers who desire a mild accent and familiarity with the product and culture.[3] Strong accents combined with a lack of cultural context can cause both customer dissatisfaction and lower productivity. In monitoring calls at a Philippines-based outsourcer, we listened to extended phone calls where more than two minutes of each call were wasted with the consumer saying, "I don't understand. Can you repeat that?" On another call, a customer living in Las Vegas called to complain about a local dealership, but had purchased his car years earlier in Florida. The CSR, who was unfamiliar with the United States, wasted time searching for the Las Vegas dealership in the Florida database. Additionally, the CSR did not own a car and was not familiar with the frustrations of the car's behavior. A few outsourcers have successfully addressed these accent and context issues. See an example in the best practices section below.

- Lack of direct control makes it harder for the company to react rapidly to marketplace changes, unless you have a flexible contract with the outsourcer. Most contracts have a length of three to five years, incorporating upper and lower volume limits.

- Lack of dedicated management and staff can occur because the outsourcer also must meet other clients' needs. When the call center is in-house, the company's interests are paramount.

- The outsourcer usually has no incentive to prevent unproductive calls or wasted calls; they get paid for effort, not prevention of unnecessary effort. In a complex health-care product company, we observed up to 30 percent of calls misdirected by the IVR or central operator. The outsourcer often gets paid for handling misdirected calls, so there is no incentive to identify the confusing marketing message that causes the misdirected calls. For example, one nonprofit organization provided members with a brochure listing over fifty toll-free numbers for different products and services. Rather than ferret out the correct number, members would call the general information number, and the call would often be misdirected. Companies should limit toll-free contact points to no more than three numbers.

- The in-house service cost may be the same as outsourcing, if all the necessary management and quality safeguards and market intelligence gathering devices are implemented.

- Significant high-level, in-house staff are still needed to support the outsourcer firm's training, as well as for quality monitoring, call content analysis, and handling difficult or escalated cases. Further, in-house management must be available to develop new responses to new issues in a rapid manner and accurately install this information in the outsourcer's KMS.

- Outsource firms have a much higher CSR turnover, primarily because there is little prospect of career advancement beyond call center supervisor or subject matter expert (SME). This leads to much higher training costs and, if not safeguarded against, poor service during training periods.

- The outsource firm's employees are not usually available for the company to hire them for other positions, even though they may have years of experience handling contacts about its products. At Toyota and Zappos, in-house contact center employees are the base of the corporate management career ladder. These employees provide the most talented, customer-sensitive operations and marketing management trainees.

Best Practices for Service System Outsourcing

It is possible to maximize the benefits of outsourcing contact centers, without risking disaster, if adequate attention is given to ongoing supervision, measurement, and the contract details. The following actions should be taken to maintain quality service and safeguard the company's reputation:

- Require the outsourcer to continuously and directly measure customer satisfaction through an email survey to a random sample of callers. Be sure to measure clarity of explanation/response, CSR knowledge, CSR authority to do what the customer needs, follow-through, and willingness of the customer to recommend your company based on the response.
- Limit the percentage of calls *not* answered by a CSR within sixty seconds. While customers will often remain in a phone queue for up to three or four minutes (after being addressed by an IVR and told the wait time), dissatisfaction grows after one minute. Companies should require reports (for each hour of contact center operation) on the numbers of calls taken and speed of answer by a CSR, for all calls encountering a longer wait. As noted in Chapter 2, sixty seconds in a queue seems like a long time to most customers. This dissatisfaction can be mitigated with entertainment. Zappos has a joke of the day if you push 5, and Aflac insurance company lets you push 7 to hear its duck quack. *Average* answer speed should *not* be a service quality metric because averages are misleading. If call volume has strong peaks and valleys, insist on implementation of virtual queue, where the customer is called back at a certain time.
- Assure the company directly receives the outsourcer CSRs' input on what they are hearing from customers. At least some of the feedback should be *direct*, not filtered through outsourcer management, and *regular* (weekly or monthly). An additional provision that many companies have with outsourcers is the ability to tap remotely (from company headquarters without notice) into conversations between the outsourcer's CSRs and customers.
- Require the outsourcer to give CSRs all necessary authority and all necessary tools to ensure that calls can be resolved on

first contact, and that the CSRs move into a soft cross-sell when appropriate.

- Require the outsourcer to capture detailed data on repeat calls and unproductive calls, including reasons for calls that were unresolved on first contact. Several companies also require that the outsourcer provide digital files of example calls illustrating each issue.

- Give your outsourcer access to both the customer information file (CIF) and the KMS, so CSRs know who the customer is, the customer's value, and enough information about the customer's circumstances to make an intelligent cross-sell offer. The KMS should include all basic and enhanced services you provide to the customer, thereby highlighting sales opportunities. Some companies contract with the outsourcer to also manage their KMS, including receiving the information from various corporate functions and formatting it for the KMS. This same system then feeds the corporate website.

- Require that initiatives be in place to prevent CSR burnout and provide a career path that encourages staff stability. An excellent strategy is to allow the outsourcer's CSRs to move to your company as permanent employees after two or three years, not just in the service area but also across the company. Several auto companies are having their outsourcer hire college graduates at 20 percent above standard call center rates and then transferring the best into the company's management trainee program after two or three years.

- One Canadian-based outsourcer established call centers in Central America, where there is intense training to mitigate accents as well as to understand the United States' culture. Career ladders have been created, and health care is provided for the CSR and partially for family members, creating high employee retention levels.

- Assure that the price you are quoted for outsourced service includes, after basic training, a "nesting" period (sheltered live contact handling with intense mentoring and little pressure) of at least two weeks (more if the product is complex). This will allow the CSR to become comfortable with the products and response guidance and gain confidence. This leads to much lower CSR attrition in the first year. Also demand CSR remedial training to *your company's standards* when evaluation results are substandard. Finally, expect formal reinforcement training on basic service skills for all CSRs at least annually. Even the best CSRs need to be reminded of best practices in investigation and response.

- The contract with the outsourcer should reflect more than operational service metrics and include a staff stability target, effective contact analysis, and input to the VOC. Both positive and negative incentives should exist for speed of answer parameters for each channel (phone, email, chat, and social media), the customer satisfaction level, CSR turnover, preventable call identification, and effectiveness of input to the VOC.

METRICS TO ASSESS RETAILERS AND OUTSOURCERS

The following metrics address the parts of the customer journey that the company's partners (whether retailer or outsourcer) impact, including setting expectations, onboarding, servicing, and VOC. The metrics for outsourcers are more detailed and demanding because the company has much more leverage with an outsourcer than a retailer.

Metrics for Retailers

- *Retailer is setting proper expectations.* An indicator of incorrect expectations is the number of calls on preventable issues and dissatisfaction on surveys associated with product functionality and performance limitations. For example, if the customer is not told that run-flat tires are more sensitive to potholes and cost more to replace, but can be driven flat for twenty-five miles if necessary, there will be unnecessary calls on this issue.
- *Effective customer onboarding (for big-ticket products and services).* The best approach is to conduct a customer survey that confirms onboarding took place and that key facts were transmitted.
- *Feedback from the retailer's frontline employees.* Direct feedback from the retailers' employees should be continuously accessible and

useful. The company's internal departments, such as product development and management, and quality and marketing managers, should rate the utility of the retailer-provided information.

- *Random surveys of customers.* The company should measure problem-levels, the noncomplaint rate, and problem-resolution rate via random surveys of customers, as well as a compilation of warranty and contact-center reported data.

Metrics for Outsourcing

We recommend six metrics that will lead to an enhanced CE in the longer term. The following describes the six sets of metrics for outsourcing:

- *Operational accessibility.* This metric reports the percentage of contacts handled within the contract accessibility standards, as well as a profile of response time to those contacts not answered within the standards.
- *Customer effort.* Two metrics of effort are required for quality: effort in reaching the contact center and the ability to find information on the website if it was accessed prior to calling.
- *Satisfaction.* Four metrics should be measured here. These include customer satisfaction, customer willingness to recommend the product, the rate of FCR by issue type, and, for problems, whether the customer felt treated fairly.
- *Engagement and cross-selling when appropriate.* These metrics should be reported by both the CSR and verified via quality monitoring. The metrics should address opportunity identification and the success in engaging or cross-selling.
- *Stable staff.* Metrics for staff stability include data on CSR retention during the first year after training completion and long-term overall CSR retention, including second-level representatives and SMEs.
- *Actionable VOC input from CSRs and aggregate analysis.* The company should evaluate the VOC input from the outsourcer in terms of preventable contacts, response rules that cause systematic dissatisfaction (therefore not working), and emerging issues. One approach to measuring effective identification of emerging issues is

to monitor the percentage of issues identified first by the contact center versus those identified by other channels—for example, media, regulatory events, or complaints escalated directly to the company.

KEY TAKEAWAYS

☞ Retailers and outsourcers can disconnect you from your customers, placing relationships at risk. A direct connection with customers must be maintained via the creation of communication channels, including the company website and 800 number, direct surveys, and company-produced literature that educates, gains feedback on, and highlights your direct communication channels.

☞ Create a joint customer journey map with your retailers, distributors, and e-commerce sellers that identifies responsibility for setting customer expectations, onboarding the customer when needed, servicing customers, and soliciting customer feedback.

☞ Create governance agreements with your retailers and outsourcers that both create parallel incentives and specify a certain service level with mechanisms to train partner employees and measure the CE.

☞ Companies must provide great, reliable service and problem resolution to their retailers, so retailers will give a company's product preference and recommendations over the competition.

☞ In addition to excellent contact handling, companies should ensure that outsourcers report all preventable contacts along with their cause. This must be given as high a priority as the basic job of answering the phone, but requires separate outsourcer incentives.

☞ Encourage outsourcers to pay above-average wages and salaries and create a strong career ladder to reduce CSR turnover and create stability.

SECTION THREE

6

MAKING THE BUSINESS CASE
FOR CUSTOMER SERVICE INVESTMENTS

A number of years ago, we worked with a leading communications company, and the new service director had trouble getting traction for process improvement. Sales were expanding, and the company's brand study showed it was the leading cellular phone company in most of the countries where it competed. The CEO and head of marketing were content with the status quo, although they admitted customer churn rate was almost 20 percent per year. We executed a customer survey that showed customer POP placed 23 percent of the company's customers at risk. Most of those customers with a POP were also dissatisfied with the prices of the company's offerings. The CFO immediately recognized the similarity of the churn rate and POP levels, and the POP's threat to maintaining a premium price.

Our analysis showed that half the customer churn rate was due to POP easily preventable via process changes. However, if no action was taken, the easily preventable attrition would continue at 1 percent per month—almost $3 million per month—as well as each customer spreading negative WOM to nine others. The CFO, CMO, and CEO immediately bought in. If you can demonstrate the monthly cost of inaction, you can precipitate action.

Organizations measure customer service performance in various ways, few of them useful. Companies seldom account for the effects of good and bad service on customer satisfaction, loyalty, WOM, and margin, let alone on profits. As noted in Chapter 2, most companies that track and analyze service metrics use the wrong measures. Some even use the results, such as talk time, in ways that can undermine the CE—for instance, by causing CSRs to rush calls—therefore systematically creating dissatisfaction.

Strategic customer service demands a new financial view of service and of investments in CE improvements. This view stands in marked contrast to the approach most management teams take, which is to view the service department and any service-related activity as a cost-center, and aim to minimize its costs. The strategic view is to see customer service as a revenue preserver and generator and to maximize its impact on revenue.

The payoffs for companies with the strategic view are measurable and significant. For example, the traditional cost-center approach argues for increasing the throughput of customer service calls; that is, to increase CSR productivity by increasing the number of calls each CSR handles per shift. However, this approach can actually raise costs, because customers who fail to obtain first-contact problem resolution often "shop the system" by calling several times, or they escalate contacts to higher-level employees. Our client studies in multiple industries show that completely resolving a customer's problem on the first call leads to an average 20 percent increase in satisfaction and *at least a 50 percent decrease in cost*, compared with second-call resolution. In our standard industry research, we ask customers how many contacts were required to resolve the issue and correlate their answer with resulting satisfaction. A second contact results in an average 20 percent drop in satisfaction, and a third contact causes an additional 10 to 20 percent decline.[1] Those subsequent calls take up additional time, and typically that of a more expensive employee.

In this chapter, we address the conversion of the impact of good and bad service into dollar terms (revenue), and the resulting financial impact on the organization (profit/loss). The analysis illuminates the true relationship between service and revenue. It also shows how to identify improvements to customer service that will have the most impact on your revenue and, on that basis, decide which improvements to fund.

This chapter combines the implications of the customer behaviors examined in Chapter 1 (satisfaction, loyalty, WOM) and the customer expectations and company goals identified in Chapter 2 (process, outcome, and financial goals), with the concepts related to problem prevention and problem solving in Chapters 3, 4, and 5. The key (and rarely asked) question addressed here is: How do we decide which problems to solve and where investment in improved customer service will give us the highest return?

As noted earlier, most organizations use extremely unscientific methods of prioritizing problems to be fixed. They either fix the most frequently occurring problems or take the squeaky wheel approach of fixing problems that customers bring to senior management's attention. They also fund fixes out of the general customer service budget, or the function responsible for the problem, rather than create a separate budget and an incentive system for fixing problems. Even where customer improvement or other quality functions exist, companies tend to focus on cost savings versus revenue enhancement projects. Most organizations don't even think of these outlays as marketing investments, despite the fact that making or not making the outlays directly affects future revenue and profit in measurable ways.

Therein lies this chapter's main mission: to show how outlays to improve customer service can be viewed as investments in future revenue generation and to analyze them as such. In this way, you will understand the financial case for these investments and be able to make that case to senior management, and particularly to the CFO and his or her staff. Only by understanding the financial payoff can service be viewed as a revenue savior and generator, rather than as a nice-to-have function funded during good times and gutted during bad times. The positive financial impact creates the economic imperative for making strategic investments in customer service *now* rather than later. That imperative arises when management realizes that, for every month these investments are delayed, $X millions in revenue is being left on the table.

THE CASE FOR GREAT CUSTOMER SERVICE

Those with a stake in customer service must make the financial case for improved service and prove that a great overall CE is the fastest, easiest way to enhance the top and bottom lines. All organizational goals ultimately translate to revenue goals and, in a business, profitability goals. Even nonprofits aim to grow their membership or scope of operations, while still meeting their budgets. So, the key questions vis-à-vis customer service are: "What financial impact do the current CE and your service function have on the organization?" and "How much additional payoff would accrue from an improved experience and service process?"

Answering such questions goes beyond tactical problem solving to examining problems in the strategic context of the CE. When the CE is imperfect, it then expands to include the customer's interaction with the service process. In either case, WOM spreads and either reinforces your marketing efforts and generates additional customers or counters your marketing efforts and leads to fewer customers.

Figure 6.1 depicts a bucket with a hole in it, with the water in the bucket representing your customers. Your organization adds customers into the top via marketing and sales. Customers who have a good experience remain loyal and attract more customers through WOM. Customers who encounter problems and are dissatisfied leak out through the hole. Problem prevention and tactical customer service reduce the hole's size. If a company experiences minimal leakage, as is the case for companies like Chick-fil-A, USAA, and Lexus, then marketing can be reduced to save costs, while positive WOM creates a continual flow into the bucket—or aggressive incremental marketing will significantly increase market share by taking others' customers. In workshops conducted over 2017–2018, we surveyed CEOs of ninety companies with annual revenue ranging from

$5 million to $50 million. We found that in B2B environments in general, and especially in professional services, WOM can be the source of as much as 90 percent of new customers. Further, a 2013 study found that customers acquired via WOM referral tend to be more loyal and less price sensitive and therefore worth 15 to 25 percent more than new customers acquired by other means.[2]

Marketing brings customers in...

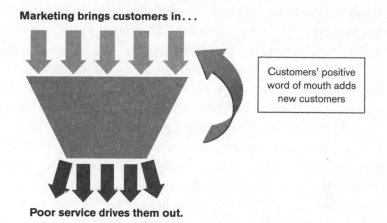

Customers' positive word of mouth adds new customers

Poor service drives them out.

Figure 6.1. Positive Word of Mouth (WOM)
Supplements Marketing Efforts

To quantify your current financial flows due to CE and customer service, you must calculate the percentage of customers who have no problem, the percentage who have a problem but do not complain to your company, and the percentage who have a problem and do request assistance from a customer service function or other department (or channel such as the retailer). Of those who request assistance, you determine the percentage left satisfied, mollified, or dissatisfied. With that information, you can calculate the current revenue at risk, as well as the payoff of three basic actions:

- Prevent problems via customer education, more accurate marketing and sales messages, and/or improved products and processes.
- Motivate more customers to complain, so they can be satisfied by customer service.

■ Improve customer service system performance, to satisfy a higher percentage of customers who complain.

The first step is to identify the three broad parameters: problem experience, complaint rate, and customer service effectiveness. Then the challenge is to identify and prioritize improvement opportunities that achieve the greatest impact on revenue and costs. In most organizations, the revenue implications of improved customer service are ten to twenty times the cost implications. Every interaction, from prepurchase to billing and repurchase, constitutes an opportunity to prevent a problem, surface a problem, or better handle a problem. Leaders like Charles Schwab, USAA, Starbucks, and Toyota view tactical service as part of the broader CE that constitutes their primary competitive edge. Meanwhile, many other companies capture and analyze copious data on satisfaction and loyalty, but then fail to compute these factors' impact on revenue, WOM, service cost, risk, and regulatory expense. These connections are what enable serious consideration of customer service investments by the resident skeptic, also known as the CFO.

HOW CFOS THINK

CFOs seek investments that will enhance the bottom line, and they support investments that will most enhance it by increasing revenue, reducing costs, or both. The investments that most enhance the bottom line are generally those that yield the highest returns, aligned with the organization's business, mission, and goals (one hopes). Investments in improved customer service typically earn returns well above those of competing investments. Returns of several hundred percent are not uncommon if all revenue impacts are included. Why, then, do CFOs and other executives often ignore these opportunities?

Historically, the financial impacts of customer service improvements have been hard to quantify. The line from cause to effect has not been drawn as clearly as, for example, new machinery to increased output, or even advertising expenditures to sales increases. Because the revenue implications of customer service improvements are not necessarily immediate or readily attributable to those improvements, CFOs often view them as speculative or even suspect. Ironically, many CFOs will admit such a link is intuitively correct, but they need hard proof.

That's why we developed the Market Damage Model and the Market-at-Risk calculation. These tools enable you to identify the revenue impact of specific experiences—that is, problems, questions, and POP, as well as delighters—by customer or type of customer. Most CFOs will be far more impressed with conservatively modeled financial data than with customer satisfaction data. The resident skeptic has long questioned the link between satisfaction and financial performance. The intermediate link is loyalty, which, as noted in Chapter 1, is measured by surveying repurchase and recommend intentions, and validating the survey data by comparing them to actual customer behavior. Therefore, the Market Damage Model translates investments in customer service improvements (prevention, higher complaint rate, and higher problem resolution) into pure financial terms. Likewise, the Market-at-Risk calculation addresses the financial impact of preventing specific problems.

QUESTIONS TO GUIDE MODELING THE CUSTOMER EXPERIENCE

A good analysis is driven by clear questions with answers that can be directly applied to the current situation. Therefore, let's be clear on the questions.

When problems occur or unanswered questions arise, the customer undergoes a negative experience. These problems, as noted in Chapter 2, can result in complaint contacts, or the customer may choose not to complain. Figure 6.2 shows example data from the B2B services environment, of the loyalty and WOM implications for the five possible outcomes of the customers' experience.

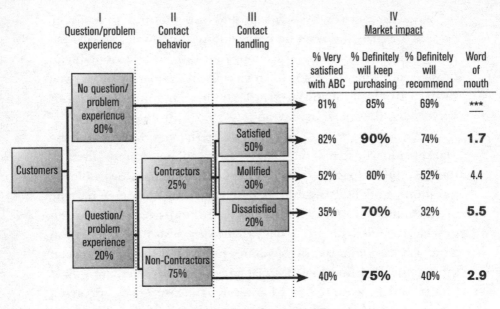

Figure 6.2. Snapshot of Customers' Experience
Highlighting Impact of Problems

Every organization must periodically ask itself three questions:

- What questions or problems have customers encountered in their recent interactions?
- What actions do our customers take upon encountering such problems?
- What are each of these problems costing our organization in terms of lost revenue and extra cost? Are some problems key POPs, and others squeaky wheels that do not deserve grease because they do relatively little damage?

Customers' pain impacts revenue, based on loyalty and WOM, in a way that can be translated into a direct financial impact, at both the overall service experience and problem-specific levels. At the service experience level, the Market Damage Model calculates the sales you lose by failing to prevent problems and to fully address them when they do occur. It even considers the effects of sales lost due to negative WOM. At the problem-specific level, which deals with the payoff of preventing specific POP, the Market-at-Risk calculation is the most precise way to measure the financial impact of specific problems and prioritize problems for prevention investment.

These calculations can become involved, so for simplicity's sake we will give one example where we first calculate the revenue damage of the status quo and then the payoff of three possible service improvement actions. Conceptually, both the Market Damage Model and the Market-at-Risk calculation assume that once you win customers, they are yours to lose if they have a bad experience. The models estimate the percentage of customers lost, depending upon the problem and the service experience, then convert customers lost into revenue lost and WOM impact.

A key component of the calculation is the value of the customer. As noted in Chapter 1, multiplying the annual revenue from a customer by the average years of loyalty enables you to calculate the customer's "lifetime value" (CLV). This value, or a more conservative fraction of that number, should be the basis for calculating the ROI in customer service investment.

It was shocking to find that many companies have not calculated the one-year, three-year, or lifetime value of a customer. *If you don't know how much your customer is worth, how can you decide how much to spend to retain him or her*—or, for that matter, to win him or her? Only with a quantified customer value can you make fact-based decisions regarding sales and marketing methods, channel partners, pricing, and customer service. Executives often fail to undertake these calculations because they believe the results would be too imprecise. Yet to-the-penny precision is unnecessary; a broad, conservative estimate of your *average* customer's value will support the Market Damage Model. Do not pursue breaking value out by type or size of customer—your service system is usually "equal opportunity," providing similar service no matter who calls. Just divide the number of customers into total annual sales and round down, and you'll have a conservative estimate based on one year of sales.

While the CLV is a widely accepted measure, few CFOs will invest based on CLV unless it is estimated conservatively. Therefore, we suggest using one sale and if, for example, that sale is for a product purchased every three years, such as a car, be really conservative and estimate one-third of a sale. In such a case you might consider that many families own two cars and in effect buy one car every eighteen months. In B2B environments, you might consider one year of a contract or the product price along with incremental services the client would buy. In addition to the customer revenue value, the second component of the financial impact from the customer's experience is WOM. Companies benefit when customers spread positive WOM and refrain from spreading negative WOM. Companies like The Cheesecake Factory, USAA, JetBlue, and Chick-fil-A get the majority of their new customers from WOM referrals. Some companies report getting more than 70 percent of their new customers through WOM, which means that sales has to bring in only 30 percent of new customers. These companies can spend relatively little on sales and promotions. When things go right, customer expectations are met or exceeded, problems and pain are absent, and satisfaction and loyalty ensue. So, minimizing problems, particularly those generating the greatest negative impact, represents a useful goal. Negative impact includes the customer's non-repurchase of goods or services, as well as new customers never won due to negative WOM.

THE MARKET DAMAGE MODEL: WHAT'S THE REVENUE DAMAGE?

The Market Damage Model calculates sales lost due to dissatisfied customers. This is a gross number, rather than one related to a specific problem. The calculation provides an overall picture of customer dissatisfaction's impact, making a case for retaining customers. The Market Damage Model originated from our White House–sponsored study of complaint handling in both business and government agencies in the 1970s. This model is also the progenitor of the Market-at-Risk model, which emerged from work for Xerox and Motorola in the late 1980s. Our research today continues to validate both models.

In keeping with the rigor we are establishing, let's first define market damage. At the highest level, we define market damage as the amount of sales or revenue lost or at risk from customers who encounter problems. To isolate improvements to be realized through customer service changes, we compare the customers at risk under the status quo to the customers at risk if an improvement is made in problem experience, complaint rate, or problem resolution effectiveness. Later, we'll show how quantifying overall damage by problem type, using the Market-at-Risk calculation, can help you set priorities planning the overall CE.

Here we're focusing strictly on problems and on how they are handled or not handled by the service process. At the end of the chapter, we will look at the effects of negative WOM and the nonservice-related customer attrition.

Data and Output

A calculation to measure basic market damage requires both internal data and external survey data. To keep things manageable, let's use simple assumptions and round numbers:

- Number of customers with problems (200,000)
- Percentage of customers with problems who complain (25 percent)
- Percentage of customers who complain and wind up satisfied (50 percent) or mollified (30 percent) or remain dissatisfied (20 percent)
- Non-repurchase behavior of each group of customers with problems (satisfied, 10 percent; mollified, 20 percent; dissatisfied, 30 percent; noncomplainers, 25 percent)

Figure 6.3 shows a sample of how the revenue damage part of overall market damage calculation works at XYZ Company, based on the above four assumptions.

The model shows that this company loses almost a quarter of customers with problems. Also, customers who don't complain cause the greatest damage. In this example, more than 80 percent of lost customers (37,500/46,000 = 81 percent) left the company without complaining. This supports our contention that it's wise to solicit complaints aggressively and to provide customers with easy access to CSRs.

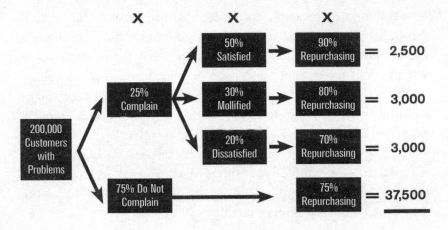

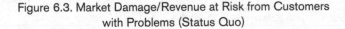

Total Customers at Risk = 46,000

At $1,000 per customer, $46,000,000 at risk

Three strategies: Prevention, Solicitation of Complaints, and Improved Response

Figure 6.3. Market Damage/Revenue at Risk from Customers
with Problems (Status Quo)

The damage in terms of lost loyalty and negative WOM comes from three sources:

- Sales lost due to the noncomplainers,
- Sales lost due to complainers who are dissatisfied, and
- Sales lost due to customers who are mollified (that is, somewhat satisfied).

On this last point, think about how often you are only mollified in service transactions. The telephone or cable company representative says, "We are sorry—the repairman will not be coming today, but I'll be happy to reschedule him for tomorrow" (so you can stay home and wait for the repairman again). Then there is the supermarket clerk who responds to a complaint about out-of-stock sale items with, "I'm sorry. We've reported it, but they're still having problems." They apologized, but you remained inconvenienced and much less loyal.

By the same token, the Market Damage Model shows the areas most likely to yield a positive sales impact if improved. In this case, at first glance it would seem sensible to satisfy, rather than mollify, complainers or to leave them dissatisfied. But the decision to fix a specific problem must take into consideration the damage caused by that problem, as well as the cost of fixing it. For that decision, we use the Market-at-Risk model, which we cover later in this chapter.

These simple, logical calculations appeal to financial mavens. Similarly, the sheer dollar amount of sales lost *every month* due to customers experiencing service problems motivates many executives to seek ways to staunch this loss of funds.

What Is the Payoff of Improvements?

The Market Damage Model enables you to quantify the current revenue hemorrhage and to analyze the effect of improvements in problem experience, accessibility of the service system (percentage of customers complaining), and service system effectiveness (percentage satisfied when they do complain). From the Market Damage Model's baseline data, you can estimate the impact on the number of customers at risk, by changing one or more of three controllable parameters:

- Increase the instances or levels of satisfaction when customers complain.
- Increase the percentage of customers who complain when they encounter a problem.
- Reduce the number and severity of problems.

Below we will show how to quantify the revenue stream response to the above actions: increasing complaint resolution rate, increasing complaint rate, increasing both resolution and complaint rates, and reducing the basic number of problems encountered by customers via problem prevention.

The Impact of Increased Effectiveness of Problem Handling

The Market Damage Model consistently demonstrates that increasing the percentage of customers who are completely satisfied after complaining will decrease the number of customers at risk of being lost. The example in Figure 6.4 shows the impact of increasing the resolution rate from 50 percent to 70 percent. This increase could be achieved, for example, by empowering the CSRs and giving them better access to information.

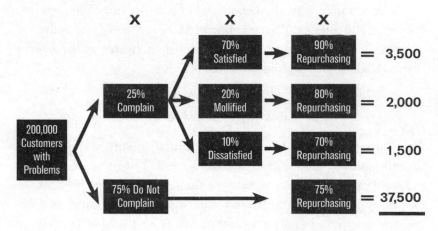

Total Customers at Risk = 44,500

Figure 6.4. Impact of Increasing Complaint Resolution Rate

Figure 6.4 shows that increased resolution rates save 1,500 customers who would otherwise be lost and reduce revenue at risk by $1.5 million.

The Value of Increasing the Complaint Rate

Let's increase the complaint rate from 25 percent to 40 percent. If a company aggressively solicits complaints, contacts rise to 40 percent or 80,000 customers, an increase of 30,000. Operations and finance executives often view this as unnecessary work. However, if the company satisfies the customer, it gains significantly more revenue than it spends on the service transaction. Figure 6.5, on the following page, assumes a ten-dollar service cost per incremental complaint handled.

The ROI in receiving 30,000 more calls from dissatisfied customers is surprising. Assuming a gross contribution of 25 percent

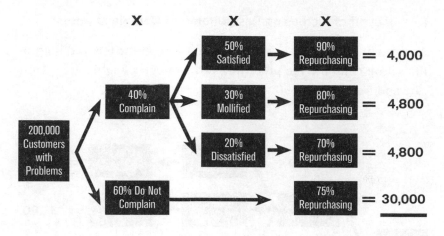

Total Customers at Risk = 43,600

Figure 6.5. Impact of Increasing Complaint Rate

of sales, the gross profit for each customer retained is $250. The ROI is 100 percent after paying $300,000 for handling the incremental calls.

The calculation details are outlined below.

- 30,000 more calls at $10/call (includes cost of remedy for some calls) = $300,000.
- $2.4 million incremental revenue.
- At 25 percent gross contribution, the incremental profit is $600,000.
- ROI is 100 percent, allowing for $300,000 incremental cost of handling calls.

The marketing, finance, and operations departments will often say, "Why get extra calls?" The above analysis shows that incremental calls from unhappy customers who would otherwise leave provide a positive ROI. Another response is to ask the marketing department for the cost of winning a new customer. In the above example, if the cost exceeds $20 per customer, it is more cost effective to keep a customer via effective strategic service than to find and win a new one.

Payoff of Increasing Resolution and Complaint Rates

An even more significant impact is achieved on the top and bottom lines if we combine the preceding two strategies, higher complaint rate and higher resolution rate.

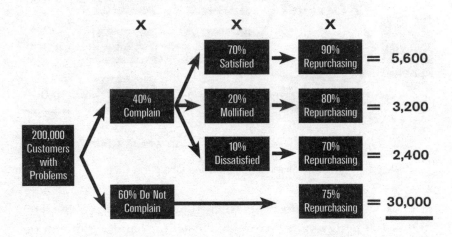

Total Customers at Risk = 41,200

Figure 6.6. Impact of Increasing Complaint and Resolution Rates

Figure 6.6 shows that a 40 percent complaint rate and 70 percent resolution rate will produce $4.8 million in additional revenue.

Payoff of Investing in Problem Prevention

The third broad strategy is to prevent problems via proactive customer education, honest marketing, and improved operations. In Figure 6.7, reducing problems by 25 percent significantly reduces the number of customers at risk. Spending $1 million on prevention activities, such as customer education, produces a large ROI.

This strategy of problem prevention provides the greatest impact and is usually the most cost effective.

All of the above strategies are based on positively impacting sales revenue. The customer service department cannot directly change the sales process to set correct expectations or change the packaging process to reduce damage complaints. Here again, strategic customer

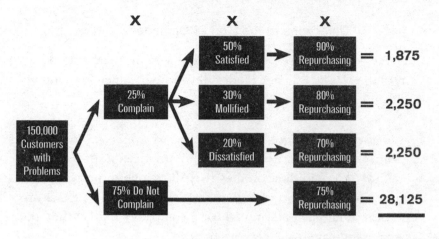

Total Customers at Risk = 34,500

Figure 6.7. Impact of Investing in Problem Prevention

service looks at which action—prevention versus handling after the fact—will be the most cost effective. To do this, you must understand specific problems' impact on overall customer revenue and WOM.

It also may make sense to create the correct economic incentives to enhance the CE, by charging the responsible department's budget for productivity or revenue lost due to problems they know of but did not correct. After all, if a department incurred damage and expense due to a chemical spill, they would pay for it out of their departmental budget. So why not apply that logic to a misleading sales promotion that causes $500,000 in extra service costs and loses $2 million in revenue? Such a "charge-back" system provides a financial incentive for taking corrective action. Several major consumer goods companies now have service departments that routinely charge the cost of unnecessary calls about sales issues back to the product manager whose program caused the problems. Likewise, at Amazon.com, the customer service department is expected to manage its dependencies beyond the boundaries of its role, using service-level agreements and active management of communications.[3] However, charging the cost of solutions to an account created for that purpose, rather than to the function's operating budget, might provide even greater incentive to eliminate root causes.

Objections to the Market Damage Model

Over the years, we have heard several objections regarding the validity of the Market Damage Model. The primary objections and our replies are as follows:

- *"Customers don't act in the ways they say they will on surveys."* Delta Airlines, Frito Lay, Cisco Systems, and American Express have all conducted longitudinal studies that show a large proportion of customers actually do what they say they will do. The exact proportion should be determined for a company's market, but a 50 percent estimate is usually conservative.
- *"The more valuable customers are the ones who complain, and we satisfy them when they do."* Our data from various markets—including high net-worth investors and aircraft purchasers—show that 20 to 40 percent of customers do not complain, even about problems that severely damage loyalty. Valuable customers' behavior resembles that of average customers.
- *"We will not realize the projected benefits that the model promises."* When organizations measure baseline loyalty and then make improvements, they see immediate increases in both process metrics, such as quality rate and reduced customer-reported problems, as well as stated intention to buy and recommend, as measured by surveys. This usually tracks closely to future purchase behavior. The key is tracking the actual behavior of customers who have experienced the improved service or experience, ideally using account numbers, like frequent-flyer identifiers in the airline example discussed in Chapter 2.
- *"Even if the service system increases loyalty by* X, *there's no guarantee that sales will increase by* Y." That may be true because market factors other than service can impact customers and purchases. However, sales will still be proportionately higher than they would have been if loyalty had not increased by X.

Skeptics of customer service investment abound, which is good because this doubt ensures rigor in the analysis. In making the financial case for investments to improve service, it is best to review the model with the CFO's staff in advance. Involving the CFO or his/her staff in the original determination of customer value, the impact of negative and positive WOM, and the data collection methodology leads to greater buy-in and acceptance. It can also decrease the rigor with which the case will have to be made. If you can get the CFO talking about his or her last bad service experience and the resulting market behavior, he or she will often quickly accept the Market Damage Model because it mirrors his or her personal experience.

The Word on WOM

Given the importance of WOM as a marketing tool—and the ill effects of negative WOM—it's remarkable that most companies have not attempted to quantify its impact on sales. Developments ranging from new theories of "viral marketing," to books such as Malcolm Gladwell's bestseller *The Tipping Point,* to firms dedicated to "buzz marketing" and "social marketing" evidence a growing understanding of its power.

In the past, our research simply quantified how many persons were told, and we then made an assumption about how many would take action. Our recent research suggests that both the extent of the WOM and whether it is positive or negative will impact purchase behavior.

In CCMC client research on WOM impact, we asked customers how many people they told about their experience and, to their knowledge, how many of those told acted on the recommendation. The analysis of the responses suggests that about half of survey respondents feel comfortable answering the question of how many acted. Across five client studies we have found that the percentage of customers who acted ranged from 10 percent to 50 percent. A conservative estimate would be to assume that one consumer acts for every twenty who hears either positive or negative WOM.[4]

An additional dimension of WOM impact is whether WOM is online or face-to-face. A study of over 186,000 consumer conversations found that "offline WOM" has a stronger purchase intention impact than "online WOM," and resulted in higher retransmission to others.[5]

Negative WOM will have greater impact in constrained oligopolistic markets, such as telecom carriers, where the consumer probably has only three or four options, and a persuasive negative review will eliminate the company as an option to be considered. In more diverse markets, like yogurt, banking, or shoes, the impact will be less because there is a good chance the consumer was not considering that brand to begin with. For detailed positive WOM, the impact per person told now appears to be greater, because a positive story will motivate shoppers to consider that brand. Our client research suggests that, for people who hear positive WOM, at least one in ten—and in some cases one in two—takes action, showing the ever-growing impact of others' recommendations.[6] WOM calculations can and should be factored into the Market Damage Model. As reported in client customer surveys, the actual number of negative WOM messages (and lost sales), based on the actions of customers told, can be included in the calculation. For example, in one recent insurance industry client survey, we found two persons were told a positive message from a satisfied complainer, four were told a negative message from a mollified complainer, six from a dissatisfied complainer, and two from a noncomplainer. If you add the conservative assumption on action taken, you can estimate WOM's impact on sales, as in Figure 6.8.

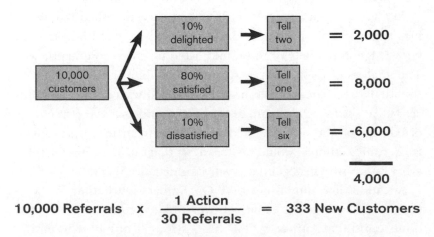

Figure 6.8. Impact of Word of Mouth (WOM) on Sales

As Figure 6.8 shows, negative WOM can be more robust, even from a small number of unhappy customers. The 10 percent dissatisfied, versus the much higher 80 percent satisfied, generate a much higher negative impact on a per-transaction basis. If one out of twenty customers hearing negative WOM would have purchased, but now will not, the loss is 300 customers (6,000/20 = 300). However, the positive referrals also generate significant sales. Even if only one out of thirty customers hearing a referral acts on it, positive WOM produces over 300 new customers per month. While this appears to be an ambivalent overall outcome, if you shift the balance toward more positive WOM, the company will experience a significant increase in net new customers. If these cases of positive WOM consist of compelling stories (as opposed to perfunctory comments), the one out of thirty hearing the story (3.3 percent) and taking action can increase to one in six (17 percent). In B2B environments, at least 60 percent—and in many companies, 90 percent—of new customers come from WOM referrals. Thus, it is essential to satisfy as many dissatisfied customers as possible, while maintaining the highest possible overall satisfaction rate.

THE MARKET-AT-RISK CALCULATION: IDENTIFYING THE RELATIVE DAMAGE OF CUSTOMERS' POP ACROSS THE WHOLE EXPERIENCE

We have found that most executives have no idea how much business they are losing in the normal course of operations, until they think in terms of the Market Damage Model. When they consider the financial impact even in gross terms, they start seeing the strategic value of customer service in terms of problem prevention, service system accessibility, and better problem solving. Usually, the next question is, "Which specific problems should I attack?" That's where the Market-at-Risk calculation comes into play.

The Market-at-Risk calculation, as the name suggests, enables you to prioritize problems for correction based on the portion of the customer base or market that may be lost. Typically, organizations are aware of the problems their customers face in doing business with them. However, surveys seldom provide enough detail to identify the specific problems customers encounter, and the surveys provide management with little guidance about a problem's impact on revenue. In addition, "trained hopelessness" ensures that complaint data will only indicate the tip of the iceberg.

On the other hand, if you present customers with a list of issues and problems and ask them to indicate the problems encountered, you can bring to mind forgotten issues related to the sale, account setup, installation, product features, use, maintenance, repair, and billing. Customers can indicate which problems were the most serious and did the most damage to loyalty. At a copier company, breakdowns prompted the most frantic phone calls, but our analysis of damage by problem type revealed that sales representatives' broken promises on installation did four times as much damage, although customers seldom complained about it. In practice, most organizations prioritize problems on the basis of frequency—how often customers complain about them—or on the basis of issues escalated to senior management levels. But neither frequency nor escalation indicates the most costly problem. Chapter 7 provides more detail about this approach.

As shown in Figure 6.9, the Market-at-Risk calculation for each problem considers frequency and damage as measured by impact on loyalty, increased risk, and negative WOM. For each problem, the necessary data includes the overall percentage of customers experiencing any problem, the percentage of interactions in which they experience a specific problem, and the percentage of customers who say they definitely or likely will not buy the product or service again. These data are usually gathered by surveys, and can be verified or refined with internal records.

Overall %		% of Specific		% of Customers		% of
Experiencing	x	Problem	x	Not Likely/Not Willing	=	Customers
Problem		Frequency		to Buy Again		at Risk

Figure 6.9. Market-at-Risk Calculation

The goal of this approach is to enable the organization to allocate its limited resources to fixing problems that have the most impact on loyalty, and thus on revenue. Again, as noted in Chapter 1, loyalty is best measured by continued purchasing intentions and behavior. As Table 6.1 demonstrates, the calculations gauge the percentage of the customer base put at risk by a specific problem and permit comparison of the relative impact of a given array of problems.

Problem Experienced (40%)	Problem Freq. (%)	Percent Who Won't Buy Again		Percent of Customer Base Potentially Lost	
		Will Not	Likely to Not	Minimum	Maximum
Product on back-order	55	20	45	4.4	9.9
Missed delivery times	40	20	30	3.5	4.8
Accuracy of invoices	28	40	90	4.5	10.1
Product availability within desired time frame	18	5	10	0.4	0.7
Availability of sales rep to discuss product failure	11	50	80	2.2	3.4
Ease of obtaining credits/adjustments	11	20	35	0.9	1.5

Table 6.1. Market Damage Estimates for Top Six Problems

The data in Table 6.1 show that the three most frequently reported problems at this company are back-ordered products (55 percent), missed delivery times (40 percent), and invoice accuracy (28 percent). Although customers experience back-orders about twice as frequently as inaccurate invoices, the latter problem places a similar percentage of the customer base at risk. The percentage of customers potentially lost due to back-ordered products ranges from 4.4 percent to 9.9 percent, while the percentage due to inaccurate invoices ranges from 4.5 percent to 10.1 percent. The second most frequent problem, missed delivery times, puts just 3.5 to 4.8 percent at risk.

In this case, the third most frequent problem, inaccurate invoices, places as much of the customer base at risk as the most frequent problem, back-ordered products. But when prioritizing problems, the cost of fixing them must be considered as well. We can assume that fixing the back-order problem, by reengineering the production process or expanding inventories, would cost dramatically more than producing accurate invoices. Therefore, the third most frequent problem, inaccurate invoices, would be the one to fix first.

Other costs and effects are also worth considering. For instance, missed delivery times could be addressed either by speeding up deliveries, which may require significant capital investment, or by having sales reps provide honest and accurate delivery times. After priorities are set, there is the question of whether to prevent problems by making process changes or to solicit complaints more aggressively and resolve the problem more effectively when it occurs.

The Market-at-Risk calculation makes the financial case for customer service in the best possible manner: by isolating the relative performance of various customer service areas and linking problems to customer loyalty. This analysis quantifies the portion of the customer base that is at risk and provides a customer-driven, financial indication of priorities. Again, as with the Market Damage Model, you can calculate the financial impact of lost sales, as long as you have a conservative estimate of customer value.

WHAT ABOUT CUSTOMERS WITH LIMITED OR NO CHOICE?

Some customers have little to no choice but to use a service. These include customers of many government agencies, utilities, and government-granted monopolies (such as railroads). It can also include internal customers of "utilities," such as an organization's IT or HR department. Such customers experience "forced loyalty" in that they more or less must continue their purchase behavior regardless of their dissatisfaction level.

In such situations, customer expectations may be low relative to situations of choice, yet most expect reliable basic services. When that expectation is not met—for example, when the electric bill increases tenfold, or the package is repeatedly delivered to the wrong address—customers will register complaints and demand additional service via escalation to executives or to regulators, both of which cost the provider. In one venue, we found that a complaint to the state regulator cost a California utility 600 times more than responding to a complaint sent directly to the utility.

Customers may also exercise choice when they finally have the opportunity, perhaps due to changed circumstances. For instance, they may switch from oil to gas heat or vice versa when the burner dies, or buy a car when they can afford to and forsake public transportation. In a technology market where a key vendor gave relatively poor service, we warned the vendor that over half the customers said they would migrate to a competitor as soon as one appeared. Two years later that happened, causing significant damage to the original market leader, as the captives escaped with glee.

With customers within an organization, such as those who rely on its IT department, the direct revenue impacts may appear to be nil. However, when we looked at issues that flow through to external revenue-producing customers *and* escalations to supervisors, staff time wasted, and staff burnout, we could calculate the cost of poor service to internal customers just as for external customers. Even when captives can't switch brands, they often find a "workaround." In one case, an oil company's operating unit was unhappy with headquarters IT and used part of its budget to hire dozens of its own programmers. They received more responsive service, but coordination and overall efficiency were damaged. Further, we have estimated that when front-line service staff are burned out and disengaged, they cause revenue damage equal to twice their annual salary before they leave.[7]

Such costs can be calculated, or at least estimated, with good accuracy, and the damage they create can be quantified. With that information, the utility, agency, or internal department with a captive market can prioritize problems based on unnecessary cost and revenue at risk. Though in absence of the profit motive, the economic imperative is often less compelling, but the estimate compels action, given that no one is immune from competition nowadays.

EDUCATE YOUR PEERS THAT CUSTOMER SERVICE IS A REVENUE GENERATOR

The financial impacts described in this chapter should galvanize most managers to at least examine the complaint and purchase behavior of customers who encounter problems. Our key point is that revenue and WOM impacts on the customer experience can be quantified. This requires collecting an ample amount of data at least once, but the return on these efforts usually exceeds the cost by a huge multiple.

On the subject of data, the departments for customer service, market research, customer insights, and operations all have reservoirs of underutilized, and often untapped, information from customer interactions and their impact. Strategic customer service requires that data from all touchpoints be collected, analyzed when appropriate, and distributed to the proper parties. This should take place as part of the ongoing VOC program *and* when problems occur. We discuss that subject in Chapter 7.

KEY TAKEAWAYS

☞ Even the best companies are leaving large amounts of revenue on the table (which can be estimated) due to customers not complaining about problems and instead quietly going to a competitor.

☞ When calculating revenue at risk, be so conservative that even the CFO says you are being too conservative. Use a customer's lifetime value carefully, if at all, because it's often not considered credible.

☞ Calculate what a 10 percent increase in satisfied complainers will be worth and try to achieve that improvement by empowering the front line to resolve more problems.

☞ Estimate current levels of positive and negative WOM and the net payoff; then find ways to both decrease negative WOM and increase positive WOM.

☞ Enhance the calculation's credibility by periodically comparing purchase-intention findings from surveys to actual behavior from sales data.

☞ Problem prevention provides the highest ROI when compared to handling problems after the fact.

SECTION FOUR

BE ALL EARS: CREATE A UNIFIED VOC

A major auto company was spending over $10 million annually surveying customers, compiling and reporting the VOC data. The joke was, "If it moves, we measure it." However, almost all the effort and reporting focus were devoted to the dealer organization, while many systemic problems in field management, headquarters customer service, product design, and warranty were ignored. One mid-level executive noted that it is easier to assign blame to the dealer base than to make hard decisions that would require corporate-level operational and cultural changes.

Contrast this company to a like-sized industrial company that spends less than one-fourth as much on the VOC, including surveys. This company harnesses speech analytics technology to analyze and report on conversations the call center has with customers in real time. It draws on multiple data sources, including operations data describing outages, field service visit failures, and surveys. The company integrates reports and interprets the data to create actionable information, used by every corporate function to improve the CE.

The company's robust VOC process enables employees to report frustrating interactions and suggest improvement opportunities for products, processes, and policies. This company spends less on the VOC process than many other organizations do, but gains dramatically more impact from technology to provide a complete view of the CE by combining surveys, customer contacts, customer preferences, operational data, and transactions.

Customer service directors often embrace a limited VOC view. They use it primarily to evaluate their CSRs' response to individual contacts and occasionally to assess whether the response guidance for a particular customer issue might need revision. If this is your approach, you are missing most of the fun. Your company must have a highly visible, aggressive customer insights function that gathers CE data from across the entire company. If not, the customer service director has an opportunity to create the VOC, to guide continuous improvement at the corporate level, and, in doing so, significantly reduce the customer service department's workload.

In this chapter, you will gain a more detailed understanding of how to create an effective VOC program or improve an existing one. Specifically, the chapter explains:

- Appropriate objectives of a VOC process,
- Key attributes of an effective VOC,
- Sources to enhance VOC data,
- VOC best practices in the customer service environment, and
- Metrics for evaluating VOC operations.

THE OBJECTIVES OF A VOC PROCESS

VOC processes can have different objectives for different company functions. For engineers and quality professionals, the VOC helps determine the requirements for creating the ideal product for the customer. For marketers, the VOC uses survey and research tools to understand how to attract new customers and enhance sales. For customer service executives, the VOC process provides feedback on the service process's tactical success. But for executives concerned with the overall CE, the VOC must describe the entire, end-to-end CE, not just the quality, marketing, or customer service component.

A VOC process will help companies achieve the following six goals:

- Identify emerging issues to improve products and processes in the short and long term.
- Set priorities for addressing new opportunities to improve the CE, based on an understanding of the cause (employee, product design, marketing, delivery, or customer use).
- Track progress on previously identified ongoing problems.
- Create the economic imperative for action on the CE by the whole organization.
- Assign ownership of CE improvement projects.
- Quantify, in a credible manner, CE improvements' financial impact.

While surveys and focus groups provide important CE information, they provide little data on the internal causes and operational details of customer experiences. What is needed is a panoramic view of the CE, provided by data from myriad sources.

VOC data should be timely and in a detailed enough manner to intervene, when it makes sense, while the problems are happening. For instance, if speech analytics detect the phrase "you people"—a strong signal of customer anger—the supervisor can be notified to possibly intervene.

One final caution—VOC refers to systematic information on the experience of *current customers*. A separate sector of market research focuses on winning *new customers*. Yet many managers and professionals view market research surveys as the mainstay of the VOC program or *as the* program. This is a mistake for three reasons.

First, the majority of market research is aimed at winning new customers. Therefore, combining market research and VOC confuses the study of existing customers with the noncustomer market, which is usually much larger.

Second, surveys taken days, weeks, or months after a purchase or experience are lagging indicators. An electronics firm we worked with discounted surveys, rationalizing that the company had already moved on to making new models by the time the surveys were done. Thus, they did not need to apply consumer feedback received about the old models.

Finally, surveys about prospective or hypothetical products and services can be quite unreliable. A classic example occurred in the late 1970s. Customers overwhelmingly rejected the idea of automatic teller machines (ATMs), saying they would not trust machines with their money and wanted to interact with real people. Yet once customers had round-the-clock access to cash, they quickly became fans. We saw a similar progression with online check-in for airlines.

KEY ATTRIBUTES OF AN EFFECTIVE VOC

The VOC process must incorporate input from all CE phases. It is far more than feedback from contact management (what most people call customer service). The VOC process also includes customer feedback on the access strategy, the service activities, and DIRFT for product design, marketing, sales, and delivery. The VOC process should also include CE descriptors that are not directly from the customer, such as operations that will adversely affect the customer—for example, missed deliveries, bounced checks that will produce a service charge, and higher water utilization that may mean a water supply leak.

As noted in Chapter 3, few organizations have effective VOC programs. A 2012 study found that only one-third of the VOC processes fixed the majority of issues raised by customer feedback.[1] We have confirmed our 2012 findings through assessments of fifty different customer service operations and the VOC over the last three years. The four attributes most associated with an effective VOC process with positive impact are:

- The VOC process gathers data on the end-to-end CE, from setting expectations to final product use, assuring that all CE phases are examined.
- The VOC process draws upon and integrates multiple data sources to enhance data credibility and impact, as well as findings and

recommendations. Sources include surveys, complaints, employee input, customer contacts (both service and sales), social media, and operational metrics describing what the company has done to, or for, the customer (such as warranty claims, missed appointments, invoice adjustments, late charges, and missed shipment dates).

- The company uses a unified view, meaning a single, agreed-upon reality based on multiple data sources describing all customer life-cycle phases.

- The finance department and CFO have buy-in and accept the validity of VOC analysis and output. This is crucial to the VOC having an impact and getting the majority of issues fixed.

Also, the study found that, of the more than 160 responding executives, 20 percent *did not even track* the percentage of issues identified by the VOC process that were resolved. You cannot have an effective VOC process if you do not track the percentage of issues identified that get fixed. Therefore, an effective VOC process provides an *end-to-end, unified picture* of the CE and its financial implications, which are CFO approved.

Unfortunately, data input from multiple sources to most VOC programs does not fit together. Given a choice, each department will collect the data and use the formats that are easiest and most useful for their respective functions. We have found as many as seven "owners" of different data sources feeding the VOC program, resulting in fragmentation and inconsistency in data collection and analysis. However, this messy organizational issue can be overcome if the following eight success factors, shown in Figure 7.1, are accepted and implemented at the company. They are all logical and usually accepted and endorsed by management.

One Executive in Charge

One executive should be responsible for coordinating the overall VOC effort. This will reduce fragmentation and provide guidance on how everyone collects data in their area of responsibility, thereby ensuring VOC data compatibility. This leadership role can vary from a limited, part-time, voluntary VOC coordination role up to

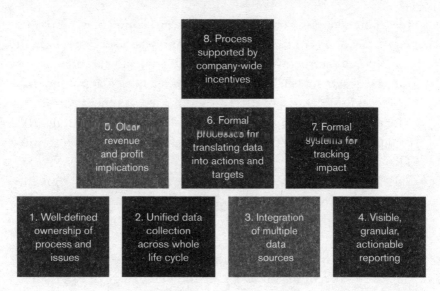

Figure 7.1. Key Factors Supporting an Effective VOC Process

the senior executive role of the CE leader. Where this position or role does not exist, the heads of customer service, quality, and the COO, or the CMO are all candidates.

Unified Data Collection Plan

Not all VOC data must be collected by one functional area or unit in a company, which would be impossible in a large organization. The data collection must be guided by a plan that allows the data to be pieced together and reconciled using a unified classification scheme, or at least coordinated across all silos. The VOC manager must create the scheme and enforce the plan.

A unified data collection plan ensures that all departments describe customer problems the same way, to validly quantify and understand the problems. At an automobile manufacturer, the factory engineers, sales and marketing functions, customer service, and the dealer service technicians all had different methods to describe the same customer problems. The engineers talked about subassembly failures and customer maintenance failures, while the service writers and service technicians talked of symptoms such as brake pulsation and engine hesitation.

In contrast, a number of years ago, Ford Motor Company began to collect consistent descriptions of problems and symptoms. One aspect of this plan recognized the importance of the way customers described problems to the service writers, when cars were submitted to dealers for repair. Ford created a small brochure to assist customers in describing the symptoms of their problem with the whimsical title "Is it a Rattle or a Click?" This helped customers use the right terminology and assured the correct diagnosis and repair.

The data collection plan must also use data collected by the latest technology, such as social media and the IoT. Traditionally, all data input to a VOC process consisted of problem codes and technical entries by service writers, CSRs, and service technicians. Now, a flood of information describes problems, product behaviors, and experiences from new sources, such as online reviews and social media. These data are textual in nature and typically would not even be considered data. Yet screen scraping and text/voice analytics can transform this free-form flow of customer and independent reviewer input into easy-to-analyze data, using the same classification scheme.

Data Integrated into a Unified Picture of the CE

Data from all sources and channels must be combined and reconciled to create an end-to-end, unified picture of customers' unfulfilled expectations and the disappointment sources and impact.

There are three challenges in creating an integrated picture from multiple data sources. First, the data from surveys, complaints, social media, and operations must all be compatible in terms of categorization of expectations, problems, causes, and impact on loyalty. Second, data that are not directly representative of the whole market, such as customer contact and social media postings, must be extrapolated to the entire marketplace to be comparable to the survey and operational data, which tend to describe the marketplace as a whole. An example of how the multiplier can be used to integrate data is provided in the best practices section below.

A third challenge is structuring the VOC data so it can be used for multiple purposes across different parts of the organization. Common purposes include identifying emerging issues, intervening on the spot to restore customer satisfaction, taking action to prevent or mitigate current issues, and tracking progress on previously known issues. Further, the analysis should highlight the highest priority issues, based on actual or potential market damage.

To do a job effectively, people need the right information at the right time. Given employees' workloads and the pace of organizational life, this means proactively distributing not only data, but also actionable analysis that "connects the dots" for operational managers who are positioned to take rapid action if informed of the problem or opportunity. Interested parties should be able to access data and proactively push the information and "connect the dots" for others, especially those who may need the data to take action. One of the more depressing occurrences at any company is learning that a problem could have been avoided if one department or group had been given information that another group already possessed. Sharing data with all who need it is a huge opportunity through technology. In the future, technology's role of "connecting the dots" could be as useful in customer service as it is in national security.

Issues Must Be Actionable

It is neither helpful nor necessary to distribute all data to everyone. Data overload creates more problems than it solves. Those in charge of the VOC program must know who needs what, take the risk of filtering and tailoring the information to their customers' goals and needs, and proactively distribute a summary. The description of issues must be granular enough to be actionable. For example, "billing issue" is not granular; "incorrect late charges on premium accounts" is granular. The top issues, along with the monthly cost of inaction and a recommended course of action, presented in a one- or two-page summary works best—ideally in at least two mediums, written and in person or video.

Chip Horner, former Worldwide Director of Global Consumer Affairs at Colgate Palmolive, told us he always follows up on the report with a face-to-face meeting. He wants to assure the information is understood and accepted and that any questions get answered. While tailoring reports to each function and reinforcing them via meetings is more labor intensive, the effort leads to higher impact.

Create an Economic Imperative for Action

Unmet customer expectations and poor service experiences impact revenue, WOM, risk, and profits. Quantifying these issues' monthly bottom line impact, and the monthly cost of the status quo, transforms inert data into actionable information creating an economic imperative. Unless the economic imperative to act is highlighted on the first page, the VOC program is just a feel-good exercise. Making the cost of inaction obvious compels action!

Another major weakness in the VOC economic analysis presentation is that most analysis simply outlines the out-of-pocket company cost of customer problems, such as warranty service expense or the immediate lost sale. This implies that if complaints could be reduced, costs would decrease, and the bottom line would improve. In fact, the revenue damage is probably ten to twenty times greater than the potential cost savings.

Consider two examples of the problems' real cost. When finance managers look at retail out-of-stock complaints, they think the lost sale is offset by the saved cost of carrying the inventory. But when customers cannot buy what they came for, they are less likely to buy other items *or* return for anything in the future. Likewise, if they cannot get replacement parts quickly, customers are less likely to re-purchase the brand. Low inventory has a significant future negative revenue impact.

In a second example, progressive finance executives view an investment in better quality and complaint handling as protection against regulatory action. One medical device company spent $100 million responding to a Food and Drug Administration (FDA) warning letter. The company's regulatory and risk executives now view an extra $5 million annual investment in enhanced quality and patient relations as an insurance premium against the disaster of getting another warning letter that could damage the brand.

Define Targets for Improvement and Suggest
and Test Potential Action Plans

Once an issue has been identified and the cost of inaction has been calculated, two other common factors impede fixing customer problems. First, the manager assigned to the issue must often start from scratch while continuing to perform his or her regular duties, so fixing the problem is a collateral duty. Second, the manager is rarely told what a successful outcome would look like in terms of movement in quality, operational, or satisfaction parameters. In many cases, complete problem elimination is not practical, but it might be reasonable to expect a 50 percent reduction in complaints. Suggested actions and achievable targets must be part of the VOC process. Some VOC analysts fear violating line managers' prerogatives, but most managers are thankful if the VOC analyst provides a preliminary action plan as a starting point and suggested achievable targets.

On the subject of setting targets, one of the silliest exercises we've seen is "satisfaction planning" for the upcoming year. A company that has, for example, a 76 percent loyalty level will select a target level of 80 percent for the next year. Why 80 percent? The rationale usually is that 80 is higher than 76. This is irrational target setting. A better alternative is to use the Market-at-Risk analysis from Chapter 6 to identify the high ROI improvements, assign responsibility for implementation, and use this information to suggest the expected increase in loyalty and satisfaction. Further, process metrics should be identified that lead to the desired outcome improvement. An improvement in the process metric will imply a similar improvement in the outcome metric. For instance, a reduction of calls requesting invoice adjustments could logically be expected to be a precursor to a decline in customer dissatisfaction with invoice accuracy. This analysis equips management with actionable plans for hitting satisfaction goals.

The customer service director should work with continuous improvement when acting as an internal consultant to the rest of the company. The action plans should allow for experimentation with multiple messages and strategies for setting and meeting customer expectations, accompanied with appropriate process metrics. A/B testing should be a habit. Ed O'Day, senior vice president of member communications at AARP, says, "At AARP, we are aware we have many diverse types of members. We have created a continuous improvement process that is constantly measuring, listening, experimenting, and innovating with a variety of communication channels. We build on what works and discard what doesn't. This approach has lifted member satisfaction with service to record high levels."[2]

Track Results

Once actions linked to improving both the CE and the organization's financial performance are assigned, identified issues need to get fixed. Most companies file an action plan and then consider the matter closed, rarely checking to see if someone moved the needle. Effective organizations require process tracking and measure the percentage of issues raised by the VOC that were addressed. Key questions include: Did the issue get fixed? For ongoing issues, what is the proposed action plan's status? Are we making progress?

The key metric for evaluating the VOC process performance is the percentage of issues identified by the VOC that are fixed in a timely manner. The information should be reported to the CFO and other senior management officials. Otherwise, the VOC process will have little or no impact.

Establish Incentives Tied Directly to the VOC Issues

If the VOC is to both proactively respond to customer needs and increase loyalty, then the VOC process must be linked to both strategic and day-to-day decision making. This connection occurs when senior management accepts the VOC's strategic importance, ties incentives to suggested actions, and funds those incentives. The VOC manager must also have a seat at the decision-making table and be able and willing to generate buy-in across functions. We generally find that for the VOC to make a positive impact (meaning that management addresses the identified issues), at least 10 percent of managers' incentive compensation must be linked to taking action on VOC initiatives.

SOURCES TO ENHANCE VOC DATA

When you look at an object with one eye closed, you cannot see how far away it is because you have only one source of input. Likewise, when you look at only one type of customer data, your view can be dangerously skewed. The following seven information sources, many of which are ignored or go untapped in most organizations, will enable you to perceive the CE more accurately. We lead with a discussion of survey data, followed by customer contact data, for two reasons. Survey data are the primary means of determining both customer satisfaction and customer service impact on loyalty and WOM. Second, surveys and complaint data are the two primary sources used in most companies. We strongly feel that these two data sources are critical but often insufficient to create a compelling VOC. Further, we have found that surveys are so poorly executed in most companies that we have devoted Chapter 8 to how surveys should be properly managed.

Survey Data

Surveys can include complex relationship surveys, follow-up after contacts, pop-up surveys on websites, and pulse surveys to explore a particular aspect of the CE. Surveys are the most reliable data source on loyalty and WOM impact and can also provide a view of the end-to-end CE from the customer's perspective. If based on statistically sound samples, surveys are more representative of the CE of the entire customer base than complaint and contact data.

Survey data, as noted, have limitations. Drawbacks include:

- The potential for bias created by survey design and sampling techniques. For example, phone surveys to landlines miss consumers who only have cell phones.
- The cost per completed survey can be high when conducted face-to-face or by telephone.
- Most surveys require time to collate and process the data, although surveys associated with many CRM systems now produce results in almost real time.

- Customer surveys cannot necessarily explain why something occurred within company processes.
- Surveys are ineffective at measuring hypotheticals.

On balance, surveys are an important VOC component, but are insufficient by themselves to support a best practice version of the VOC process.

Customer Contact Data

Many companies triage all customer contacts into complaints and inquiries. Complaints are usually coded separately and given more weight than inquiries. Often complaints and inquires have the same content. Complaints are often just slightly more forcefully presented. On the other hand, customers' problem statements are rarely recognized as complaints. For example, when a customer questions a service charge, is that an inquiry or a complaint? If they say they cannot find a product and ask what retail location has the item in stock, is the communication a question of where to buy, or is it a complaint that the product cannot be found? A further subset of these contacts is escalated complaints—for example, when someone asks to speak to a supervisor or calls the company president's office.

Customer contact data are often produced in real time from customer interactions with the service system, mainly by phone, IVR systems, chat, and email. These data have the advantage of being timelier than surveys and often have palpable emotional content. Recordings of customer complaints, played when presenting statistics to management or manufacturing plant floor staff, have far more impact than numbers. Unstructured data, whether recordings or CSR case notes, can be converted into coded descriptive data either manually or with speech/text analytic software.

Contact data are harder to interpret since they only represent a small percentage of customers with questions. Most questions go unasked. Some issues (whether defined as a question or problem) are less critical (e.g., late charges) and less likely to result in calls than other issues, such as missing parts for a birthday toy. The multiplier for contact data, first introduced in Chapter 2, can be as low as 2 to 1 (implying a 50 percent contact rate) and as high as 100 to 1, or even 2,000 to 1. For any problem or question, only a small percentage of customers will complain. Those who complain will voice their issue to several different touch points. Thus, it is important to extrapolate contact data from each major touch point to the customer base and the marketplace, so the data can be tied to survey and operational data.

Escalated complaint data include not only what the original problem was but also a reason for its escalation. This second data element indicates where the primary response process is inconsistent or flawed. Customer contact data from all sources—call centers, internet, and technical self-service—provide timely and robust input on the CE.

In addition, contact data can provide valuable clues about the problem causes, including customer expectations and actions. All of these can help you prevent problems from recurring. For instance, a former client that is a packaged foods company received complaints about mold in spaghetti sauce, shortly after it eliminated preservatives, for marketing and health reasons. Analysis of discussions with consumers revealed that complaints increased when consumers left the opened jar of sauce in the fridge for over two weeks. Adding a note to the label that said, "May be refrigerated for up to seven days after opening," dramatically reduced complaints.

Finally, positive comments can be used as staff motivators. Numerous survey devices exist to obtain and provide immediate feedback to management on great staff performance (as well as complaints) with one touch of their mobile phone. Some of the tools are location based, and Google Maps and background tools do the work of finding and delivering the message to the business's management within two minutes. Positive feedback can *immediately* be given to employees and celebrated in daily stand-up meetings, which is a huge motivator.

Operations Metrics

Internal operational and operations exception metrics tell you what is happening to the customer, often before the customer is aware of it, and thus can serve as leading indicators. What happens internally to the company then happens to the customer. For instance, FedEx and UPS know when package deliveries will be delayed due to airport closures. These metrics portray the cause-and-effect relationship between a company's actions and customer reactions. The internal metrics include, for example, the number of orders processed. Operations exception metrics include instances of operational failures, such as returned mail (signifying the company has a wrong address), website crashes, failed credit card transactions, and missed deliveries—all of which enable you to predict customers' negative reactions in advance. Other useful internal exception metrics include returned products, warranty claims, and invoice adjustments—each of which implies a customer disappointment.

Operating managers tend to trust operational information derived from their own systems more than survey and complaint data. Given that operations departments produce the operations reports, the operations manager finds it hard to refute the data. Yet internal metrics in exception and error reports, like those on late deliveries and inaccurate orders, are rarely viewed as actions that affect customers negatively, even when they do!

For example, consider the metric "retail items out of stock." If you have data on short deliveries of chicken legs to your store, and you know the average number of customers who buy this product when on sale (for example, 300), you can estimate how many customers will be disappointed when on-sale chicken legs are out of stock for two days (600). Reporting that 600 customers were disappointed sounds a lot worse than saying chicken legs were out of stock for two days. When you combine data from internal metrics with survey data quantifying the impact on customer loyalty, you can estimate the revenue lost as a result of such a "minor" logistical error.

Internal Quality Metrics

Internal quality metrics include inspection of products and services as well as evaluations of service access and service delivery. Product inspection data only look at physical product quality issues, such as no scratches and proper assembly. Product quality and inspection does not measure or even consider design issues or unmet expectations due to misleading marketing. Service quality metrics can include customer wait time on hold, evaluations of call content, and how interactions were handled.

The big opportunity for contact centers comes from evaluating the service delivery calls, but with a different objective. Most evaluators listen to calls to determine whether the CSR followed protocol and was courteous, and possibly to ask if there was a better way of responding to the issue. Evaluators seldom try to understand the call's underlying reason. There is great opportunity in asking, "Could this call have been avoided and/or anticipated?"

Mobile Contacts and Interactions

Mobile contacts (beyond phone calls) include text messages and GPS check-in apps. The text messages are increasing but are not a major channel for inbound customer service, though they are becoming a medium for outbound confirmation of service calls and medical appointments. The mobile check-ins take place when a customer enters or walks close to a retail location, and the company recognizes their phone. The customer is then sent a promotional offer to encourage purchases. Yes, you need the capacity to handle a mobile workload, but it is like phone, email, and web interactions. They are all part of your existing workload, but come with higher expectations of immediate response and reaction.

Social Media, Online Reviews, Communities, and Other Unstructured Data

This information extends from the actual text of social media and online community interactions to emails and online reviews. When manually reviewed or, more practically, analyzed using text/speech analytics software, this information can provide valuable insight to a broad range of issues. Examples include problem frequency and causes, how often certain words are used, customer expectations, emotion levels, company response effectiveness, and damage to loyalty.

Social media and call recordings are also invaluable in "humanizing" the data. Saying, "Eighty-five customers had a problem," is interesting, but attaching an emotional quote dramatically enhances the impact. One of our clients, a New York utility, used a report entitled "The Mood of the Mail," which included customer comments, complete with swear words and sarcasm. It was one of the most widely read company reports.

As noted in Chapter 2, contrary to popular perception, most consumers do not turn first to social media. In general, consumers want to complain in private, which is where mobile apps that convey the complaint directly to the retail location come in handy. A 2011 IntelliResponse study found that less than 1 percent of consumer interactions with companies via social media were complaints.[3] This number exactly matched the finding of CCMC's *2011 National Customer Rage Study*.[4] The *2017 National Customer Rage Study* found that this number only rose to 5 percent, even for consumers' most serious problem of the year, technology involving cable, cell phone, and computers. So social media is still NOT a major channel for complaints, even in 2017.[5] On the other hand, a 2012 study by Argentina-based Proaxion found that 25 percent of Argentinians complained first via social media.[6] Two CCMC/LearningIt studies in Japan found that for products as diverse as cosmetics and bathroom fixtures, more than 10 percent of consumers commented on social media.[7] Suffice it to say, in this fast-evolving space, no consistent rule can be applied across different cultures.

Online communities, especially among business users, are good sources of intelligence on customer problems and attitudes. Intuit, the maker of popular finance and accounting software programs, sponsors an online community of thousands of accounting professionals. These users readily report problems and advise each other. In many cases, Intuit's customers are more comfortable telling others in the network about issues, rather than complaining to the company. Intuit facilitates forums and can observe and learn from the conversations. While many companies get most of their input from Facebook pages, General Motors only gets 7 percent of its social input from that source. The vast majority of social input for General Motors comes from online communities of car enthusiasts.

Likewise, online review sites such as OpenTable and TripAdvisor are great sources of diagnostic information about the CE, even though bogus reviews, both positive and negative, are on the rise. This is another reason for using social media as just one of multiple sources. When reviews are positive and specific, they can also motivate staff. The challenge for using social media community and review site data is the same as that of customer complaints and contact data: You must decide how to extrapolate the data to the marketplace as a whole.

Employee Input

There are two major types of employee input on the CE: employee surveys and information from employee input processes using email or instant messaging systems. Employees often see customer issues when customers see them. The question is how to inject this insight to the VOC process. Employee surveys are traditionally focused on employee happiness with pay, benefits, and supervision, with some attention to training and advancement. This is not very helpful in understanding the CE. However, a survey that asks employees about the specific issues that frustrate them, their causes, how often they arise, and how much time is wasted each time they occur *does* provide valuable information.

Rapid issue input processes can be a great source for identifying emerging issues, since they can often highlight problems not found in surveys and inspection mechanisms. For example, one airline has a feedback system that requires the lead flight attendant to send an email within thirty minutes of landing that summarizes the three top customer issues encountered on the flight. Three issues per flight times 2,000 flights a day provides 6,000 in-flight issue data points per day, almost in real time.

Summary of Data Source Strengths and Weaknesses

Each data source describing the CE has its pros and cons. We recommend collecting and integrating all seven types of data, in spite of the cons, because each source provides a different and unique perspective. Table 7.1 summarizes their strengths and weaknesses.

Source	Strengths	Weaknesses
Internal operational metrics Transaction and system records of what the company did and did not do to/for the customer	Credible to management and useful in problem solving (to the degree that they describe factors that are important to the customer) because they are operations data	Provide a limited view of the customer experience based on only the aspects of operations that management measures (such as billing errors, late deliveries, etc.)
Internal quality metrics Inspection data on defects Call monitoring data Service access data	Allows identification of cause of original contact/problem Provides data on effectiveness of service access and process	Human review labor intensive Often focused on script compliance vs. broader issues Speech analytics are expensive
Customer contacts and complaints Description of CE from customer perspective including expectations and product use Good source of positive feedback on employees	Very timely and descriptive of the actual customer experience Provides root cause and emotional impact	Data are fragmentary, unrepresentative, and must be extrapolated to the customer base
Mobile transaction data While growing rapidly, basically the same as contact, survey, and complaint data via other channels	Like contact data, very timely Volume increasing rapidly	Due to restricted input, often cryptic and incomplete
Customer surveys Broad information on CE based on specific questions for relationship and specific transactions	Data can be projected to the customer base and markets (with proper sampling), and ongoing comparable measurements are possible Best analysis of drivers of loyalty	Significantly more costly and often less timely than data from internal metrics and customer contacts
Social media, reviews, and communities Public postings from small segment of total customer base Community input can include thoughtful input from super-users	Very timely feedback Community members provide thoughtful input and reaction to company proposals	Information incomplete and hard to get additional details from customers Quality of data is variable
Employee input Can be real-time input via email as well as advisory boards and larger surveys	Can identify process and customer-based causes Can quantify amount of wasted effort due to problems	Surveys often not aimed at service; employees not given results of input to feedback mechanisms

Table 7.1. Summary of Data Source Strengths and Weaknesses

To hear the voice of the customer, you need to question, and listen to, the employees involved in the processes that affect the CE. Comprehensive analyses of CE also show that the single best predictor of loyalty is whether the customer had a problem and how it was handled. Thus, data from customer service interactions describing problems must find their way into any VOC program worthy of the name.

In sum, the factors that create or erode customer satisfaction and loyalty are complex and therefore cannot be captured by any single method. Furthermore, every data source has its strengths and weaknesses. Thus, every organization that aims to build and maintain customer satisfaction and loyalty needs an effective VOC process that draws upon multiple information sources, usually with data from customer service as its central foundation.

VOC BEST PRACTICES IN THE CUSTOMER SERVICE ENVIRONMENT

Used in conjunction, several best practices will assure an impactful VOC that meets the eight success criteria listed at the beginning of this chapter. Each practice enhances the ability of the analysis to create organizational impact.

Integrate the data using a multiplier for contact and social media data. The multiplier—that is, the ratio of the number of problems in the marketplace for each contact received at the contact center—should be estimated either for overall complaints or, ideally, for major complaint types—for example, billing, sales, and marketing. The multiplier will be presented as a ratio, for example, 10:1—that is, there are ten problems in the market for each one that has been reported to customer service. This allows translation of contact data into instances in the marketplace, strengthening the business case for action.

As noted in *The Amazon Way*, experience metrics should exist for every major transaction and problem across the entire customer journey.[8] The experience metric should be based on complaint and survey data bolstered with operational data confirming the frequency of issue occurrences, such as transaction failures.

Figure 7.2. Understanding Where Customers Complain

Source	Contacts	Multiplier	Total Estimated Events in Market	Best Estimate of Late Shipments
Complaints to Customer Service	25	8	200	
Complaints to Sales Representative	15	12	180	
Complaints to Website	7	20	140	175
Instances of Late Shipments (from Logistics Dept.)			100–Direct Report from Logistics	

Table 7.2. Calculation/Estimate of Customers Encountering Late Shipments

The integration is done by extrapolating the contact data to the marketplace, using the multiplier, and then comparing that estimate with the problem frequency, based on any available survey data and operational data. For instance, the frequency of late shipment deliveries can be estimated based on operational data that show late shipments, as well as the number of customer inquiries about status and complaints about missed deliveries. Figure 7.2 provides an illustration of how the multiplier is estimated for missed delivery dates, and Table 7.3, on the following page, shows how the multiplier is used to estimate the number of customers affected and the potential revenue impact per month. In Figure 7.2, a onetime customer survey asks customers if they have encountered late deliveries and, if so, whether the customer complained, and, if so, by what channel. The survey results show that 25 percent of customers complained, but they spread their complaints across three channels: customer service, sales representatives, and the website. The multipliers for the three channels are eight, twelve, and twenty, respectively. These multiplier magnitudes are common in industries where service is mediocre across most major suppliers. This same survey could assess the loyalty of customers who have encountered late deliveries, and compare it to those customers who have not, to determine impact on loyalty.

Table 7.2 shows how the multiplier is used to scale up the contacts to the total estimate of problems. The three estimates vary, as the multiplier is a rough ratio. Therefore, the best practice is to take the three estimates from the three communication channels and compare the estimates to any internal operations data. In this case, the logistics department provides estimates. The VOC estimate is significantly higher than the logistics department estimate.

Customers Encountering Problem per Month		Damage to Loyalty		Value of Customer		Monthly Revenue Damage of Late Shipments
175	X	8%	X	$100,000	=	$1,400,000

Table 7.3. Calculation of Estimate of Monthly Revenue Damage
of Late Shipments

Table 7.3 multiplies the estimated number of customers encountering the problem by the impact on loyalty and value of customer to arrive at the estimated monthly revenue damage of late shipments.

Report issues at a granular level. The detail of issues measured in surveys and the classification in contact data are critical to actionability of the VOC. The actionable level of granularity is usually fifty to one hundred categories. Customer contact and social media data can be classified in the CRM using a hierarchal coding scheme that presents the CSR with a general set of categories (e.g., billing), the subset (e.g., invoice adjustment/order fulfillment), and sub-subsets (adjustment/wrong item shipped). This does not slow the process of recording the contact but does increase granularity to support a root cause analysis.

Using contact quality monitoring data in a multipurpose manner. Most companies expend huge supervisor and contact quality analyst effort listening to and analyzing calls for CSR evaluation. While listening to the contacts, the monitor almost never asks, "Why are we getting these calls, and how could they be better answered?" Most effort is spent listening to a limited sample for each CSR where, if the sample is random, 70 percent of the calls add no learning value. Monitoring activities should be focused on difficult and challenging calls rather than a sample that contains a large number of simple, easily handled calls. Further, monitoring forms should always require notes on how the reason for contact could have been prevented.

Supplement with experts. Most VOC analysis groups, especially customer service departments, have limited analytical staff. Three sources of short-term assistance are corporate operations staff, the continuous improvement department, and the IT department. Operations staff from other departments, such as sales, marketing, and brand, can provide valuable perspectives on how customers may have developed incorrect expectations. One auto company provided brand and sales analysts for two days per month to assist with the VOC report. The resulting report was more actionable and more readily accepted by executive management. The continuous improvement staff can provide insights on internal processes. IT analysts can both help in accessing internal operational exception data and suggest how IT might be able to enhance processes.

Reporting must include economic imperative, action plan, and process metrics to measure progress. Written reports should be brief, without masses of data that require analysis and interpretation. The data presented should tell a story, create an economic imperative (the cost of each month of delay or inaction), and suggest actions. These recommended actions should be informed by input from analysts with cross-company experience and accompanied by improvement targets and process metrics to understand operational progress. Many VOC managers accompany the report with a face-to-face briefing to assure understanding and acceptance.

Enhance acceptance of the VOC data and findings by:

- Leading with the positive news by highlighting two or three functions with improvements,
- Providing an action plan and pilot test design for each issue identified,
- Humanizing the data with quotes and call recordings,
- Not criticizing the current performance level, but showing how much money is left on the table, and
- Identifying opportunities to proactively warn customers of possible problems and preventing issues.

Conveying the VOC in an action-planning and accountability environment. Executive reports should highlight areas of needed action, suggest which corporate function should take the lead on each issue, and include viable process metrics and targets to allow progress to be tracked. To ensure that accountability is clearly established, the VOC team—who can explain the data in depth—should facilitate the action planning session jointly with the continuous improvement department, who can facilitate participants' strategy development, assignment of responsibility, resource needs, targets, and timelines.

Celebrate the VOC impact. Highlight successes and act like an internal consultant. Let your client take credit for the improvement. Communicate improvements to the employees via low-tech mechanisms, such as a one-page newsletter in the bathroom—variously referred to by different companies as "Flushfacts," "The Stall Street Journal," and "Learning in the Loo." Likewise, report to your customers on issues you've identified and fixed. It reinforces to everyone that you are listening and that continuous improvement is really working.

METRICS FOR EVALUATING VOC OPERATIONS

The resources devoted to the VOC only have payoff if action is taken on the recommendations made. In addition, there must be improvements in customer satisfaction and a reduction in customer problems. The following metrics are outcome metrics that will assure the VOC has a positive impact on operations:

- *Average number of data sources used to identify issues and their impacts.* At least two (ideally three) data types should be used to make the case for action on an issue. Whenever possible, operational data, in addition to customer input, should be used for recommending process changes in other parts of the company.
- *Degree to which VOC is successfully used to improve existing operations.* This metric is the percentage of changes in the contact center operation that are adopted and implemented within three months of issue identification.
- *Percentage of VOC users taking action on the VOC.* This metric addresses the VOC's impact on both recipients who are internal to customer service and users in the rest of the organization who say they read the report and took action on at least one issue the VOC raised. The simplest approach to measuring this is to biannually ask each internal VOC recipient what actions have been taken based on the VOC.
- *Degree to which the VOC leads to enhanced corporate products and processes.* This metric is the percentage of VOC-recommended changes in the processes and products that are implemented in twelve months. If issues are not addressed, it indicates that the business case the VOC made is not compelling. Therefore, the VOC should take care to make a limited number of recommendations but assure that each is strongly supported. As noted in best practices above, process metrics should be developed to measure improvement in process, so a customer survey need not be performed to determine if the process has improved.
- *Reduction in overall level of problems customers encounter.* This metric is derived from an annual relationship survey that measures customer problem levels. The survey should be consistently administered over multiple years and aid customer recall by using a list of problems across the customer journey.

☞ The customer service–produced VOC report should have three objectives: enhance the overall company offering, enhance the contact center processes, and evaluate and celebrate the CSRs.

☞ VOC data are more compelling when derived from multiple sources, including customer contacts, surveys, operational data, and employee input.

☞ The VOC process must reconcile and integrate the contact and survey data with the operational data, to assure its credibility to the company's operational and functional parts.

☞ In addition to an overall corporate report, the VOC process should provide each functional area with its own tailored report.

☞ To motivate action, the VOC report must suggest a monthly financial cost of inaction.

☞ The VOC report should suggest a preliminary action plan for top-priority issues, along with process and outcome metrics to track progress and show which functional area should take the lead in addressing the issue.

☞ The VOC process should partner with the continuous improvement department to facilitate action planning in order to assure positive impacts.

☞ On a quarterly basis, the VOC report should include the status of key issues and show where the needle has moved.

8

LIES, DAMNED LIES, AND CE SURVEYS

The disquieting CE facts from the *2017 National Customer Rage Survey* reported in Chapter 1—that problem rates are up, more than one-half of customers are extremely or very upset, and only 21 percent were satisfied with the action taken by the company— are perplexing, given the public emphasis that most companies' marketing messages put on great service.[1] Few would dispute the notion that companies have heavily invested resources to "perfect" the CE. Yet today's customers are experiencing more problems and are less satisfied with corporate responsiveness. What gives? Are CCMC's Customer Rage Study results flawed, or are most companies incompetent at preventing and resolving customer problems? Our research and experience suggest that this enigma represents a broader and more distressing circumstance regarding the distrust and impotent use of VOC data in general, and CE survey data in particular. Consider just a few examples:

- In pursuit of a better CE, a European food and beverage company "insourced" its toll-free customer care center, which it had outsourced for many years. The task force created to manage this transition established three goals: 1) improve service quality and increase customer satisfaction, 2) lower costs, and 3) expand and enhance the service. This company never measured customer satisfaction with the existing outsourced customer care center; it did not quantify its service channel's supposed brand loyalty benefits; and it did not conduct a formal cost-benefit analysis of growing and improving this service. The first official task force act, made in the name of minimizing distractions, was to postpone all customer surveys until the new contact center was opened, and the call volume was under control.

- A multinational B2B manufacturer discovered that product quality was suffering because employees were skeptical about and demotivated by the company's commitment to a target of "zero product defects." Employees weren't mocking the target, but were cynical about senior leadership's commitment to providing the resources required to meet an unrealistic, lofty standard. Locked in a boardroom for a few weeks to develop an innovative plan, a group of rather weary executives emerged with a new, improved, and customer-centric approach to product quality. Signs were printed, speeches written, and town hall meetings scheduled. The new strategy? One hundred percent satisfaction, guaranteed.

- A major U.S. retailer intended to invest many millions to enhance its national customer relations contact center. The strategy was to invite store visitors to contact a special 800-customer care number if they had a question or problem while shopping. Prior to launching this initiative, the company fielded a customer satisfaction survey. The principal finding was that awful service in the stores is a primary cause of customer dissatisfaction and decreased brand loyalty. The company dismissed the finding about lousy retail service and marched forward with its campaign for a new customer care number.

- A blue-chip, multinational consumer goods company operates two customer contact centers that handle millions of inquiries about hundreds of different products. Citing customer satisfaction as job number one, the company embarked on an ambitious study to assess the feasibility of consolidating two centers into a single center. In teeing up the feasibility study, the executive team stipulated that the study should be robust in every way, but it wasn't interested in "those satisfaction scores, which are so easy to manipulate." For four months, two accountants argued about the correct costs of operating two centers and the "real" costs of operating one center. A third accountant is added, six more months go by, and the decision to consolidate was approved.

You can't make this stuff up.

A common thread running through these and like stories is a disdain or misunderstanding of the role and value of genuine customer input and CE surveys. Alarmingly, as demonstrated in the above anecdotes, it is not unusual for some companies to view CE survey data as a distraction, an unnecessary burden, or a biased indicator (especially if the results challenge conventional wisdom).

Perhaps this discontent and pessimism regarding CE survey data is not all that surprising. Given the popularity and acceptance of conventional wisdom such as "73.6 percent of all statistics are made up,"[2] the "fake news" milieu of the day, and the ever-increasing use of misrepresented statistics, do you really blame corporate CE practitioners for their ambivalence about investing in and using CE survey data? Yet there is more than a grain of truth to the claim that survey results are frequently misrepresented. Mark Twain popularized that saying, "There are three kinds of lies: lies, damned lies, and statistics." Today he might instead say, "There are three kinds of lies: lies, damned lies, and CE survey results." One of our favorite examples is the WellCare Health Plans fiasco. Two months after J.D. Power and Associates commended WellCare Health Plans, Inc., for outstanding customer service, federal officials suspended WellCare's privilege to sign up new Medicare clients. Citing repetitive customer care problems, regulators claimed that WellCare's "performance was substandard in numerous areas" and was "one of the overall worst performers among all plans."[3]

Even at their best, most CE surveys are not especially effective in providing actionable results. They take the customer's pulse and provide a score, but surveys are often ineffectual in guiding the development of a better CE and moving the proverbial needle. In short, many companies today appear to be spending much and getting comparatively little in return for their CE survey investments.

That's a shame. Ineffective CE surveys are not a fait accompli. Done right, they offer rich, meaningful CE insights, as well as a trustworthy barometer of corporate well-being. Used correctly, such survey results offer a powerful and practical management tool for shaping and nurturing CE investments. Taken on with good intentions, rather than a desire to confirm the status quo, they facilitate the discernment and implementation of the "right" actions—those actions at the intersection of a better CE and a more profitable company.

This chapter suggests how to avoid common management mistakes and misunderstandings about surveys and their results. Second, we provide ten operational best practices for design, fielding, analyzing, and reporting that will increase survey impact and cost/effectiveness.

THE SINGLE GOAL OF CE SURVEYS: CONTINUOUS IMPROVEMENT

Achieving a better ROI for your CE surveys is simple, but not easy. Companies that reap the greatest benefit from their CE survey efforts are those that establish a North Star Goal of conducting CE surveys as a means to an end of continuous, incremental CE improvement. All other objectives must be secondary to, or vetted on the basis of their alignment with, this higher-order aspiration.

It is easy for CE survey outcomes to go sideways when ignoring this imperative. For a short time, we once worked with a major utility that lost its way by compromising this standard for its annual employee survey (employees were a critical internal customer group). Ostensibly, this longitudinal survey's purpose was to build an employee-driven culture rooted in the continuous improvement of the workplace experience. Scores in the survey's inaugural year were unfavorable. The survey firm was let go, and our firm was hired for the next survey wave. Year two results weren't much better. Our firm, believed to be focusing too much on "data and method," was replaced by a third consultant promising better results by focusing more on "employee engagement." You get the picture. Fidelity to a goal of continuous improvement begins and ends with a steadfast commitment to crafting authentic actions rooted in insightful data analysis. This company took a path of lesser resistance—change the objective, modify the goal, and shoot the messengers.

In our forty years of experience, we have observed that companies achieving the best ROI for their CE investments are flush with VOC customer survey data and resist the temptation to "dumb down" the business case for a better CE. In particular, the leadership of exceptional companies is rooted in the expression of the seven unique CE habits for survey design, fielding, analysis, and use.

Embrace Management by Facts, Not Anecdotes

Even in the emerging data-centric era, some companies are still over-dependent on the individual, personal experiences of employees or other anecdotal data sources (e.g., focus groups, comment cards, complaint records, etc.).

How often have you heard a colleague say, "I know a customer who . . . ," or "I know about this one recent complaint where . . . ," or "In this focus group we just completed . . . ," and so on? Sometimes known as the "person who" fallacy, these rich, vivid anecdotes quickly become truisms that have an almost hypnotic effect on the organization and disproportionately influence decision making. As a senior executive of a large trade association once lamented to us, "If one member expresses an opinion about his needs, it's a trend; If two members share that view, it's a mandate." Worse yet, falling victim to the "person who" fallacy is self-perpetuating and can lull a company into a sense of complacency about its need for a more intentional, empirical approach to listening to the VOC.

Would you manage your sales pipeline, marketing campaigns, product development efforts, or financial forecasts by such anecdotes? Of course not. And neither should CE outcomes be left to chance. Companies that are built to last recognize that unduly using intuitions, gut feelings, and anecdotal data about the CE is a risky methodology for sustaining predictable, enduring, and profitable relationships with customers. Instead, among other VOC listening posts, they institutionalize some type of formal, robust customer survey process capable of rendering reliable, valid, and ongoing insights about the CE and its impact on loyalty, WOM, sensitivity to price, and share of wallet.

Table 8.1 illustrates a somewhat oversimplified but pragmatic framework for rethinking your CE survey approach. Two axes bind this multidimensional matrix: the survey purpose axis and the survey range axis. A brief set of definitions is necessary to demonstrate the value of such a matrix as a strategic corporate CE survey tool.

	Survey Focus			
Survey Purpose	Transactional Survey	Relationship Survey (across whole customer journey)	Competitive Survey (for existing customers)	Market Research (to win new customers)
Baseline Survey	Key drivers, economic imperative, and setting priorities			
Tracking Survey	Measuring progress against targets			
Pulse Survey	Answer specific questions on newly emerged topic			

Table 8.1. CE Survey Context

With respect to the purpose axis, a baseline survey is an in-depth, omnibus, point-in-time survey designed to provide an enriched view of the CE. It identifies the key drivers, supports objective setting, and builds a revenue model to encourage investment in CE improvement. A tracking survey is intended to provide a progress report on ongoing CE improvement initiatives, and a pulse survey is any other special-circumstance survey (e.g., onetime survey to measure customer favorability to a policy change). When this system-oriented approach to survey purpose is optimized (i.e., the baseline and tracking complement one another), the need to field pulse surveys is limited (as is customer survey fatigue and cost to the company).

With respect to the survey focus axis, a transactional survey concentrates on a recent, specific transaction (e.g., purchase, new customer onboarding, service experience, customer service contact about a question or problem). A relationship survey is one that measures all CE aspects, across the customer journey, without regard to any specific experience or encounter. A competitive survey, which includes benchmarking surveys, is designed to tap into the customers' point of view about the competition. Finally, traditional market research surveys assess what customers and prospects (e.g., current customers of the competition) state they need and what would be needed to win them as new customers.

This simple, fill-in-the-blank model can help when you are blue-skying a survey system or rationalizing an existing survey program. Using the customer journey as your center point, name and identify all the surveys that the company is currently doing, and label and record the surveys according to the respective table cells in Table 8.1. The finished product will provide a concrete profile and visualization of your current survey approach strengths and vulnerabilities (e.g., where you are duplicating and overspending, and where you are missing certain CE points of view). For instance, a standard error of many companies is to conduct satisfaction-tracking surveys when they have not executed a baseline survey to understand what is most important to customers. At one client, we found that the company's tracking surveys measured service aspects that explained only 20 percent of the resulting customer satisfaction levels—a complete waste of time and money, as well as incorrect guidance to customer service on what to improve.

This framework becomes especially powerful when you overlay information about other VOC data sources on top of the CE survey entries (e.g., internal operational data, qualitative CE data, etc.).

One final note of caution bears mention: beware of benchmarking. Benchmarking CE survey results has been popular for at least a few decades. However, if the wrong items or inappropriate companies with different markets are benchmarked, or the results are inaccurate, bad data are worse than no data because they lead the company to pursue the wrong goals, move in the wrong direction, or, at a minimum, waste lots of money.

Set Your Sights on Improving Performance
Instead of Chasing Scores

Score chasing comes in various forms. Sometimes, companies literally beg for better scores. For example, following a car repair, one of this book's authors received a "presurvey" from the local car dealership ("Will you rate your experience as 'very satisfied'?") a few weeks before getting the "real survey" from the auto manufacturer. During a recent hotel stay, the front desk receptionist wore a button that read, "How about a 10?" (i.e., on the survey you'll receive from our corporate office). In both cases, the aim is to "coach" the customer into giving the company the highest score. Ironically, our research shows this "coaching" has a significant negative impact on the score. Mercedes-Benz recently attempted to mitigate this behavior by also asking if the customer had been coached on how to answer the survey.

Other times, companies "correct" the scores. We once worked with a domestic retailer to end a common practice whereby the local stores could request the removal of certain surveys from their overall score—usually those with lower ratings—because the customer was "unreasonable," "crazy," or otherwise "wrong." One auto firm had two full-time staff processing dealer survey appeals of bad scores. We suggest they reallocate those staff to continuous improvement analysis.

Companies getting the most from their CE surveys transform their culture from one that is score-obsessed to one that is performance-inspired. We like Andrew Carnegie's vision of philanthropic effectiveness as an allegory here. The aim is to engineer "real and permanent good."[4] Analogously, companies devoted to improving performance value a better, always improving CE, not a score. Their objective isn't solely to hit a target number tied to an "ultimate question" (i.e., Net Promoter Score or NPS), an arbitrarily imposed target, or some arcane, industry-specific benchmark. Rather, the survey leads an effort to engineer a better CE, and the scores follow.

View Bad News as an Opportunity for
Increased Profit

High-achieving CE companies exhibit a self-assured attitude toward CE survey results that manifests itself as a triangulated mindset seeing the glass as half-empty, demonstrating a tolerance for CE survey data ambiguity, and exhibiting an appetite for CE risk taking. Here are some examples:

Seeing the glass as half-empty. An abundance of decision-making research shows that behavior may be more influenced by a fear of "loss" than by a promise of "gain." Perhaps owing to a fear of presenting bad news or a need to skew the results for promotional campaigns, many companies ignore this practical consideration with their CE surveys.

Using biased scales and questions (e.g., are you very satisfied, mostly satisfied, somewhat satisfied, or only a bit satisfied?), selecting "special" customer samples (excluding those who are known to have had problems), and putting a positive "spin" on the results (combining "very satisfied" and "somewhat satisfied" respondents to get a higher satisfaction score, even when those who were "somewhat satisfied" are *three times less likely* to buy again) are a few tactics used for viewing the CE world through rose-colored glasses.

The most powerful CE survey results quantify the risk associated with *not* taking acting to improve the CE. As discussed at greater length in Chapter 6, companies earning a better ROI for their CE surveys purposefully include survey questions to ferret out areas of customer dissatisfaction and potential causes of customer defection (e.g., providing participants with a list of twenty to fifty problems they may have experienced, presenting respondents with a list of competitors, and asking which company is the best, etc.). While such practices counter conventional wisdom, the resulting data go a long way toward telling a story that compels action. Also, as several Harley-Davidson customers commented on a survey we conducted, "It looks like you really want to solve problems!"

Demonstrating a tolerance for ambiguity. Customer champions are more at ease with the uncertainty that's endemic to customer satisfaction and loyalty survey results. Everyone appreciates certainty:

facts, unequivocal outcomes, and truisms. Yet with survey results, it's fair to say it's often a murky and muddled world. Survey results may reveal one or two certainties, things essential to creating a better CE. However, most data will yield a "maybe." Leaders who are more comfortable with such uncertainty usually guide companies that consistently enjoy higher customer satisfaction and loyalty performance. When the results are equivocal, these companies neither fear nor attempt to discredit the data. Instead, they impose their wisdom of the business and a business case–mentality on top of the data. Further, they will reach out to a few survey respondents (having obtained permission to recontact respondents in the original survey) and have in-depth conversations to further understand the results.

An appetite for considered risk. CE leaders are usually *less* risk averse. They are at ease with, and demonstrate a greater willingness to take, calculated risks to improve the CE. Why shouldn't they be? They possess plenty of data and, when necessary, a maturity to work with the mixed messages that accompany customer feedback. At least part of this mindset is owed to framing their CE investments in terms of a cost-benefit calculation. Leaders know the costs and benefits of a lesser and better CE. As a result, it's considerably easier for them to connect the dots between what customers need, what must be done to meet those needs, and the cost-benefit of fulfilling those needs.

Set Credible Targets

Some years ago, a well-known consumer transportation company sought our counsel during their customer satisfaction crisis. Bad press coupled with a stagnant customer satisfaction index (CSI) made for a rather anxious board of directors. Hoping to send a message, the board set a CSI target of eighty. It was a goal that seemed defensible until you considered a current CSI of sixty-six and an average annual change that had not exceeded about five points over the prior few years.

Target setting isn't about sending messages or emotional appeasement. Those companies realizing a better ROI for their CE surveys predicate their targets on a goal of encouraging continuous, long-term, incremental improvement. Thus, targets are rationally, carefully, and methodically calibrated on the basis of current and past performance (What are the floor and ceiling? What is the observed average change? etc.), statistical considerations (What is the level of statistical significance for the proposed target?), and credibility (Will the organization embrace the target?).

A sizeable challenge endemic to target setting is designating the right metric(s). Two general schools of thought regarding a target metric have emerged among corporate practitioners. The first approach is a reliance on a single metric, such as overall satisfaction or NPS. The alternative is to construct a multi-measure target that is a weighted index of two or more metrics. Neither method is right or wrong, and both have distinct benefits and consequences.

A single metric makes it easier to manipulate for higher scores, if managers choose to try to game the system by, for instance, coaching customers on answering one question. At the same time, a single metric is much more easily understood by most operating managers and can be directly translated into financial implications.

By contrast, some academics and consulting firms have argued that a compound index of satisfaction, loyalty, and willingness to recommend can be a better indicator of true loyalty. However, an index is a much harder-to-explain metric to stakeholders and can mask movement in the overall score (without disentangling the individual metric components). We have observed three best-practice considerations regarding target metrics formulation.

First, regardless of the approach, keep it simple. Stakeholder confusion about what the metric is or how it is calculated can doom it to irrelevance. Second, if you want to earn stakeholder confidence, it's important that you scientifically validate the target metric's so-called "key drivers"—that is, those CE aspects that explain how and why the target metric moves up and down. The easiest path to disenchantment with a target metric is a number that never moves or moves in ways that defy explanation. A proper key driver analysis will help you understand the levers to pull to drive continuous improvement of the target metric. Third, contrary to prevailing wisdom, brand loyalty—and NPS in particular—is not *always* the "ultimate" metric. In fact, our four decades of cross-industry research have consistently demonstrated plentiful instances, especially in the B2B sector, where overall satisfaction is a better, more statistically predictive, and more sensitive target metric.

Moreover, when it comes to NPS, it's worth recognizing that it can often fail to precipitate action, because NPS can induce a state of complacency instead of a sense of urgency. We have often likened the NPS fallacies to the observed challenges in getting the citizenry to accept fact-based arguments about the probability of global warming.

For example, NPS as an indicator may be too general to capture the organization's attention and imagination. As the average ocean temperature or CO_2 levels are to global warming, so may NPS be to the CE. It might well be a leading indicator of impending malaise, but it's not "close enough to home" and probably doesn't apply to a particular executive's "neighborhood" or function.

Similarly, NPS may not promote accountability because it's not tied to specific customer life-cycle phases or the organization's individual functional areas. So, as many factors and processes contribute to global warming, many factors contribute to customer dissatisfaction and disloyalty. Action follows from ownership, which stems from more proper and precise diagnosis of causes. In the absence of further reliable diagnostic data about the CE, NPS permits a leader to "rationalize" that his functional area's contribution to the overall problem is small. Further, NPS damage can seldom credibly be tied to particular CE phases, although we have seen several attempts. Worse yet, the NPS calculation excludes all respondents on the 1–10 scale who assigned a 7 or 8, which in many cases can be 30 to 50 percent of the total customer base.

Finally, NPS does not create an economic call to action that is credible to the finance and marketing departments. While omnibus metrics play a role in diagnosing opportunities to improve the CE, they are often insufficient. We have observed many instances where quantifying revenue damage and negative WOM is a catalyst for corporate action. This is a fundamental NPS limitation that can be only generally tied to loyalty and has seldom been converted into quantified estimates of customers lost, revenue at risk per month, or number of negative WOM cases caused by poor customer experiences.

Concentrate on What Matters Most

Sometimes less is more. As stated earlier, better a small success than a colossal failure. Of course, when applied to the CE, these strategies work best when you focus on CE key drivers. Two of our most successful clients, one an auto company and the other a major business services provider, are extremely successful by focusing on three and four customer priorities, respectively.

All too often, CE surveys measure many things, except the *right* things. We once worked with a professional services organization to explore the validity of their CE survey metrics. Their two-page questionnaire featured a few key outcome measures (e.g., overall satisfaction and loyalty) and twenty-five satisfaction questions that were designed to help them predict satisfaction and loyalty, covering various CE aspects. Together, these twenty-five measures only predicted about 20 percent of customer loyalty. In other words, they were measuring a lot of things they assumed were predictors of their customer loyalty target metric, but comparatively few were actual predictors.

All else being equal, you will get a better ROI for your CE surveys if they help target your limited resources to improve where it truly counts. You do not need to measure everything, but at least measure those few things that make a difference.

Tell a Good Story That Compels Action

When reviewing CE survey results, people tend to have one of three reactions. Some see nothing—the data resemble a television test pattern, or the linkage between the results and their day-to-day job is muddled. Others, especially when the results are negative, express confusion or get defensive, since the data are complicated or inconsistent with their own experience; thus, something must be wrong with the data. Still others will get it but ask, "So what?"

Storytelling breaks down barriers to using the results and engages the organization in mindfully prescribing actions. The best stories help the company establish a shared narrative and business case for change. These stories create an economic imperative to act, by quantifying what is at risk from not taking action, and connect the dots between the survey results, the right actions, and the benefits of effectively executing those actions.

A longtime financial services client of ours demonstrated the value of good storytelling. Their corporate culture for sharing survey results was all too familiar. Directors from every department were shepherded into a conference room to endure an annual, two-hour, perfunctory PowerPoint briefing that almost always ended in the edict, "Things must change." They didn't, until this company reinvented the process for sharing results.

Although senior leadership continued to set improvement priorities, the broader organization was held accountable for driving change. Empowered cross-functional teams of mid-level managers were engaged in a daylong, structured, and facilitated dialogue to formulate action plans for improving customer satisfaction and loyalty. Since launching this new protocol, the company has consistently ranked first in its industry-syndicated customer satisfaction survey. The action-planning protocol will be described in more detail in the best practices section of this chapter.

Strive to Evolve CE Data Literacy in the Organization

Data literacy is the ability to collect, manage, evaluate, and apply data in a critical manner. While companies are slowly becoming more advanced in collecting and using big data to drive transactions (e.g., service, sales, marketing, etc.), more often than not, they are less skilled at leveraging "small," strategic data that offer insights into the broader CE. It is one part knowledge deficit (How do I read and apply simple statistics?), one part cultural (We just need one number, like NPS), and one part "la visual résistance" ("I can't/don't want to look at data unless they're in a colorful cartoon format").

Companies that have scaled the CE mountain and achieved great things have progressively improved the organization's data literacy. These market leaders have a thirst for the details, understand the core concepts of CE statistics, and have developed their staffs' ability to translate survey results into CE policy.

THE CHARACTER AND DESTINY OF CE LEADERS

Watch your thoughts, they become words; watch your words, they become actions; watch your actions, they become habits; watch your habits, they become character; watch your character, for it becomes your destiny.

—Frank Outlaw, Founder, BI-LO Stores[5]

Reading Frank Outlaw's modern admonition of a saying that evolved over centuries, it's worth recognizing that the seven CE survey habits can transform a company. We have seen three character traits evolve among the companies that faithfully live into these habits: possess a visionary schema for long-term CE success, know what matters most to customers, and know how to operationalize CE survey results. Together, these three characteristics distinguish the best from the rest regarding CE survey ROI.

Possess a Visionary Schema for Long-Term CE Success

One of the most frequent questions we hear from hopeful CE corporate practitioners is, "What does success look like?" We answer this reasonable and important question with the visionary—or as we sometimes call it, the success curve—shown in Figure 8.1. As it is said, sometimes a picture is worth a thousand words.

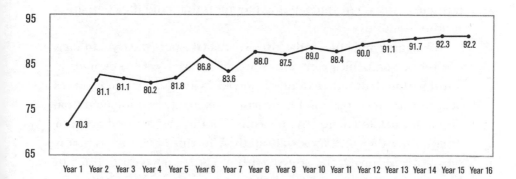

Figure 8.1. Curve of Success

This curve uses a single CE metric (in this case, customer satisfaction) and is an apt representation of the reality and aspiration of incremental, continuous CE improvement. The data shown here are from a real client that we've worked with for nearly two decades. The company name and business sector are unnecessary to appreciate the profoundly remarkable outcomes of their CE journey. Where is success to be found in this data curve? Over a seventeen-year period, overall satisfaction has increased 21.8 index points! Not surprisingly (at least to us), during this same time frame, the company also achieved unparalleled financial performance and consistently bested its competition in syndicated customer satisfaction survey results.

To fully grasp this extraordinary accomplishment, consider that, over this period, the company

- Was involved in ownership changes,
- Weathered two periods of market instability, and
- Went through various operational challenges, such as leadership, IT, location, and other changes.

The constant throughout these uncertainties was this CE story. In a sense, what makes this company truly unique and extraordinary is that its full identity—culture, operations, financial success, and competitive circumstance—is located and vested in the CE success curve displayed in Figure 8.1. The CE worth is transparent in a single, simple, elegant, and longitudinally trustworthy index score. It is one of the single unchanging elements that bind the company's various identities.

Not many companies today own such a CE success curve. In fact, not many companies can represent an invariable CE key metric, uninterrupted, over an extended period. When leadership changes occur or when scores don't conform to expectations, some companies are quick to change the measure, modify the methodology, or discontinue their CE survey altogether. In this case, the company sees value in staying the course with its CE survey metric. It is not what they do, but is part of who they are.

In short, the best companies define CE success in terms of continuous, incremental improvement. In this example, customer satisfaction increased by an average of a little more than one index point per annum. That does not seem like much in any given year, but in the long term, these smallish gains yield transformative outcomes.

Know What Matters Most to Customers

When executed properly, key driver analysis (the methodology for identifying what matters most) is central to getting executive attention. Done correctly, it calls attention to what will be gained from effective action and thereby ensures the proper allocation of finite resources for CE improvement.

Despite great advances in sophisticated analytical tools, many key driver analyses are methodologically flawed. For example, they rely on a measure of "stated importance" (what the customer self-reports as "important"), the "squeaky wheel" method (areas of lowest satisfaction), or simple correlation analysis (one-by-one association of a set of CE measures with overall satisfaction or loyalty).

Our experience suggests that a more effective methodology for key driver analysis entails using multivariate techniques (e.g., factor analysis coupled with multiple regression) that permit the CE researcher to restate key driver outcomes in the language of executives. Executives care less about "what's important" and more about understanding what can be learned by effectively acting on things that matter. In our own practice, we prefer the use of a simple key driver sensitivity analysis. For each attribute measured (i.e., each CE element measured), we ask and answer one simple question: What is gained in overall satisfaction or loyalty from a 5 percent point increase in satisfaction for the individual driver?

Assuming that the company has sufficient data to do so, you may also consider doing two key driver analyses: one for customers reporting "no problems," and a second for customers who had a recent problem. Often, this analysis will yield additional detail about key driver nuances. Customers' emphasis on service dimensions becomes significantly stronger once they encounter a serious problem.

Know How to Operationalize CE Survey Results

As part of CCMC's continuous improvement effort, we field a client satisfaction survey following every engagement. Our questionnaire includes the usual suspects, such as a set of satisfaction attributes related to the client's experience with various aspects of the engagement, overall satisfaction, and a gauge of the intention to recommend. However, the most important question we ask is, "Have you taken tangible action to improve the CE, based on the work we've coproduced?"

More than 90 percent of CCMC clients report they are using CCMC survey results to take actions to enhance the CE. Taking action on survey results is more the exception in the general marketplace. Even among companies that tick all the technical best practices boxes for increasing survey impact, many still fail in their attempt to positively influence the CE, because they have no process in place to connect the dots between the survey findings and operational accountability. Intentionally operationalizing meaningful changes in business practices is a compulsory event that CCMC refers to as *action planning*.

Assuming the ultimate goal of any survey is to contribute to a positive, incremental, and sustainable CE improvement, action planning is the magic elixir to achieve this outcome. It is the antidote to complacency. As we define it, action planning is the intentional and ongoing process of identifying, operationalizing, and implementing specific actions that affect enough customers, over a long enough period, to increase positive ratings for those selected CE elements that yield the greatest payoff.

Tactically, action planning consists of a formal, face-to-face gathering of a cross-functional group of key stakeholders (as few as eight and as many as fifty) engaged in a daylong facilitated session focused on three to five priorities for action that the survey identified. Strategically, action planning is an ideation effort; it is the connective tissue between the survey findings/recommendations and the change in organizational behaviors. The various methodologies for implementing this facilitated event are plentiful (e.g., brainstorming techniques, visualization practices, etc.).

Regardless of the methodologies used, the critical point is to ensure that an action planning effort is in place and process metrics are identified to track progress. CCMC finds that action planning dramatically increases the ROI that companies can earn for their survey investments, by ensuring that they focus finite resources on, and act on, what matters most to customers. When compared against companies that do not implement a formal action planning process, companies that engage in formal action planning are significantly more likely to achieve sustainable increases in customer satisfaction and loyalty, achieve those notable gains more quickly and at a lower cost, and ensure that the survey results are integrated into the organization's culture.

TEN BEST PRACTICES FOR CE SURVEY SUCCESS

Our treatment of CE surveys would be incomplete without identifying a few best practices for CE survey success in supporting continuous improvement. The following are ten best practices that generally apply to all CE survey types. Some of these best practices relate to survey methodology, and others pertain to how the survey results are analyzed and packaged.

Prepare the internal audience for constructive bad news. One way to lose your audience is to unpleasantly surprise them with data that they find counterintuitive to their own experience or that are threatening. The following are critical to properly setting the audience's expectations in advance:

- Stress that research often produces counterintuitive surprises and will surface some unhappy customers.
- Show that negative results highlight the causes of price sensitivity, which, when identified, can be used to facilitate better margins.
- Couple each negative result with a quantification of the upside revenue opportunity.
- Assume that the findings will focus on process issues instead of affixing blame to a particular unit.

Use a sample that yields precise and representative data. No survey practice is more tied to the proverbial warning "garbage in, garbage out" than the sampling technique. Regardless of the survey type, rigorous sampling—picking enough of the right customers to participate in the survey—is essential to producing trustworthy data. Any sample must be built to fulfill two prerequisites to produce trustworthy data. First, the sample must be constructed to yield statistically precise results. Second, the sample should be developed to produce representative data.

The statistical precision of a survey finding has to do with margin of error and statistical confidence, which are mostly a function of customer sample size and the response rate. Think of it this way: All else being equal, the more data points (i.e., survey respondents), the greater the precision of the survey results. Plenty of academic and practical resources are available to guide a determination of responsible, scientific sampling technique. The goal is to strive for a CE survey data set that yields no more than a plus or minus 5 to 7 percent margin of error, with a 95 percent confidence level. The best way to achieve this minimum precision level is to forecast and plan for this target. Table 8.2 provides a rough-and-ready reference guide to such planning purposes.

The statistical representativeness of a survey concerns the degree to which the customers responding match the customer population on some key set of characteristics (e.g., the products or services they have purchased, gender, income, etc.). While statistical precision and representativeness can be related, they are not identical. For example, a company could possess a precise data set of 1,000 survey respondents that is not representative of all customers (e.g., includes only men, is skewed toward customers only using one type of product or service, etc.). We typically perform a "congruence" test on any data set, to determine whether the survey respondents are representative of the customer population. For example, if Product A is used as the criterion characteristic, we compare the "match" between the percentage of customers in the population using Product A and the percentage of customers using Product A in our CE survey data set. This congruence test will be repeated for a variety of indicator characteristics. The representativeness of the data set is based on the relative difference between these two percentages across the chosen set of variables. The closer the average

Sample Design: Sample Size				
Sampling Tolerances (95 In 100 Confidence Level) Approximate Sampling Tolerances for a Survey with Percentages at or Near These Levels				
Number of Returns on Which Results Are Based	10% or 90%	20% or 80%	30% or 70%	40% or 60%	50%
2,500 interviews	1.2%	1.6%	1.8%	1.9%	2.0%
2,000	1.3%	1.8%	2.0%	2.2%	2.2%
1,500	1.5%	2.0%	2.3%	2.5%	2.5%
1,000	1.9%	2.5%	2.8%	3.0%	3.1%
900	2.0%	2.6%	3.0%	3.2%	3.3%
800	2.1%	2.8%	3.2%	3.4%	3.5%
700	2.2%	3.0%	3.4%	3.6%	3.7%
600	2.4%	3.2%	3.7%	3.9%	4.0%
500	2.6%	3.5%	4.0%	4.3%	4.4%
450	2.8%	3.7%	4.2%	4.5%	4.6%
400	2.9%	3.9%	4.5%	4.8%	4.9%
350	3.1%	4.2%	4.8%	5.1%	5.2%
300	3.4%	4.5%	5.2%	5.6%	5.7%
250	3.7%	5.0%	5.7%	6.1%	6.2%
200	4.2%	5.5%	6.4%	6.8%	6.9%
150	4.8%	6.4%	7.3%	7.8%	8.0%
100	5.9%	7.8%	9.0%	9.6%	9.8%
80	6.6%	8.8%	10.0%	10.7%	11.0%
60	7.6%	10.1%	11.6%	12.3%	12.7%
50	8.3%	11.1%	12.7%	13.4%	13.9%
25	11.8%	15.7%	18.0%	19.2%	19.6%

Table 8.2. Sampling Tolerance at 95 Percent

difference is to zero, the greater the probability that the sample is representative of the customer population.

While there are no guarantees of obtaining a representative data set by chance, a few methods can increase the probability of securing one. First, before fielding the survey, the CE practitioner should validate that the sample itself is generally representative of the customer population. Second, any gross discrepancies between the sample and the population, as well as any underrepresentation of particular segments (both for the purposes of representativeness and any segment-specific analysis), should be addressed as needed, by using a supplemental sample (i.e., by adding more participants from certain segments to the sample).

Design a CE survey that identifies the key drivers of satisfaction and customer problems, at a granular level. The key drivers of CE satisfaction are critical to setting CE priorities. At the same time, the best way to complement a more prescriptive understanding of the CE priorities is to granularly describe the associated types of customer problems. For example, if the CE key driver was "product quality," what types of customer problems diminish product quality? The CE survey best practice here is to ask the customer to review a list of potential problems across the entire customer journey. The problem list should contain twenty to fifty problems. While such a list may look intimidating and negative to executives (especially marketing), aiding the customer usually identifies three times as many problems, compared to simply asking the customer, "Have you had any recent problems?" Further, the list can include critical issues many customers are afraid to mention, such as "being misled by the sales representative." In this instance, once the issue is on the list, the customer has "permission" to flag the problem.

Use a survey invitation that convinces customers to invest their time to respond. Regardless of the survey methodology, an invitation to participate in a CE survey should provide two specific examples of how the company used survey feedback to improve the CE. For example, a delivery company we once worked with indicated that it was enhancing its claims and invoicing processes, based on customer feedback. A quick-serve restaurant we collaborated with announced it had brought back BBQ sauce, as customers requested. In both cases, customer feedback was strong, positive, and served as a catalyst for enhancing survey response rates.

Use customer-convenient survey channels. Web-based surveys that customers can take at their convenience are more effective than telephone-based surveys or forcing customers to respond immediately after calling customer service with a question or problem. For B2B relationship surveys, schedule an appointment with the customer, send the questionnaire in advance, and enlist an account manager to follow up and encourage nonrespondents to participate in the survey. These techniques can yield B2B survey response rates between 50 and 95 percent.

Package the survey results for ease of use by executives. CE survey results should be tailored to each audience, and describe the top issues in no more than one to two pages. Complicated data tables that require study and analysis (e.g., top ten complaints by top fifteen products, giving the reader 150 data points to analyze) are a barrier to consumption of the results. When using data tables and graphs, proactively conduct the analysis for the reader, and list the four key problems that most need attention. For maximum impact, estimate the monthly cost of inaction for each key issue and provide a suggested action plan with process metrics to measure impact.

Present data in a positive tone and with creative ideas. While we noted in the first best practice that the CE survey audience should always be prepared for constructive bad news, the survey results should strive for balance and also highlight positive accomplishments. For example, point out where previous initiatives had a positive impact or show how a process metric has improved. Blame should not be assigned to individual units, but dissatisfaction and its accompanying financial opportunity can be associated with particular cross-functional processes. Communicate to the operating manager, "You are doing well, but look how much more money you are leaving on the table that you would accrue if you did X." By nature, processes are cross-functional and therefore less threatening. Also, if you add creative ideas suggested by customers and your customer service CSRs, the report is repositioned as an idea source. One company's customer service department had a section of the satisfaction tracking report titled, "The Wacky Ideas Section." The marketing, brand, and product development departments viewed the section as an innovation source.

Create an economic imperative that the CFO accepts. The monthly cost of inaction on each CE priority should be quantified, according to the Market-at-Risk approach outlined in Chapter 6. The Market-at-Risk methodology and the customer value should be validated in advance with the CFO or the resident financial cynic. Remember that CFO buy-in significantly increases the VOC impact on customer satisfaction improvement.

Present the data at a granularity level that makes them actionable. Define CE priorities in as detailed a manner as possible. Issues such as billing or sales unresponsiveness are too broad and likely to cause defensiveness. The CE practitioner can greatly enhance the prescriptive value of the survey findings through three survey design practices: 1) offer, as previously described, an aided list of between twenty and fifty problem categories, and ask respondents to indicate all problems experienced, as well as the most important problem; 2) provide an analysis of a limited number of open-ended questions—for example, in an open-ended question that follows the survey's problem list, ask for a description of the most serious customer problem; and 3) provide an analysis of a set of special survey questions, included in the survey, to uncover insights about known priorities.

Measure, communicate, and celebrate progress. As noted in Chapter 7, many VOC processes are not systematically monitored to determine whether the plans made in response to the VOC reports ever achieve the promised improvements. Lack of accountability is a serious impediment to achieving action. Creating accountability by measuring progress is one of the most important functions the CE leader can perform.

Another key part of this process is recognizing and celebrating successes and ensuring all the involved actors receive accolades. If anything, spread the glory too wide. Those who were not strong contributors on the current project will work harder next time.

Communicate the process changes made, based on customer and employee feedback, to the entire employee base. Most companies communicate via the website, emails, and supervisor briefings.

Unfortunately, many employees do not read everything, and many supervisors filter and truncate communications (see VOC best practices, "Celebrate the VOC Impact," in Chapter 7).

Be sure to include your customers in the communications. They are excited that you are paying attention to their input. Gary Furtado, president and CEO of Navigant Credit Union in Rhode Island, relates that when he communicated the results of Navigant's Member Experience Survey and his intended action plan to the membership, he received over fifty emails from members congratulating him on his courage to ask about problems and his follow-through on conveying the results and action plan to all the members.

KEY TAKEAWAYS

☞ Customer research should focus on the key drivers of customer satisfaction and be supported by supplemental data, such as problem experience, delighters, and the additional needs of current customers (while market research focuses on how to win new customers).

☞ Conduct an end-to-end relationship survey, including all sales and marketing touches even to noncustomers, at least every two years, and use the results to guide the focus of the CE key issue tracking surveys, which should be conducted quarterly or monthly.

☞ To have an impact, surveys must provide unvarnished guidance on how to continually improve the CE. Management must welcome any bad news because that is where the additional profit lies. Focusing on good news lulls you into complacency and provides little return on your survey investment.

☞ CE and satisfaction measurement must be credibly linked to financial opportunities, if it is to create action.

☞ Survey reports must be tailored to each audience, by function and level of the company. Conducting even a thirty-minute meeting with the audience will greatly increase their understanding and buy-in.

☞   Action planning must create buy-in to the value of improvement and accountability for results. It is necessary to have granularity in the problem statement, action plan, and process metric, to measure progress and assure that everyone knows what they are signing up for.

☞   Tell customers and employees what the company has learned and what you're doing with the survey results. Communicating these actions enhances satisfaction and motivates both groups to provide additional input.

SECTION FIVE

IMPLEMENTING PSYCHIC PIZZA: TECHNOLOGY AND ITS APPROPRIATE ROLES

When implementing functionality with technology, the question of what comes first—the chicken or the egg—has a definitive answer. Appropriate functionality must drive technology selection, not the opposite direction.

Here are two examples. I attempted to buy tickets for a highly publicized, popular event on the website of a nonprofit I have supported for years. The tickets were to go on sale at 8:00 a.m. At 8:01 a.m., I went on the website and tried to select two seats, only to have the website freeze. I exited the website and tried to enter twice more. By 8:10 a.m., a new banner appeared on the home page saying all tickets were sold and to call their office with any questions. I called and got voice mail and left a frustrated message. Ultimately, a staff person called back to say I was now on a waiting list. Technology did not contribute to a good experience.

On the other hand, one Sunday morning, my home-delivered *New York Times* was missing. I called the delivery 800 number, and the voice recognition system asked if I was calling about a delivery issue. When I said yes, it then asked if the paper was damaged or missing. When I said missing, it apologized for the problem, confirmed my address, said a new paper would be delivered, and asked if I wanted a text confirmation. I said yes, and the confirmation arrived within two minutes. I then received a call from the delivery person saying she would deliver the paper within thirty minutes, and fifteen minutes later she cheerfully handed me the paper. This encounter was successful because of the company's use of voice recognition, linkage of the phone system to the CRM, confirmation of the transaction via the text channel, linkage to field delivery, in-process confirmation by the field staff, and timely follow-through.

This chapter first outlines the customer service functions described in Chapter 3 that various technology modes can facilitate. We address the major technology types a customer service director must be conversant with to work effectively with IT and, when appropriate, with the director of digital marketing (DM), to implement the technology across the CE. This chapter will not train you to implement the technology, but will tell you what technologies to consider for each function, as well as a few key issues to raise with your IT department. It will also help your CIO to understand all the ways that customer service and the CE can be enhanced. Finally, we suggest several metrics for diagnosing and managing technology's impact on the service experience.

HOW TECHNOLOGY CAN BE LEVERAGED ACROSS THE SEVEN SERVICE FUNCTIONS

Technology is critical to customer service—from when the customer becomes aware of your company through the customer's receipt of a reply. It also facilitates input of the VOC insights and reporting to other parts of the company. We suggest how technology can be leveraged across the service functions described in Table 3.1 in Chapter 3: awareness, intake, reply, evaluation, customer insights/reporting, and staff support. Customer onboarding (part of proactive communication) is addressed as part of awareness. In many companies, customer service is not responsible for this activity, but a) it should be, as part of proactive communication, and b) if not, customer service must provide strong input to the onboarding process.

Awareness—Motivation and Facilitation, and Customer Onboarding

The website and internet search, as well as product and literature labeling, are the usual means of motivating customers to contact the company for customer service. The company website home page and social media sites must highlight the complaint solicitation message. The home page should also highlight key issue hyperlinks, as well as all other communication channels available to reach the company.

Technologies should also facilitate the customer connecting with the right department to receive effective customer service. When the customer calls, ideally the inbound telephone system IVR (supported by the CRM) will identify the customer's phone number, recognize the customer, and move immediately into the intake process. The phone number and key options for any IVR must be highlighted on the website, in product literature, or on the product itself.

An additional aspect of awareness entails education and onboarding once the customer has purchased a product or service. Onboarding might involve a targeted "push" of information to the customer tailored to their previously noted preferences and the sales channel used in the purchase. If the customer bought online, onboarding is most effective online. If the purchase was made in a retail location, the customer may want in-person education or other educational options.

For instance, Tesla provides twenty-eight minutes of video about the automobile, divided into sixteen segments. Audi's most effective car salesman educates customers on the three most important issues and strongly encourages customers to return in two weeks for education on what they have not figured out on their own. This approach maximizes customer satisfaction and provides the staff with presentation flexibility. In another example, a major consumer association sent an eighty-page welcome package that covered all the benefits and programs available to members. After our assessment that the large amount of material was overwhelming and not useful, the association reduced the onboarding packet size by focusing on the enrollment data in the CRM. Materials are now tailored to the consumer's reason for joining and subject of greatest interest (among five possible topics ranging from political advocacy to travel benefits). Such tailoring increased satisfaction with the welcome process by 20 percent.

Customers with a question or problem go first to the company's website home page, or for products, to YouTube videos. SEO will assure that company videos are high on search results, to safeguard the brand and ensure consumers get the latest information. Education must be delivered in small segments, like three or four bullet points or sixty seconds of video at a time.

Intake—Routing and Logging

Customer service contact intake is usually through a company's website (including email and chat), mobile device, or traditional phone. The routing process can be a major frustration, especially if an automated routing process (including touch-tone and voice recognition IVR systems) is poorly designed or if a regular customer is not automatically recognized. To recognize the customer, information requirements should be limited to reduce bureaucracy and encourage input. Mechanisms such as ANI can eliminate the need for authentication. Credit card companies see that the customer is calling from their designated phone number when activating a new card, acknowledge that fact, and require only the input of the new card number, making the transaction painless.

Easy intake may, on occasion, require sacrificing security for ease of communication. Allow customers to ask questions or make comments without having to log in or create passwords. In high-security environments, companies should establish a consumer query site outside the firewall, so consumers are not required to negotiate complex barriers to ask questions not specific to their account or make input on operational issues.

Customer recognition can be based on an email address, cookies, or an account number. When requiring customers to complete online forms, the customer should be warned via a banner of the

most prevalent mistakes and include edit checks as well as prepopu-
lating information as much as possible.

Simplicity also applies to automated systems and social media.
Part of intake must include monitoring customer comments on
social media sites and logging of customer comments and complaints. In the ideal world, the company can link customer social
identifiers with the customer account. It is acceptable to ask for account identification, noting that it will allow provision of seamless
service. Though only customers who are very active will likely provide such information, they are probably the most important from a
damage-control perspective.

Reply—Assessment, Investigation, and Classification

The CSR traditionally handles assessment and issue classification
after listening to the customer's description. Now these activities
can make use of speech recognition/text analysis, coupled with artificial intelligence (AI), to identify the customer's issue and suggest
or assign a classification. Technology must allow both the consumer
and the CSR to efficiently and accurately classify and investigate the
issue. The two primary tools for classification are the CRM coding
functionality CSRs use and a text and/or speech analysis tool applied to recorded and real-time conversations.

The CRM classification process should be structured in a hierarchical manner, so the CSR first selects a general reason category and
is then presented with up to ten subcategories. Older CRM systems
tend to provide CSRs with a list of codes to scroll down until they
find the appropriate code. The difficulty is that CSRs seldom scroll
down more than twenty codes, so coding has significant inaccuracy.
Therefore, the use of scroll-down coding should be avoided.

The second approach to classification is using text or speech recognition converted to text, which is analyzed to assign the customer's statements into a reason-for-contact category. This second tool,
while helpful, must still be confirmed by the CSR, except for simple
statements like "reservation," "delivery," or "missing paper."

Investigation is driven by the reasons-for-contact code, product
identification, and customer history. In service industries, the CRM

provides the functionality to use the customer identification to retrieve the three most recent transactions with that customer—for example, claim filed or purchase made, and any relevant documents based on the reason for contact code. For instance, if the code is "claim status," the system accesses the claims workflow to determine where the most current claim lies in the claim workflow process.

In product industries, time is often wasted identifying the product model number or type. The customer must either look for it or describe the color and shape. Photo analysis apps, using AI, now allow the CSR or the chat function to identify the model, often eliminating several minutes of conversation. For instance, Moen is experimenting with a chat function that uses AI, applied to an uploaded picture, to identify complex models of fixtures and automatically suggest parts. The cost of the AI-driven process is much less than the cost of conversation.

Reply—Resolution, Confirm and Coordination, and Tracking

Resolution identifies solutions to the customer issue. If it is a straightforward issue, resolution can be a single process. If the issue is complex, a solution space may contain multiple solutions (housed in the KMS) based on parameters, such as customer value and information on the root cause. The fundamental hub is the CRM system supported by AI and the KMS.

Once the classification is noted, the CRM system automatically retrieves any pertinent information (e.g., orders, claims, account history) to support the resolution process. Meanwhile, the CRM tracking process keeps tabs on the issue status.

The resolution, whether by CSR or automated process, is guided by the KMS based on the classification of the issue. If the source of the contact is the online community, community members submit their responses directly to the other members via the forum. The KMS can contain procedures, methods, and policies as well as videos and video links.

Once the response is provided, the CRM will store the response, launch the evaluation, confirm and coordinate the process, and close out the issue in the tracking system.

Reply—Knowledge Management System (KMS)

The KMS supports responses to issues and ideally is automatically accessed by the reason-for-contact code, to provide the CSR with guidance on the decision rules. Two key aspects of the KMS are how it is maintained and updated and whether it also drives content on the public website. Both activities are underestimated in most companies, but when done correctly, can lead to dramatically more cost-effective service and CE. KMS maintenance requires a formal process for each time a new issue is identified, researched, and handled. Making the KMS a key driver of the website CMS dramatically reduces the number of calls that need to be handled.

Evaluation—Appraisal

The two appraisal levels require several technology types. First, CSR appraisal requires real-time call, email, and chat monitoring capability, as well as contact recording. Further, monitoring assistance tools can allow recording of evaluations and the process the CSR used to investigate the issue. These systems are often part of the phone-switch call recording system.

The CSR appraisal also consists of the customer satisfaction survey process. This process includes an after-call intervention via recording, email, or phone call or a separate email or phone survey launched by the CRM system. While some analysts have argued that immediate feedback is more valid, we believe that forcing the customer to respond immediately after the call (at the company's convenience) leads to a significant response bias. Customers who are unhappy or in a hurry will tend not to respond. A better approach is to provide an email survey that can be responded to later. This also allows the customer to evaluate CSR follow-through on promises.

The second appraisal level is evaluation of the overall response process. This appraisal is also better achieved for both consumers and business customers by email surveys launched by the CRM system after the issue has been closed.

Customer Insights, Reporting, and Proactive Communication

The insights function consists of storage and retrieval, statistical generation, and analysis. Many CRM systems include the capability to integrate data from customer records, surveys launched by the CRM, customer information files, operational databases from the Enterprise Resources Planning (ERP) system, and appraisal and recording information from the telecom system.

Proactive communication is the cornerstone of prevention. For every transaction, customer service should ask themselves what the customer might request and provide an answer in advance. Proactive confirmation and education can be programmed for at least 80 percent of all customer communications. If proactive confirmation is built into the software, after the original investment, it is free. Likewise, when a transaction failure occurs, the same principle applies: It is cheaper to proactively communicate than to wait for the customer query, research the issue, then reply. The FedEx/UPS tracking approach is now expected in tracking everything from individual takeout food deliveries to railroad carloads in a B2B environment. The communication must be tailored to the issue and the customers' preferred channel.

Staff Support— Hiring and Training, Development, and Incentives

With respect to supporting the customer service staff, the key technologies are workforce management (including workload forecasting), training and development, and gamification. Workforce management software is viewed primarily as ensuring an adequate number of butts in seats for each half-hour increment of operational time. The software also highlights opportunities for freeing up frontline staff for career-enhancing activities, such as a detail to other functional areas and developmental training.

Online training is now heavily tied to appraisal results. When a weakness is identified, a training module is recommended. However, care must be taken not to focus just on weaknesses, but to continuously offer training that moves the employee to the next expertise level and enhances development.

Gamification software takes performance data and provides feedback and recognition to staff to both compete with other team members and with their own previous performance. Some systems also suggest specific training that will help employees enhance their effectiveness.

FOURTEEN TECHNOLOGIES THAT CUSTOMER SERVICE DIRECTORS NEED TO KNOW

The following technologies all have a role in customer service and customer feedback. As a customer service executive, you must be familiar with how these technologies contribute to service activities. The following sections summarize the functionality that technology delivers from a service perspective and, when appropriate, highlight examples of best practices that enhance CE.

CRM Systems

CRM systems range from simple logging, tracking, and reporting systems to more complex systems that incorporate most of the twenty processes outlined in Chapter 3. The five critical aspects of CRM systems often lacking are easy logging and classification, linkage to the KMS and artificial intelligence, inclusion of a survey process, integration with operating systems to support proactive communication, and monitoring CSR use of all functionality.

The CRM system should support logging and classification of contacts received via any channel, linking the contact to the customer's history using the customer identifier. Classification can be supported by a hierarchical coding system or speech/text analytics confirmed by the CSR. The system should be able to code three separate reasons for contact, because one-third of all contacts have multiple underlying reasons.

The CRM must have linkage to the KMS, which provides solutions and talking points based on the nature of the customer's contact information, identified during classification. This reduces the need for CSRs to memorize the proper factual response to every problem or question.

The CRM system must link to, or contain, a customer feedback process, so the customer can be sent a survey after the contact. The best practice is to email a satisfaction survey that can be responded to at the customer's convenience, as opposed to an immediate follow-up survey call.

CRM systems now provide the capability to monitor the CSRs' use of the system's functionality. This allows identification of CSRs and customers who are not making effective use of all the available functionality. Those who are not using much of the functionality can then be retrained. For example, Salesforce.com, GM, and Charles Schwab now all have the capability to monitor how their customers are using the technology provided. A detailed description of the ideal CRM system functionality is provided in Appendix A.

Operating Data Systems Such as ERPs Are Key to Delivering Psychic Pizza

Integration of the CRM system with other systems incorporates operational information to facilitate proactive communication, what we have called Psychic Pizza. This is probably one of the most important and least common functions. For example, the CRM must tie to the order/fulfillment/logistics system in an e-commerce company environment, and tie production scheduling in a manufacturing environment. When the process fails or has a delay, the failed transaction is transmitted to the CRM and thence to the customer.

CuriosityStream provides a good example of linking operations systems to the CRM, to prevent and rapidly acknowledge customer issues. CuriosityStream is a leading supplier of educational films and documentaries on science, history, wildlife, and other cultural areas to millions of viewers all over the world. Buffering or video chatter during download is the most important cause of consumer dissatisfaction. CuriosityStream employs three proactive, preventive strategies for enhancing the CE. The company monitors video download quality for each customer and maintains a buffering log for every instance of buffering for all customers. By analyzing the root cause of each buffering instance across multiple content delivery networks, CuriosityStream reduced such problems by over 90 percent, significantly improving customer satisfaction and retention. Further, they are proactively preventing customer buffering for videos by beginning each video stream at a moderate visual quality level and increasing it until maximum visual quality is reached for each customer and his or her individual circumstances—for example, the customer's internet speed. Finally, when the company's sensing system identifies that the consumer has a lower capacity internet provider/system that can cause buffering problems, CuriosityStream proactively notifies the customer that their network will not support higher-speed download. The company then downgrades the customer's subscription to basic service and refunds the cost of the premium service that the consumer will not be able to enjoy. If CuriosityStream subsequently detects an upgrade in the consumer's network, they will reoffer the enhanced subscription.

KMS

The KMS is critical to effective cross-channel response and proactive customer education. A good KMS can capture each newly discovered solution to an issue and catalog the solution, so the next CSR, root cause analyst, or customer will not need to reinvestigate the whole problem from scratch. This collective intelligence dramatically reduces training time and reduces customer service workload, if the database is partitioned and common troubleshooting methods and error code translations are made available to customers via the website. A partitioned database is one where some users can see all the data and other users can see only partial data. For example, a database could be divided into employee-only view and customer/employee view.

The biggest problem with KMS is that companies do not maintain the information in the system and fail to share it with customers. The KMS should be a resource for both internal and external customers—it is a core knowledge repository. Even in small organizations, at least one full-time person should be maintaining the KMS.

This investment will be more than offset by service cost savings, since customers will be able to find their own answers, if the KMS is partitioned, and the bulk of the database is made available on the website.

A best practice for the KMS is to continuously update the information in the database via input from the frontline staff, based on their research, resolution of new problems, and knowledge of issues. For example, at Harley-Davidson the service manager encourages frontline staff to pursue new issues to resolution and report the issue in a standard format to the KMS administrators for final formatting and entry into the KMS.[1] The service manager also recognizes and congratulates the team members who make the most input. An additional best practice is to monitor the KMS effectiveness by team members, to identify both employees who need more training and topic responses that appear ineffective.

Company Website

Customer service should co-own the website content with the data management department, because most visitors are existing customers trying to find information versus potential new customers. Customer service should demand five website aspects:

- The home page should highlight the top five to ten issues that existing customers will encounter, providing hyperlinks to complete answers. The number of calls received on those issues will drop dramatically as customers' self-service rates skyrocket.
- The home page, and every other website page, should highlight the search, contact us, FAQs, and website map at the top of the page. Also, a banner should state, "We can only solve problems we know about!"
- If the website provides significant self-service and account management functionality, a new customer portal should be provided that includes friendly graphics, short videos, and an index to key FAQs.
- Customers should be able to easily access large parts of the customer service content without having to log in or use a password. At least one-third of all contacts are not account specific, where authentication is required.

- The search field should be equipped to provide useful responses to all standard inquiries and problems, including guidance for "problem" and "complaint." Many websites provide no solution when those words are typed into search fields. The website should also capture data on any searches when the outcome is "no answer," or the customer indicates the answer is unhelpful. This data should be provided to customer service in a monthly report, because many of those outcomes will probably result in a preventable contact.

Telephone-Switch System and IVR

The telephone-switch system should provide several key functionalities, along with enhanced reporting (which is critically important). While each of the nine key functions may seem obvious, each has nuances that are clarified below.

- *CTI.* The telephone-switch system should not just provide screen pops but also report talk time for each call in a manner that can be linked to reason for contact in the CRM.
- *Multiple messages played while on hold.* One of the biggest frustrations customers encounter is hearing the same message over and over while on hold. The messages should progress as the wait time lengthens.
- *Reporting by thirty-minute increments.* Most telephone-switch systems report in one-hour increments. The workload should be analyzed and forecasted by thirty-minute increments that require reporting by the half hour.
- *Recording of calls, ideally connected with speech analytics.* The cost of recording has declined to the point where all calls should be recorded. The calls only need to be stored for thirty days, or as long as the appraisal or compliance functions require.
- *Longest call on hold.* Few telephone-switch systems capture the longest call, but this is an event that likely creates the most dissatisfaction. This parameter is also useful for creating metrics for call center performance beyond the simple average speed of answer.

- *Provision of current wait time.* Customers are given more control over their lives if they are told the current wait time. The customer can then do a cost/benefit on whether to continue waiting.
- *Provision of virtual queue.* The virtual queue, combined with reporting of current wait time, can dissipate much of the dissatisfaction created by call center queues. This should be a requirement.
- *IVR driven by voice recognition.* Voice-driven IVRs are very effective when correctly designed and tuned. It creates much less dissatisfaction than push-button queues. However, making voice-driven IVRs accurate and well designed is still more of an art than a science.
- *Ability to listen to customer interactions with the IVR.* The satisfaction and market intelligence received is worth the investment. For example, American Express uses the technology to analyze IVR experience by listening to customers using the IVR.

Search and Search Optimization

Search is important to customer service because a significant percentage of customers simply use a search function like Google and YouTube to find an answer to their question rather than going to the company website or contacting customer service. Therefore, customer service must work with IT to enhance SEO to ensure that the desired company information is high in any search result. Periodically, customer service callers should be asked if they went to the website or searched online for the answer. If a significant percentage of customers were unsuccessful, they should be further interviewed to learn how to enhance the company's SEO protocols.

YouTube and Video

Videos, including YouTube recordings, are effective tools to educate, provide directions, and deliver shareable entertainment. Production quality is not important in most environments. In most cases, a company could have the customer service staff produce the video using smartphone videography.

Video is now the easiest way to educate and instruct customers. The more complex the task, the more effective video is, especially when compared to phone (verbal) or text-based instructions. A key advantage is that the consumer can retain the video link and refer back to it. Videos can also be used to describe limitations on product performance and use.

The most prevalent use of video is entertainment, a key tool for customer engagement. In late 2014, more than two million cat videos had been uploaded to YouTube, and they had more than 25 billion views.[2] While some consumers view videos for educational purposes, most are looking for entertainment, and the most entertaining videos are shared with others. A second source for entertaining videos, beyond your own staff, is the online community. Both Intuit and the American Association for Clinical Chemistry post member-submitted videos (only available to logged-on members), which often include humor.

Online Communities

Online communities and review websites are both important tools for companies, even though companies cannot control the sites. User-community websites provide mutual support for customers and are a great source of both VOC and customer engagement, but again are beyond the company's control. Some companies are creating their own review websites. Even here, the company cannot completely control the site because reviewers will act independently, and the company should not be perceived as "managing the news."

The biggest pitfall of company-sponsored online communities occurs when companies do not invest in community monitoring and support. The worst thing you can do is throw a party and have lame refreshments and no music; people walk in and immediately walk out. The online community moderator must have a naturally enthusiastic personality and enjoy moderating. In a good example, a nonprofit organization in Washington, DC, that sells used clothing recruited an employee who became their "Vintage Clothing Fashionista" and quickly attracted over 5,000 followers, contributing to a significant increase in store sales. When this person moved on to another organization, the company found it hard to replicate her verve and wit, and the community following declined.

The next two biggest errors that companies make are failing to analyze the comments and reviews in aggregate (for policy purposes vs. individual situations) and failing to respond to legitimate criticism where appropriate. Analysis of the review content is an ongoing task that text analytics does well. On the other hand, such tools are still somewhat expensive, and a daily visual scan can pick up most important issues. This same daily scan will identify issues that need action, such as offering to fix the situation for the customer or responding in a low-key manner.

Review Sites and Social Media Monitoring

Customer service directors must be conversant with two types of functions. First, the company can sponsor and administer review sites, or the site can be independent. Second, beyond review sites, social media must be monitored. In both cases, the company must be comfortable with the customers' right to freedom of expression. When a negative view is presented, the company has a right to provide its point of view but should not attempt to block, delete, or impede discussion. The company should view such discussion as a valuable information source.

In B2B environments, many executives worry about a negative review damaging their business environment. However, there are three arguments for welcoming all reviews. First, a review site or reviews contained within the context of an online community ensure that the company is aware of an issue early. Second, the company can engage in a nondefensive manner, to mitigate the damage. Third, in any busy online community, a negative comment is rapidly "pushed down" the screen by other comments, so it is not prominent for long. On balance, we suggest sponsoring or participating in online communities rather than ignoring or avoiding them.

Mobile Phones

The mobile phone revolutionized customer service. First, an increasing percentage of customers initiate their contact via their smartphone. Second, customers receive text and voice notifications via their phone. Text is especially welcomed, since the customer does not need to answer a phone call. There is also the ability to co-browse and have video chat interactions. Intuit has found that video chat enhances customer confidence in the recommendation by 30 percent.[3]

For example, the smartphone camera allows customers to video stream to their insurance company pictures of damage, which assists in insurance claim reporting and adjustment. This functionality dramatically reduced the cost of small and moderate damage claims adjustments in the past two years, by eliminating the need for an adjustor to go on-site. As noted in the investigation process description above, a photo of a faucet can be analyzed to provide the CSR or the chat system with the model number and link to replacement parts. Further, smartphone cameras enhance the effectiveness of technical support for products in a manner similar to what co-browsing does for IT support.

Speech and Text Recognition Analysis

Speech and text recognition analysis tools allow written or spoken conversation to be converted into structured knowledge. If performed correctly, this is helpful for telephone and email intake because much of the logging, assessment, and classification can be done using AI. The problem is that, beyond a small number of predictable inputs, the analysis tools still have a relatively high error rate that causes serious customer frustration. First, the speech recognition tool that identifies the words spoken and converts them to text can be inaccurate. Second, the analysis of a text's meaning/intention can be misunderstood. Misunderstanding a customer's email or chat request leads to inappropriate responses or ineffective triage. Even when the customer's inbound query is not detailed enough, or the text recognition tool is not exact enough for the query to be clear, most automated response processes keep trying to respond even after the customer has expressed frustration with the answer. The "smart" tool, powered by AI, will quickly acknowledge that it has failed and transition the customer to a human. Another approach is for a recognition tool to hear the ambiguity and ask two more diagnostic questions, to avoid providing an array of inaccurate responses. The tools should be required to report all errors and customer opt-outs, and endeavor to achieve a 97 percent successful transaction completion rate.

Two additional aspects that will help enhance speech recognition effectiveness are the provision of key words that will be recognized, printed wherever the 800 number is provided, and customers' ability to "break in" and override the system to go directly to the desired option, if a customer knows what he or she wants. This avoids forcing the customer to listen to the rest of a twelve-second message. An additional ten seconds seems like an eternity when the customer is upset and knows what option they need.

Internet of Things (IoT) and GPS

The IoT already has a huge impact on customer service, by moving service calls from reactive to proactive. For example, if a General Motors automobile is in an accident, the vehicle notifies the OnStar security and safety system, allowing the company to dispatch road service and proactively reach out to the customer to show concern and determine whether medical attention is needed. In another example, Cisco Systems is notified by its server that a component is about to fail, allowing a service call to be scheduled in a non-emergency time frame, thereby reducing service expense. Also, Uber and Lyft show the customer the driver's real-time location, eliminating uncertainty, a primary cause of dissatisfaction.

Smartphone GPS allows proactive communication of offers and acknowledgement and recognition of customers who arrive at a retail or travel and leisure location. The challenge for the customer service director is to ascertain at what point the knowledge of location goes from being helpful (e.g., check-in apps at a hotel) to creepy (knowing you just walked into the gym). This can only be evaluated via soliciting customer feedback.

Gamification

Gamification was first used in airline and gaming loyalty programs, to motivate customers to buy a little more to achieve the next reward level. The technology now takes performance data on *employee* activities and provides feedback to motivate, recognize, and engage employees.

The two biggest challenges in gamification are to go beyond recognizing the top 10 or 15 percent of employees who perform well and provide thoughtful feedback to every employee on how to improve. Many systems focus only on the top few employees but provide little improvement recognition among the bottom two-thirds of employees, which is where the bulk of improvement and greatest impact can be achieved. Therefore, assure that any system addresses the lower employees with as much intensity as the top employees. Second, the feedback cannot just be the employee's rank-order position but must provide specific suggestions on where improvement is needed and links to online training that address weak areas.

A question for the customer service director is, "Are the measurement, feedback, and rewards viewed as a positive to be looked forward to by CSRs, or is the whole process feared?" Finally, the system should assure that feedback and incentives are focused on only one or two performance dimensions at any given time. Providing feedback on twenty items is overwhelming.

The Edge of Technology:
Artificial Intelligence and Biometrics

Two types of interrelated technology have now moved from experimental stages to mainstream use to revolutionize customer service: AI and biometrics such as voice, facial, and fingerprint recognition.

AI differs from the many KMS applications that currently exist because the KMS simply consists of a set of rules based on key words and information about the customer. If the customer is calling about

X topic and has *Y* characteristics, a specific response rule or process that is deemed the most relevant should be used. On the other hand, AI tools obtain feedback from customers concerning adequacy of their suggested responses and "learn" over time to improve the response content. Therefore, the KMS is not static but continually improves using feedback.

AI can also search massive databases to support customer application for products like insurance. For example, the traditional process for purchasing flood insurance took forty-five to sixty minutes to fill out the application of up to fifty-four questions and then two weeks for underwriting and processing. Neptune Flood, an insuretech company, has disrupted this industry using AI. Jim Albert, Neptune's CEO, reports that the simplified application process now requires about two minutes. Approval is provided the same day. Most of the questions, such as property elevation, can be derived from generally available databases. Further, serious errors in the data provided in the application, which traditionally is at least one error in every two applications, has decreased by 90 percent.[4]

Biometrics are used in some smartphones for authentication and security. Fingerprints have also been used for years by the Transportation Safety Administration Global Entry program. Facial recognition is now being pilot-tested at airports as a substitute for airplane boarding passes. At United Healthcare, voice prints of adult children are kept on record, so they can discuss their parents' health accounts instead of getting authorization from the parent each time, to comply with health information privacy requirements.

The two key questions for the customer service director are, "How often is the technology wrong?" and "How easily can the customer reach a human?" In recent reports on using facial recognition for airline boarding, some articles suggest that error rates around 4 percent exist, especially for ethnic minorities and passengers with glasses or scarves.[5] At this time, a biometric system is more disruptive and creates greater customer dissatisfaction than the traditional process of presenting picture identification.

SUCCESSFULLY WORKING WITH THE CIO AND DIGITAL MARKETING DEPARTMENT

I was so impressed with the *New York Times's* handling of my missed home delivery (described at the beginning of this chapter) that I interviewed Ben Cotton, the newspaper's executive director for retention and customer experience to learn more. Cotton explained that his team includes dedicated IT developers and designers, so there is no requirement to justify every service improvement initiative to the CIO. Reporting and replacing missing and damaged newspapers was a high-volume, basic function, and making the process painless and convenient was a win for both the subscriber and the company. Cotton mentioned that the newspaper's app recently implemented "vacation stop," which allows subscribers to pause their home delivery with only a few clicks.[6]

Most customer service directors do not have dedicated IT staff; thus, they must work with the CIO and the director of DM. DM now designs/controls a significant part of the entire technology budget and infrastructure, often including the website and social media. There are seven best practices for working with the CIO and the DM director.

Use a customer journey map as a basis of joint action. The detailed customer journey map, annotated with current customer POP, is an effective basis for conversation between customer service, IT, and DM. Such a map will highlight opportunities for enhanced functionality to IT, who can then identify current or available technology that can cost-effectively deliver the needed functionality. Dan Wakeman, vice president and chief technology officer at Educational Testing Service, notes, "Smart CIOs are now using the detailed customer journey map as their guide to technology investment. If the investment does not enhance the quality of the customer experience, it is not contributing to the bottom line."[7] This map will also highlight where DM can/must capture electronic addresses and preferences and manage customer onboarding, to help them adopt the company's technology.

Assemble a list of the top ten customer service issues/POPs. These ten issues should be analyzed by customer service, IT, and DM to determine if there is a single simple technological fix, a process fix, or a better way to avoid the issue via proactive communication. For example, at Aflac Inc. insurance company, the head of service mandated that the corporate joint IT/service task force not automatically implement the latest technology, but to listen to customers and provide the key things customers want. One of the first things the task force noted was that customers asked for the ability to print their invoices. The IT department told the task force that printing invoices was already possible; pointing out where the link was, five clicks from the home page. The continuous improvement department suggested moving the link to the home page. Clicks rose from 30,000 to over 100,000 the first month, and the results of the next customer satisfaction survey rose several points, in part due to that change.[8]

Acquire the customer's email or text/cell phone address to support proactive communication. A company must have an electronic address for customers to proactively communicate with them. Getting an email is often a challenge because consumers don't want to receive spam. Assuring customers that they can choose to only receive notifications on key transactions will entice more to provide you with their electronic contact information. A second problem most companies encounter is that email addresses frequently go stale. LinkedIn has a weekly painless check-in process that presents customers with their main and backup email addresses and cell phone numbers, asking, "Is all this current?" You simply click yes and move on.

Capture the customer's channel preferences. A company must know the customer's preferred channel and communication intensity—for example, "Call me for *A* and *B* but not for issues *C* and *D*"—so you do not irritate the customer with too many communications. This is critical in B2B environments, where there may be dozens of shipments per week. Many businesses also change the communication channel depending upon the severity of the service failure being communicated. At one logistics company, an oil refinery customer indicated that they wanted an email if a chemical feedstock shipment was going to be more than two hours late, a text if more than four hours late, and a personal cell phone call if more than six hours late.

Onboard customers to assure technology acceptance. The onboarding process is the best time to capture customers' electronic addresses and communication intensity preferences. It is also the best time to ensure that customers adopt the basic technology that will make both their lives and the company's life easier. For instance, One Nevada Credit Union in Las Vegas stresses how critical the mobile app is to receive services because they have few tellers—and they charge five dollars to speak with customer service. A branch staff person spends more than thirty minutes with each new customer, first loading the app on the customer's smartphone and then drilling them on how to use it for three primary functions. This initial thirty- to forty-five-minute time investment assures that One Nevada members are comfortable and happy using the technology.

Use a common customer identifier across all databases. For the company to identify and report process status, failures, or confirmations to the customer, the transactions in the operational databases must be linked to the same customer identifier as the one in the CRM system that initiates the customer notification. This common identifier across all data systems presents a major challenge, but is critical for achieving proactive, problem-preventive customer service.

Partner with the CIO to eliminate minor customer and employee POP. In one of the most successful examples of this partnership, Jim Albert, former CIO of Bankers Financial Corporation in Florida, worked with customer service, HR, and field employees to identify the top minor systems issues that were frustrating or time wasters. He then shut down all large systems projects for one week (calling it "Do it! Week") and had the IT staff fix, confirm the quality of the fix, and roll out fixes for over four dozen minor systems aggravations. In many cases, these fixes enhanced the CE as well as employee satisfaction.

METRICS FOR TECHNOLOGY

Several metrics should be applied to technology as it supports customer service.

Technical adoption by new customers. If new customers do not use the company's mobile app, or call to place an order rather than use the website, the customer onboarding process is ineffective in both training and incentivizing customers to use the technology.

Percentage of service transactions that are self-service. The first step is to obtain information from IT on how many customers are using each technology type. For example, we examined the profile of the percentage of transactions that customers executed by phone, branch, desktop, mobile app, and ATM for two similar financial institutions. One had 20 percent of its transactions executed by the mobile app, and the other had more than 65 percent of transactions via the app. A key factor in the difference was the approach to onboarding new customers, as described for the Nevada credit union in the earlier section on "Onboarding customers to assure technology acceptance." If existing customers are not using the most appropriate technology, the transaction effort is harder, and the company is expending more resources than necessary.

Two possible actions are to make the technology easier to use or to more aggressively educate customers on the technology's use. In an example in Chapter 5, Charles Schwab provides consulting and training services to independent financial advisors who are not fully using Schwab interface and fulfillment technology. The incentive communicated to financial advisors is that transaction quality and speed will increase and, over time, back office fees will decrease because less effort is needed to process and provide interim status reports for electronic transactions (as opposed to manual, phone, or paper-based transactions).

Calls to help desk and customer service per X orders, by issue type. This is a metric used to diagnose the clarity and ease of technology use. It is critical that the trouble ticket has high granularity in the classification of issues—for example, at least one hundred categories— to allow identification of exactly what aspect of the technology is confusing.

Transaction failures by transaction type. The good news is that these data do not need to be collected; they already exist in every system and simply need to be reported. The majority of failures are not aggregated and reported in most companies because IT does not care about the orders or shipments that do not arrive. They only care about the successful ones that drive the order-to-cash workflow.

Website search failures. Each search failure is an issue that either results in an unhappy customer or a phone call to service. Again, less than 10 percent of companies even get reports on search failures. The search failure is either reported by the customer as "not helpful," or the system records the "no results found" message that some customers receive.

Percentage of visitors to home page who are new visitors versus current customers. This metric is critical because it will show, in almost every case, that many fewer new visitors are coming to the home page than existing customers, who are trying to conduct a transaction or find information on an existing order. For frequent visits from existing customers, a device-based memory should allow auto login, so the customer need not type in a password and identifier each time.

Percentage of visitors coming from search engines versus coming directly to website. This metric allows understanding of the effectiveness of WOM referrals versus SEO sources. In most successful B2B environments, more than 50 percent of new customers are acquired via referral from existing customers.

KEY TAKEAWAYS

☞ Customer service should make IT a full partner in enhancing the CE.

☞ Customer journey and simplified transactions should drive the selection and priority for technology implementation.

☞ Proactive service is not possible without an electronic communications channel to the customer, such as email and/or text.

☞ Linkage of the CRM to operational systems and ERPs is mandatory if proactive communication/Psychic Pizza is to be achieved. Customer service should have a strong influence on—and ideally ownership of—at least one-third of the website home page, to ensure that solutions for key customer issues are easily accessible.

☞ While the website is critical, mobile apps with distilled content and just-in-time emails and texts are now needed as well.

CREATING A CAN-DO, CUSTOMER-FOCUSED CULTURE

Upon check-in at a major chain's budget hotel at 7:00 p.m., the reception desk clerk looked troubled and said, "Your reservation was cancelled yesterday through the corporate system, and we are booked solid." After determining that the cancellation source was murky, he then said, "Let's find you a room nearby," and did so right away. I was unhappy with the problem, but will stay at the hotel again because the problem was quickly fixed even though the hotel was not the cause. This clerk exhibited a skilled, can-do attitude, despite the hotel not receiving any revenue for his effort. This chapter focuses on creating and maintaining a can-do, customer-focused, risk-taking culture in a tight labor market.

We first look at three underlying motivators for frontline service employees, beyond monetary compensation. Second, we focus on how companies create such a culture via the staff support and evaluation functions, which include the hiring, training and development, incentives, and appraisal processes. Third, we look at the role of supervisors and executives. Last, we explore ways you can shift toward a more strategic customer service role, thereby raising your status.

WHAT DO SERVICE STAFF WANT?

Attracting and retaining service staff is more complicated now for two basic reasons: the tightening labor market in most areas of the country and the advent of social media sites where employees rate their employer. The labor market requires higher wages at the same time many companies are bringing contact centers back to the mainland United States. Also, social media sites like Glassdoor.com provide detailed feedback on companies of all sizes. A Glassdoor.com contributor has even blogged about the characteristics of seven company types employees should avoid.[1]

In evaluating the service environment of over 1,000 organizations, we find that employees want four things: competitive compensation, job success, recognition, and career progress.

Competitive compensation. Employees need a living wage that recognizes their skills in the regional marketplace. One of our basic questions to HR and the customer service director is whether the company provides a competitive wage and where the compensation lies relative to comparable customer service positions in the region. Over half of companies have no solid data; we immediately recommend a quick benchmarking study. In almost every case, the results surprise the HR executive. The primary recommendation is to pay at least 10 percent, but ideally 15 percent, above the current median wage for each position.

We can hear the groan from finance at such a recommendation, but the cost/benefit is clear. Traditional analysis of turnover costs (including recruitment, interviewing, and training) is one half-year's loaded salary. And this is a painfully conservative estimate. When you also include the damage to revenue in the three months before a good employee leaves—in other words, when the employee has decided to leave and becomes disengaged—the cost is five times the out-of-pocket cost of the turnover.[2]

When firms make an investment in staff, the payoff in reduced turnover is apparent within a year. A major auto firm raised its call center wages by four dollars per hour, going from 10 percent below the median to 15 percent above the median, and turnover dropped 75 percent. The customer service director reported that the company could hire much better, more committed employees. He also attributed a significant part of the double-digit increase in the NPS to the staffing improvements.

Job success. Employees want the tools, training, and empowerment to succeed. This includes the technology discussed in Chapter 9, as well as the authority to make decisions on their own in all situations, without fear of penalty. They also want to feel good about the company, its mission, and how they relate to the customers they serve.

Recognition. Individual recognition must be public and include peers. It can be verbal, but also must be substantive (e.g., tied to career progress). Group recognition, such as the standard pizza party at month's end when the call center's performance targets are met, promotes relationships and team building but does little to recognize individuals.

Career progress. Career progress is a priority for almost all employees, and lack of it is cited in most exit interview data that we have reviewed. Employees must be able to see a tangible career path, ideally out of the contact center into other parts of the organization, but at minimum, up the contact center hierarchy. The word *tangible* is used because employees should be able to model other staff who have made that progress. Another important aspect is to provide a mentor who can advise and assist the employee in advancing his or her career. This could be a supervisor or a trusted employee outside the command chain. Employees also need to see how they contribute to company success and how the company's operations and purpose contribute to a greater good.

Investment in each of these is a win-win-win for the company, the employee, and the customer. This premise is supported by some exciting data Paul Zak reports in his article "The Neuroscience of Trust."[3] In a set of studies, some projectable on U.S. working adults, Zak identifies eight management behaviors that enhance trust. Over the past two decades, he has shown the neurophysiology of how trust enhances oxytocin output that, in turn, enhances empathy while reducing stress.

Five of the eight management behaviors Zak says contribute to trust are: recognize excellence, give people discretion on how they do their work, share information broadly, intentionally build relationships, and facilitate whole-person growth. These factors track perfectly with the latter three factors we mention above: job success, recognition, and career progress. Zak also reports that high trust has a .77 R-squared correlation (a very strong correlation) with employment joy, as measured by the question "How much do you enjoy your job on a typical day?" In relation to the HR department, which worries about salary expenses, Zak reports a 2014 Citibank survey where nearly half of employees would give up a 20 percent raise for greater control over how they work.[4]

CREATING A CAN-DO CULTURE

An employee environment that fosters an empowered and customer-focused culture requires the four components in Table 10.1: job description, hiring, training and development, and appraisal and incentives. The table provides a checklist for customer service directors to create a can-do, customer-focused culture. If you can say yes to each of these twenty-four dimensions, you will have the foundation for empowerment. The two other requirements for empowerment are supportive supervisors and supportive executives, which are discussed in a later section, "Managing Up and Down to Create the Culture."

You need to hire the right people using a job description that highlights empowerment, and then train, develop, and motivate the employees to think of the customer at every decision point. CSRs and frontline service staff should not be afraid to take risks and innovate. You may be surprised that appraisal and incentives are not separate components—that is because they are heavily intertwined.

The customer service staff support function is complicated by the fact that HR may be leading this activity, while the customer

Component	Explicit Attributes	Evaluate Your Structure (Y or N)
Job description	Use flexible solution spaces	
	Use authority to take action	
	Take time to connect	
	Make input into VOC and CI	
Hiring	Interview via primary channel	
	Peer interviews for confidence and empathy	
	Require examples of taking action and innovation	
Training and development	Convey vision and purpose as well as systems & skills	
	Focus on handling tough issues	
	How and when to connect	
	How and when to make input	
	Career ladders and requirements	
	Provide intensive nesting	
	Provide mentoring	
	Train for the next career step	
Appraisal and incentives	Self and peer appraisal	
	Frequent supervisor feedback and recognition	
	Focus on challenging contacts	
	Survey challenging contacts	
	Include connection & input	
	Combine surveys and internal measures	
	Public recognition	
	Recognition for improvement for all levels of performance	

Table 10.1. Checklist for Creating an Empowered, Can-Do Service Staff

service director must live with the results. This is an area where the customer service director must be aggressive to ensure that staff are hired and molded into a can-do, customer-focused workforce.

We now examine the four components that lead to a can-do, empowered culture.

Job Description

The job description for frontline employees is usually operational and only touches on CE by requiring courtesy and responsiveness. An effective job description explicitly creates accountability for the use of empowerment, an emotional connection, and input to the VOC process. Conners and Smith describe creating accountability as "defining results that will get you the desired results."[5]

If you want empowerment, put it in the job description. The mandate should be to "ensure customer satisfaction by handling difficult and atypical situations using existing guidelines as well as individual creativity without the need for supervisor approval." The Pointe Hilton in Phoenix, Arizona, has a culture statement that directs employees to anticipate the customer's needs and to ensure that the guest will return and recommend the resort. It states, "We trust your judgment—we will stand behind your decision," and "The only wrong thing you can do is to do nothing."

Likewise, if you want connection and input to VOC/continuous improvement (CI), these attributes must be in the job description. Accountability is also created in the call center job description that states, "Employee will select X customers per shift and attempt to connect with them and successfully connect with at least half of them." While this is painfully explicit, it meets the Connors/Smith criterion of specificity. Likewise, for input to VOC/CI, the job description will have two parts. First, CSRs must enter accurate coding of the reason for contact. Second, they are expected to identify and suggest opportunities for process improvement.

A warehouse general manager at Ryder Trucks Logistics makes input to CI part of every employee's job. Employees must meet with him every six months and present an idea for a process improvement. The employees, including the janitor, get the general manager's undivided attention at each meeting and thoughtful consideration of the idea. Productivity and employee morale at that facility improved dramatically.

Hiring

Interviewing is critical but can be a huge resource sink for supervisors. Empowering frontline CSRs to carry much of the interviewing load is a solution. The initial interview can be short and over the phone, to see how the candidate presents via that channel. Innovative companies like Zappos and GE have frontline CSRs conduct both the phone and the first face-to-face interview. CSRs have great incentive to hire strong team members since they will be dependent on the employee once he or she comes on board. Also, candidates are more open with a peer than with a supervisor. One CSR told us of interviewing a candidate for the evening shift, and the prospect asked if there was time to do schoolwork between calls. The CSR noted that the candidate was not coming to the job to work full-time and rejected that person's application.

An interview must identify self-starters who can provide examples of thinking out of the box and innovating, and self-confidence is crucial. A 2017 Corporate Executive Board article showed that "controllers" who have strong opinions will confidently tell the customer what the best path forward is and are much more successful than CSRs whose main strength is empathy.[6]

Training and Development

Empowerment is most useful in atypical situations—what customer service often calls "the difficult conversation with the customer." It also applies to identifying opportunities for process improvements, knowing when to create connection with the customer, and making input to the continuous improvement process. Many companies view the latter two activities, connection and input to VOC/CI, as discretionary activities that are harder to evaluate than the use of empowerment with difficult contacts. We believe that CSRs and frontline employees should be intensively trained on all three.

Steve Curtin suggests that most training activities address "job functions not job essence."[7] While important, the job functions are insufficient to achieve customer focus. All training should be purposeful and customer focused in terms of delivering service to the customer in particular situations. Training should include:

- The company vision, purpose, history, heritage, and how it makes the world a better place.
- Systems and skill training to handle the basic transactions that comprise 70 to 90 percent of the workload.
- Handling the more difficult situations, which includes soft skills (empathy and diffusion of anger) and flexible solution spaces for handling ten representative difficult issues.
- Creating emotional connection and rapport with customers.
- Making input to VOC/CI.

Zappos begins its training with a video from its CEO, Tony Hsieh, who describes the company's history and purpose. He stresses customer focus, giving back to the community, and doing what is right at all times, for customers and employees. Like Dan Gilbert, CEO of Quicken Loans, who moved the company's headquarters to downtown Detroit, Hsieh moved the Zappos headquarters to a struggling area of north Las Vegas to help the community. He encourages the employees to participate in and patronize the community, as well as contribute to many other charitable causes. This conveys the company's "higher purpose," doing well while doing good.

As noted in Chapters 3 and 5, guidance on handling atypical, difficult situations must be provided with two caveats. First, for any type of issue, there should be built-in flexibility—what we call flexible solution spaces. Second, there should *not* be an attempt to anticipate every situation; the resulting guidance would be too voluminous. The best practice is to provide flexible guidance on the top ten issues and tell employees to use their best judgement for all other situations.

A flexible solution space outlines multiple solutions (typically no more than four) to the same general issue. It is accompanied by a range of factors the employee should consider in selecting the solution and negotiating a resolution acceptable to both the customer and the company. Such solution spaces will win the compliance and legal departments' support, since the solutions circumscribe broad limits but allow employees to tailor the solution to the individual customer situations. The employee can "break the rules without breaking the rules." During training, each solution space is accompanied by storytelling and practice. Employees should also practice using ten benchmark issues as a basis for extrapolating or interpolating, so they are comfortable going beyond the guidance.

Ron Zemke, author of numerous landmark books on customer service, found that when employees were given five to ten sets of benchmark guidelines, they felt comfortable extrapolating to other solutions as needed. The willingness to take such risks is contingent upon clear reinforcement, first by role-playing during training and then from supervisors and executives, as described below.

The employee empowerment policies should be presented in a four-part format. The first section is the basic response and the "standard" solution. The second part is the range of factors that might affect the resolution, and alternative scenarios with any necessary limits on the resolution or remedy. When needed, guidance on how to take the actions implied by the resolution or remedy is also included. A key point is that neither the range of factors nor the limits of the resolution are presented as definitive or complete. They are presented as examples—the CSRs are told it is fine to use their best judgment. If CSRs are flummoxed, they should ask for help or guidance from their mentor or supervisor.

The third section of the solution space is a list of the half-dozen probable challenges and arguments the customer may bring to the situation, such as, "I was never told that," or "Why was I told this?" or "Do you have a known defect in this part of the car?" The employee is armed with the best clear and believable response to each anticipated challenge. The final solution section provides the employee with background and reference materials as well as a list of internal contacts for when a customer wishes to escalate the issue.

Employees need the time and training to connect with the customer and express creativity, what Steve Curtin calls "job essence versus job function."[8] Planning a connection involves two strategies.

The first, like the earlier PetSmart example in Chapter 4, is to create a number of inherently high-involvement transactions that, if executed well, will probably provide an opportunity for connection. If an owner brings his or her dog in for grooming or pet day care, and the employee relates well both to the pet and the owner, there is a high probability for a positive connection. If the employee sends two emails during the day-care period, with a picture of the dog playing with new "friends," connection is almost certain.

The second approach is to take a plain vanilla transaction that would not normally be memorable, and make it memorable. For this to work, the employee either spends enough time engaging with the customer, or has enough information to create a connection. This is much more opportunistic and depends upon how well the employee reads the customer but can also be planned to a degree. For instance, some airline flight attendants are trained to focus on and compliment men's ties (for the 4 percent who still wear ties) and women's scarves and shawls. This creates delight in fifteen seconds.

Another example of good training, empowerment, and connection with the customer that leads to a great CE is my local MotoPhoto. The company's website states, "Each location is independently owned and operated by a team of photo enthusiasts who proudly serve their community." People of all technology levels—or with practically no experience—come to this small shop in Bethesda, Maryland, for assistance. Noting their can-do and patient attitude with customers, my wife asked for help to create a cookbook. Although the store was busy during the holiday rush, an employee spent two hours assisting her, including downloading software on the company's computer to handle the recipes. The customer connection in this transaction resulted in major positive WOM for the business.

Some customers do not want connection—maybe because of their personalities or circumstances like being in a rush. The employee must first read the customer and then decide if connection is appropriate. Also, if the customer is in a long line, providing timely service to everyone may be more important than creating connection with each customer. The employee must decide whether connection is appropriate, both from a time investment and customer desire perspective.

The time needed to connect with a customer is one of the most uncontrollable factors that employees and management face. For example, to the degree that weather results in five flights being cancelled in a twenty-minute time span, the six airline gate staff do not have time for in-depth empathizing and connecting. If some of the ramp workers and other airline back office staff are mobilized (and are trained to rebook customers), the six employees could be twenty. Deciding when time is available to create a connection is a key area of employee discretion.

An additional aspect of empowerment is the ability to make input to change the process. Remember in Chapter 2, we noted that customers want assurance the same problem will not recur. Employees have the same desire that the company avoid preventable problems. Therefore, an important aspect of empowerment is the ability to make input to the VOC/CI. A best practice is for several veteran CSRs to tell the new class their experiences in identifying opportunities and how they formulate and transmit their process improvement recommendations. This participation also provides public recognition to the veteran CSRs for their input—again a win-win for everyone.

Training does not stop after the initial training period. As the Corporate Executive Board study shows, self-confidence is critical for creating and using empowerment.[9] The best approach we have seen to create self-confidence is a nesting process where the newly trained CSR is placed in a unit with intense access to mentors, who act more as trainers than supervisors. The workload should not be demanding, so the CSR can receive feedback at least hourly. When difficult contacts come in, the CSR can obtain guidance for and confirmation of their proposed course of action from the trainer or their mentor. Nesting time varies but often extends for two weeks. The result is CSRs who are confident about using their empowerment and asking for help when they need it. Ford Motor Company has an innovative variation on this approach: If CSRs need help from a technical specialist while responding to a call, they conference the customer in with the specialist and stay on the phone and listen, thereby learning how to address that issue in the future.

Development is a win-win for the employee and the company. The supervisor is key in helping employees create an individual development plan (IDP). Rick DuFresne, former head of service at Toyota Motor Sales USA, would ask employees, "Where do you want to be in five years?" and use their answer to develop a skill acquisition plan. Such a plan assures the employee there is hope of making career progress. This ties nicely with Paul Zak's "Whole Person Assessment Question" that he believes supervisors should ask: "Am I helping you get your next job?"[10] This IDP is the basis for planning future training for the employee. If the company provides an employee with training on topics necessary for his or her next career step, this shows the company values the employee, and he or she has a good chance of taking that next step.

The final part of development is provision of a mentor. The mentor provides specific tactical advice as well as encouragement on how to navigate the corporate world. Employees with mentors are more confident and successful.

Appraisal and Incentives

Appraisal, like hiring, can be labor intensive. Ironically, appraisal procedures that require the least management time often prove to be the most effective. More traditional, structured appraisals focus on weaknesses and negatives rather than recognizing excellence and opportunities for development to the next level. Below are seven appraisal procedures ranked, starting with the most cost-effective.

1. CSR self-evaluation—CSRs select one or more challenging calls and evaluate their own performance on a few key criteria and brief their supervisor or peer.
2. Peer evaluation—CSRs select a peer or are assigned one randomly, and that person listens to and appraises a call.
3. Supervisor spot evaluation—supervisors dip into a call or an email and give the CSR on-the-spot feedback.
4. Supervisor conducts formal evaluation using evaluation protocol.
5. Customer satisfaction survey is sent to the customer immediately after the contact.

6. Customer satisfaction survey is sent within a week after the contact.
7. Quality team conducts evaluation by selecting a limited number of calls to monitor.

This is not to say that survey and quality teams should be completely disbanded. CSR self-evaluations, especially associated with empowerment, need outside validation. In each of the above procedures, the cause of the declining effectiveness for each feedback approach is the time distance, focus, and relevant context to CSR empowerment and its relation to customer satisfaction. While customer satisfaction is critical, the customer may be unhappy because of process constraints rather than the CSR's ability. However, combining call assessments with customer surveys is more convincing because they often confirm each other and are credible to the CSR.

Appraisal of customer connection is based on the small percentage of calls during which the employee attempts connection. In most cases the employee needs to flag the contact, or speech analytics can search through calls to find them. Connection in retail customer service environments is best appraised via observation, compliments, and survey data. Recognition for even one success will motivate others to work at it.

Appraisal of input to VOC/CI is best achieved via monitoring the ideas emailed to a customer service root cause analyst or the customer insights analysis process. We find that supervisors can filter too much out and pour cold water on ideas because they are thinking tactically and view the passing of ideas up the line as additional effort. Credit must be given not just for ideas that are accepted, but also for going to the effort of submitting even partially thought-out ideas. Positive feedback can spawn the next idea that might be much better and more actionable. This point on feedback is a perfect bridge to what Zak says is the most critical part of empowerment: incentives including recognition.

Research by Gallup, Inc., as well as our own experience, suggests that lack of recognition from supervisors is the top reason for turnover of good employees.[11] What is ironic is that recognition costs almost nothing to provide. Even the lowest performers are doing their jobs well most of the time. Great supervisors make recognition a priority for both daily individual public feedback and group meetings.

A best practice for reinforcement is to hold what we call victory sessions. In these sessions, held once every two weeks, each team member talks for sixty to ninety seconds about the toughest situation they *successfully* handled in the last two weeks. Each employee receives *peer and supervisor* recognition for a job well done. Also, everyone receives education and ideas on how to handle similar situations. Empowerment and risk-taking should be recognized and celebrated, reinforcing both behaviors. Victory sessions create the incentive to "go the extra mile" when a truly difficult customer is encountered—the employee knows that a successful response to the situation makes a good story for the next team victory session. One company is considering video-recording such sessions and, with employee permission, putting selected stories on the company intranet—most people love seeing themselves on YouTube– type platforms.

Everyone needs recognition for personal improvement on operational skills and habits. This is where gamification plays a role. Gamification uses software to monitor individual performance on a range of dimensions. It then provides feedback to individuals and, if appropriate, their supervisor or mentor, on their performance, highlighting any improvements. The beauty of this approach is that the positive recognition can be communicated to the individual employee and the group, but only the employee and the supervisor know how the employee is ranked. For example, an employee might be ranked nine out of twelve but have improved significantly. In many cases, gamification is the most positive contribution to the performance of the bottom half of the workforce. UPS used gamification for driver training to help drivers identify and avoid obstacles and accidents. The cost of driver injuries declined 56 percent.[12]

The customer service director should meet with HR and review each of the twenty-four items on the checklist in Table 10.1, to first validate understanding and agreement. Next, the right-hand column is completed to note gaps. Where gaps exist, set priorities on easy fixes and the more difficult issues. Then get started!

MANAGING UP AND DOWN TO CREATE THE CULTURE

Leadership will make or break any culture. Executives set the direction and tone, but supervisors, who are the customer experience army's sergeants, assure actual delivery of the CE. Both groups are important and must be aligned.

Supervisors, the Sergeants of Your Army

Supervisors are *the* critical factor in successful empowerment of frontline employees. The supervisor's job description must specify the results expected. The four key components are the mirror image of the CSR job description. Supervisors must recognize employee successes, delegate authority, provide positive coaching, and encourage employees' input to the VOC/CI.

Recognition

Employee confidence in their empowerment and skill in connecting with customers is enhanced by continuous reinforcement of the employee's specific actions and willingness to take risks and try new approaches. Recognition is a no-cost, easy reinforcement. A compliment highlighting a specific action is informally given to the CSR immediately after the selected transactions as well as in periodic team sessions. The good news for supervisors is that we suggest they spend less time on the onerous task of formal monitoring and appraisal, which most supervisors hate.

At Blinds.com, a full-service window blind company, the supervisor's goal is to recognize every employee's behavior at least once a day. Supervisors monitor one or more calls and make at least one positive comment about some aspect of the call. While walking among the CSRs, if supervisors overhear an employee's adept handling of a customer, they mention it. And all of these comments are made in front of the group. Supervisors conduct weekly drills for skills reinforcement training. The training focuses on one of a dozen specific skill sets, either flagged as a weak area by recent evaluations or a skill set that has not been addressed in the previous three months. Even the best staff get sloppy without reinforcement.

Delegating Authority

Delegating is hard for some supervisors, but has a large payoff if done correctly. When delegation works, the employee and customer are happy with an efficient, satisfying transaction and the supervisor saves the time of involvement. Lisa Dandeneau, COO of Navigant Credit Union in Rhode Island, recounts: "When we empowered and trained our front line to decide when to waive the check hold policy, there was great concern among frontline supervision and the risk department that losses would rise—but losses remained at the same low level, our supervisors had many less interruptions for decisions, and our members are happier."[13]

The reason supervisors do not delegate is that they distrust the employee or the customer—neither of which makes sense. If they distrust the employee, supervisors fear employees will give too little or too much. If the employee is trained to satisfy the customer, the former will *not* happen, and it is almost impossible to give too much.

Michael Ellis, former director of rooms at the Pointe Hilton in Arizona, says the toughest action a front desk staff member must take is telling a guest with a good reservation that the hotel is overbooked, and the person must go to another hotel at the Hilton's expense. Dealing with a tired, angry customer is difficult. Convincing the front desk supervisor to allow staff to manage the situation, when they feel equipped and ready, is even more difficult. Ellis counsels supervisors to encourage staff members to handle the situation, knowing that the supervisor is observing in the back room via video camera and will immediately rescue them if they need help. Once an employee successfully resolves this most difficult situation, the employee's self-confidence and the supervisor's confidence in the employee soar.

Coaching

Chris Blair of Blinds.com makes this savvy observation: "Telling is not coaching." If you just tell an employee what you think, you are not supporting self-discovery, and you are not coaching. If you say, "What do you think you did well, and what do you think you could have done differently?" you teach the employee to practice self-improvement. The supervisor champions daily coaching and feedback based on a preceding service interaction rather than on weekly or monthly feedback. This feedback, which stresses a high ratio of positive over negative, is given in front of other team members, so there is peer recognition as well as learning.

Encouraging Input to VOC/CI

Feedback provided by the frontline staff on company process and policy has a large impact on employee morale. While we recommend the frontline staff have direct email to the root cause and CI analysts, the supervisors still have a major influence on the amount of input made and how often it is given. As noted earlier, recognition for providing input is critical, even if the employee's idea is not implemented. When an idea is implemented and a process improved or an avoidable problem mitigated, the supervisor tells the results to frontline staff. When this process works well, employees have a stronger sense of control over their environment and lower frustration levels. The example in Chapter 4 of a one-page internal monthly newsletter published by VOC/CI staff, such as "The Stall Street Journal," also applies here as a method of encouraging input to the VOC.

EXECUTIVE ACTIONS NEEDED TO CREATE A CUSTOMER-FOCUSED CULTURE

To foster a culture of empowerment and connection, executives must take four specific actions: emphasize CE in communications; walk the talk; make CE a key attribute for accountability, appraisals, and incentives; and break down barriers to frontline success.

Emphasizing CE in Communications

When executives communicate, they tell everyone what is important by the order they address issues. The CEO of a major communications company always starts his quarterly financial analyst calls with a discussion of customer satisfaction metrics before talking about financial results. His logic is that if satisfaction is rising, financial performance will also rise over the long run. In another example, Fred Smith, founder of FedEx, stresses the Purple Promise: "Make every FedEx experience outstanding." In his letter to stockholders at the beginning of a FedEx annual report, Smith highlighted four frontline employees who gave stellar service, complete with their photos. One highlighted a courier who spent his own money to have a special box built to ship a fragile item. He took a risk to help a shipper who was so impressed that the shipper transferred the bulk of his business to FedEx. Devoting 30 percent of the chairman's letter to highlighting these employees sent a strong message to both employees and the market that FedEx encourages a can-do culture.

Zappos enables employees to give rewards to other employees who go above and beyond or show extreme creativity in solving customer problems. A trophy case on the first floor of the headquarters building highlights recent winners.

Walking the Talk

At Disney, everyone, including executives, is expected to interact with guests and pick up a piece of trash if they see it. At the Pointe Hilton, every executive spends time in the lobby interacting with customers and inspecting suites for cleanliness and calling both recent guest arrivals and survey respondents. Frontline employees should see executives stop their "important duties" to deal with a customer who has an issue.

Making CE a Key Part of Accountability, Appraisals, and Incentives

Insisting that HR list empowerment, connection, anticipation/prevention, and VOC input in the job description is a prerequisite to establishing accountability. If it is not explicit, it does not exist. Blinds.com has a great approach to accountability, appraisal, and incentives. The job description and appraisal sheet have two parts. One part is objective—it states what behaviors are expected. The second part addresses how well the behavior is performed. Our point is that all the behaviors must be in the job description, but the nuances can be left to the appraisal and incentive process.

Frontline supervisors must be accountable for making the staff accountable for the full range of responsibilities in the job description. Executives should review the job descriptions of frontline supervisors to ascertain if a culture of service, whether to internal or external customers, is fostered. If it is not supported at the supervisory level, it will not happen!

Breaking Down Barriers to Frontline Success

Marissa Mayer, CEO of Yahoo!, talked in a recent speech about "get[ting] obstacles out of the way," so employees could be successful. In pursuit of this goal, she created a PB&J internal website that asks employees to highlight "process, bureaucracy, and jams" that are impeding their progress. If more than fifty employees vote for an issue, management commits to fix it quickly. Frontline employees have been convinced that anything can be changed if it is getting in the way of better serving customers and company success.[14]

BECOMING A STRATEGIC CUSTOMER SERVICE DIRECTOR

A customer service director asked how to approach the recent emergence of CE in her company. She was concerned CE was the latest fad and fraught with pitfalls, while customer service "would always be needed." A two-part strategy was suggested for the short and intermediate term. First, she should become more strategic in her current role and lay the foundation for an enhanced CE within her customer service organization. Second, she should approach the marketing and quality executives, who were being tasked with CE enhancement, and offer to work with/for them.

Laying the foundation for CE consists of creating a customer journey map and identifying key POPs and their financial impact. Also, you should enhance the internal services processes. Build analytical capabilities by having several staff trained in quality improvement processes and analysis. Each of these skills can be learned in three- to five-day courses, often online. Work with IT to make customer service more proactive and preventive, reducing contact workload and costs. Use careful measurement and A/B test models. This approach provides quantifiable, quick wins from service improvement without violating anyone else's turf.

The customer service director should offer to act as the analytical support group for executives who are tasked with the strategic CE initiative. Customer service is the natural focal point for all CE data—sales and operations are in the beginning of the customer journey, while customer insights and surveys are often at the end of the journey. Information is power, or at least makes you indispensable to the CE initiative, because you are integrating and reporting the data on the whole end-to-end CE.

Over the longer term, the customer service director can move into the CE executive role, since neither the marketing nor the quality professionals usually want to leave their professional lane. Many CE executives continue to manage both centralized and decentralized customer service.

On the other hand, if another executive is appointed to the CE executive role, the best strategy to maintain and grow a customer service career is to define customer service as broadly as possible. The strategic customer service role can legitimately include acting as the data source for all CE information, leveraging technology to become more proactive and anticipatory (which will also allow you to help manage the website content, social media interaction, and KMS content), and taking over the customer onboarding process. You can leave the broad CE strategy and advocacy to the CE executive, while still expanding the customer service portfolio and influence.

Table 10.2 is a checklist for getting started with career-enhancing activities and becoming a strategic customer service director. Check off your status on each item.

Action	Difficulty	Done	In Process	Not Done
Create a Customer Journey Map	Moderate			
Quantify the value of average customer and attrition rate	Simple			
Create a simple estimate of the revenue damage of the status quo	Moderate			
Create compelling business case for service	Hard			
Identify and quantify the volume of three top service issues	Simple			
Measurably fix at least one of the issues in the action immediately above	Moderate/ Hard			
Train at least three staff on basic quality methods	Easy			
Assist another function in fixing an issue	Moderate			
Work with IT to implement one proactive service function	Hard			
Create tailored, actionable VOC reports for marketing and quality	Moderate			

Table 10.2. Checklist for Career-Enhancing Actions

The checklist in Table 10.2 mirrors the advice given to the customer service director above and is drawn from previous chapters of this book.

1. Create a customer journey map. The map is for the primary customer or product group, highlighting key POPs internal to customer service, as well as across the whole journey. Illustrate each POP with a story. Be as hard on customer service as on all other departments.

2. Quantify the value of average customer and attrition rate. With data from marketing and finance, determine the average customer's value and the customer attrition rate. This should take two or three interviews at most.

3. Create a simple estimate of the revenue damage of the status quo. Using the output of step 2 above, the attrition rate times number of customers times their value will be a big number and deserve attention.

4. Create a compelling business case for service. Fine-tune the above model, using either estimates or actual survey data, to build the more detailed Market Damage Model outlined in Chapter 6.

5. Identify and quantify the volume of the three top service issues. Use the journey map and the internal service data to select three significant, but fixable, problems. This will demonstrate that customer service is fixing its own processes and cleaning its own house.

6. Measurably fix at least one of the issues in number 5 above. The fix positions customer service as a competent internal consultant.

7. Train at least three staff on basic quality methods. Staff who know the quality methods and terminology enhance the department's credibility and potential impact. The staff gains experience by applying the quality methodologies to internal department problems.

8. Assist another function in fixing an issue. Customer service should offer to help another department with a POP that service is currently handling and provide the staff to assist in analysis. The customer service staff also assists with measurement, which is important as well. Position the project as a win-win, but let the other manager get the bulk of the credit.

9. Work with IT to implement one proactive service function. Using the Aflac example from Chapter 9, identify three possible simple functions that can be automated or made easier, and work with IT to identify the easiest to implement. Measure the reduction in workload and increase in satisfaction. Again, let IT get most, if not all, of the credit.

10. Create tailored, actionable VOC reports for marketing and quality. Interview a brand manager and a quality manager and

ask what VOC information they need. Tailor a report for each, meet with them and your analyst, and understand how they can use the report to improve the CE. As in items 8 and 9 above, help the internal customers take at least one action that has measurable impact.

At least six of ten items on the above list have proven relevant for every company that we have suggested this methodology to. Take one or two of the above items and Just Do It! You will be on your way to becoming a strategic customer service director.

METRICS FOR MEASURING AND MANAGING EMPOWERMENT, CONNECTION, AND INPUT

Metrics measure empowerment, connection, and input at the individual and departmental level. Some metrics are the same and others differ between levels of measurement (e.g., individual CSRs, supervisors, and the department).

Empowered Action for Difficult Issues

The volume of customer surveys indicating dissatisfaction with actions taken, and the percentage of contacts requiring multiple contacts, are traditional indicators of the effective use of empowerment. Customer surveys and complaints often indicate that individual employees did not use empowerment. These data are typically analyzed across all contacts handled by the CSR. The challenge is that 80 to 90 percent of contacts do not require the application of empowerment. Therefore, an analysis of the results for difficult issues alone is more enlightening. When identifying interactions to review or observe for assessing empowerment, the supervisor strives to find the exceptional situations, as indicated by the reason for the call (difficult issues) or calls with excessive talk time. Likewise, the manager looks at satisfaction and escalation rates by team, to identify supervisors who are not delegating authority and encouraging use of empowerment.

Escalations to Supervisors or Other Departments

With proper empowerment, few if any transactions are escalated. Unnecessary escalations are a useful process metric for measuring empowerment but can be misleading. Most escalations to a supervisor indicate the employee's lack of empowerment or lack of confidence in their skills to use it. But minimal escalated complaints do not guarantee that an employee is using empowerment effectively. Employees can simply say no to customers or stonewall until customers give up. Therefore, you should also observe customer contacts or survey customers to confirm that complaints are being handled correctly.

One useful approach is to require employees to indicate in a field on the CRM system why the contact is being escalated—for example, lack of authority, skill, or information. A customer's refusal to accept the employee's response may indicate either a communication training issue or an unreasonable customer. The escalation and survey data are a flag for possible issues. Monitoring of telephone and email/chat conversations can focus on fully understanding the root cause. Technology can assist this activity via speech and text analytics.

In a retail environment, escalation to a supervisor is easy; otherwise the employee indicates to the customer that there is a wait time, and most customers abandon the transaction or complain. Supervisors make a serious error when they jump into the retail transaction pool and start handling the clerk's duties, rendering themselves unavailable to handle escalations. While assisting the front line will always be necessary, it ultimately creates more damage. At the end of each shift, there should be a discussion of what employees felt uncomfortable handling on their own. Any potential escalations are reviewed, and the supervisor reinforces that what the employee did is acceptable.

Connection

Routine transactions are often the best opportunities for employee-customer connection, so there should be at least some review of how often connection is attempted, even during simple transactions (this can include preventive education). As connection happens sporadically, supervisors are dependent on either CSRs flagging attempts and successes, or using voice/speech recognition to identify occurrences in a telephone environment.

Compliments indicate that employees took the initiative to be creative in solving the problem. Two survey questions that are useful for measuring connection are:

- Did the staff member genuinely care about your issue? (Yes, Somewhat, No.)
- What one word would you use to describe our company and how you feel about it? (Open-ended answer.)

In retail settings, the manager considers how busy the location is. Even in busy situations, the quick "microburst of emotional connection" is still possible. Employees are reminded to deliver one or two microbursts per hour. The good news is that both the employee and the customer feel better when this is done.

Input to VOC/CI

Individual CSR and supervisor effectiveness are measured by the quality and volume of input to the VOC process. The first metric is the accuracy and completeness of the reason for contact codes. Usually, an audit finds that 96 percent or more of CSR entries are complete and actionable. With CRM coding assistance, that percentage will rise. The second metric is the number of process improvement inputs individuals and teams make. This is much smaller and can be reported by the VOC root cause analyst within the customer service department.

Organizational effectiveness of input to VOC/CI is measured by the decrease in number of specific problem types reported by the service system or surveys. Where initiatives have had impact, you should see decreases in calls over the short term and reduction in dissatisfaction, as measured by surveys over the longer term.

KEY TAKEAWAYS

☞ Frontline employees must have four things: better than average pay, the empowerment and training for job success, individual recognition, and career progress.

☞ A culture of customer focus and employee success cannot happen without empowerment and management trust, which allow frontline staff to successfully handle at least 95 percent of issues.

☞ Frontline service staff job descriptions must explicitly build in empowerment, time for connection, and input to VOC/CI.

☞ Supervisors need to focus on coaching and positive recognition that shows trust in the employee, assists in employee development, and enhances the service system process.

☞ Executives should signal their strong support for empowerment, trust in the front line, and connection. Supervisors must be trained and evaluated on their active support of empowerment, connection, and input to VOC/CI.

☞ Companies must measure the success of empowerment and connection actions to manage these activities. Escalations are a key indicator of weak empowerment.

☞ Measurement of empowerment focuses on nonroutine transactions and escalations.

☞ The customer service director focuses on supporting the corporate CE champion and acts as an advocate for the enhanced CE.

APPENDIX A

Customer Relationship Management Systems

Recommended Functional Specifications

Through research with hundreds of companies exhibiting best practices for customer relationship management, we developed the framework of contact management functions and processes that is described in Chapter 3. Effective execution of these functions ensures that customer service achieves its four overarching goals:

➤ Provide an appropriate response to the individual customer that maintains/increases his/her satisfaction and loyalty.
➤ Create emotional connection when appropriate.
➤ Prevent future complaint contacts via anticipation and education.
➤ Sell other products and services to the individual customer, when appropriate.
➤ Collect and analyze data to identify the root cause of customer problems/unnecessary questions.

The twenty processes in Table 3.1 are clustered into seven logical groups that are slightly different than the assignment of processes in the table. This is because the clusters below are usually executed at the same time during the customer journey. The staff support function is not addressed in this appendix because it is peripheral to the primary contact-handling role.

➤ Awareness (motivation and facilitation) and proactive communication
➤ Intake (routing, logging, and classification)
➤ Reply (assessment, investigation, resolution, confirmation and co-ordination, storage and retrieval, and knowledge management)
➤ Reply (tracking)
➤ Evaluation (appraisal)
➤ Customer Insights (statistical generation and analysis)
➤ Reporting (input into organization)

The CRM system should include the following functionalities:

Awareness (motivation and facilitation, and proactive communication)

The awareness function, which includes the motivation and facilitation processes, communicates that the company wants to hear from the customer and provides the channels for communication. The CRM system should:

> ➤ Periodically feed messages to the email marketing system to encourage the customer to contact the company about their satisfaction and to relay that the company is there to serve the customer.
> ➤ Make the customer aware of all the communication channels and ensure availability whenever customers are using or thinking about the product.

The proactive communications process consists of communicating to the customer based on opportunities identified through the customer insights analysis function and based on information fed from the ERPs on transaction failures and/or confirmations. Necessary functionality includes:

> ➤ CRM linkage to operational systems to identify and flag significant transaction failures that impact the customer, and provide confirmations of transactions if requested
> ➤ Criteria specifying the severity of failures that will be communicated to the customer
> ➤ Criteria specifying the customer's preferred channels of communication
> ➤ A mechanism for automatic notification of failures, opportunities, and engagement communications to the customer
> ➤ Customer options to manage the level of intensity of proactive communications, including opt out

Intake (routing, logging, and classification)

Intake includes the ability to route, log, and classify the appropriate data for contact handling, future relationship building, and data analysis. These processes are dependent on having the right data in the right form. Further, the system must allow the data to be efficiently collected by the CSR. The CRM should have the following functionalities:

> ➤ Single sign-on (versus signing in to multiple systems)
> ➤ Flexible addition of data fields with edit checks

- Allow hierarchical coding of data fields up to three levels—for example, reason for contact, root cause, product, location/unit.
- Ease of adding new classification codes by administrator
- Links on the website to web chat, and call-me buttons to facilitate routing
- Website email template allows customer to classify contact as well as input text.
- Website email template allows customer to specify desired time frame for reply.
- Customer record allows CSR to use drop-down menus to reduce entry errors.
- Auto-population of data fields where possible—for example, town entry based on zip code
- Intuitive screen layout to facilitate "talking and typing"
- Ability to designate certain fields as required fields
- Ability to have text fields for further CSR explanation of customer issues
- Web access to allow remote and flexible entry of cases by field sales reps
- Use of CTI so customer information prepopulates CSR's computer screen based on incoming caller ID or when a CSR enters an account number
- Easy customer identification by CSR for those who previously contacted the organization
- Ability to link multiple customer records of same household or to link multiple product records
- Ability to add "flags" based on business rules to quickly identify customers who require special handling (e.g., customers with a credit-hold or "Gold" status)
- CSR ability to note cases that were preventable and where the CSR attempted engagement
- Flexible search capability (e.g., search by name, phone number, or account number)
- Ability to spell-check and correct text data fields

Reply (assessment, investigation, resolution, confirmation and coordination, storage and retrieval, knowledge management)

The reply function supports assessment, investigation, resolution and confirmation to the customer, coordination with other internal units, and input to storage and retrieval. In a phone environment, assessment, investigation, accessing the KMS, resolution and confirmation, are all likely to happen during the call—although some contacts may need to be routed to another area for response. For the written environment (letter, email, or chat), there are more distinct steps involved in determining, developing, and sending the correct response along with any appropriate follow-through.

An effective contact tracking system will have the following features to facilitate reply:

> Facilitate assessment and investigation by automatically accessing the last three contacts or submissions (e.g., claims) by the customer (the existence of such data should be flagged at the top of the screen so the CSR can click on them if needed)
> Easy access to FAQs or response guidelines driven by reason, product, or location codes
> CSR has ability to send/receive emails to the field and other units.
> Ability to receive photos and video streams from the customer (if necessary, the CSR must be able to send the customer a link for the video streaming app)
> Integration with, or easy access to, company ERP system for reference to customer accounts
> Provide links to useful parts of the KMS based on the classification code entered by the CSR to provide response guidance—this includes the flexible solution spaces discussed in Chapters 3 and 10
> Ability to print customized letter or email responses, fulfillment letters, and shipping labels using stored paragraphs/letters/templates
> Suggested template responses based on reason code, product, location/unit
> Ability to send useful videos links to the customer
> Ability to refer the case to another unit for response
> Ability to use electronic signatures
> Ability to use different letterheads
> Ability for CSRs to chat with other staff and supervisors to obtain guidance
> Mechanism for CSRs to submit new issues to the KMS for issues requiring investigation by the KMS maintenance staff where there is no information in the KMS
> Mechanism for CSRs to submit suggested responses to the KMS for issues that are not in the KMS; the KMS maintenance staff will vet the suggested response and format for inclusion in the KMS.

> Transmission of case information and ability to reply to the other departments for coordination or for information based on reason for contact.
> Storage of scanned documents and photos that are linked to cases or viewed within FAQs and/or response guidelines
> Ability to easily export data to other programs (e.g., Excel)

Reply (tracking)

This function ensures that the action required is taken, whether by the customer service unit or another unit, and the appropriate data are properly stored for ease of future retrieval, handling, and analysis. *Internal* tracking involves monitoring the disposition of contacts handled within the department. *Referral* tracking involves a closed loop system of monitoring contacts referred to the field or other departments to ensure handling in a timely and appropriate manner. Necessary functionality includes:

> Automatic "cc" (email or voice message) to appropriate personnel based on pre-coded business rules
> Tracking and feedback on cases referred to another unit that are closed or resolved to ensure the other unit closes the case and the CSR knows the details of the resolution if the customer calls back
> Tracking the time to close a case, regardless where that contact was received or whether it was handled within the department or referred
> Automatic escalation or flagging of cases not closed within a designated time frame
> Ability to run reports on action taken, including adjustments and dollar amounts, by reason for contact, product, unit, etc.

Evaluation (appraisal)

Evaluation dispatches surveys to the customer according to specified parameters and collates the data for use in appraisal of the CSR, the team, and the contact center response processes. Effective functionality includes the ability to do the following:

> Email surveys to customers after a case has been closed
> Designate certain types of cases to be sent surveys

➤ Link survey and case data to call recording (including key strokes) and talk time, and report cross-tabulations of these parameters by CSR and by issue

➤ Calculate average time (in hours or days) for CSRs to close cases overall, by type of issue and by unit where cases are referred to for resolution

➤ Tally number of cases, by CSR and unit as a whole, that are open longer than the standard

Customer Insights (statistical generation and analysis)

The customer insights function consists of aggregation/tabulation of customer contact data and analysis of the data to identify systemic opportunities for product, service, and marketing improvement. The analysis also includes the potential impact of the information on company policy and procedures. CRM functionality should include:

➤ CSRs input to the VOC process immediately after each contact via a chatter or email capability, and setting a flag that the call was preventable

➤ Entry of transaction data that can be used to normalize contact rates (e.g., number of customers per branch, products sold)

➤ Robust analysis that easily integrates with other reporting packages, which should include:

  ➤ Frequencies, cross-tabs, and analysis by product, unit, reason codes (at various levels), normalized frequencies, means, standard deviations, and other basic statistical analysis

  ➤ The talk time reported from the telephone switch to identify issues leading to long talk time due to ineffective response guidance or ponderous information searches

  ➤ Identification of process failures from other systems and opportunities to proactively notify customers

  ➤ Analyze ordinal data and the verbatim text comments from surveys

  ➤ Speech and text analysis that identifies emerging topics and successful response patterns

  ➤ The ability to establish and enter thresholds and alerts (e.g., if the complaint frequency exceeds a predetermined threshold, the system produces an alert to a supervisor/manager)

Reporting (input into organization)

Flexible reporting capability includes the ability to do the following:

- Produce tailored reports by pre-designated recipient groups
- Produce reports in written, email, or online display
- Display graphical and tabular data
- Run reports on demand and/or on a schedule
- Allow input of analysis (satisfaction and productivity by type of issue) to be a gamification tool to flag CSR performance and improvement
- Monitor whether report recipients have opened and examined the reports to assess who is using them and who is ignoring them

APPENDIX B

List of Acronyms

AI	artificial intelligence	ETDBW	easy to do business with
ANI	automated number identification	FA	financial advisor
		FCR	first-contact resolution
ATM	automatic teller machine	FDA	Food and Drug Administration
B2B	business-to-business		
CCMC	Customer Care Measurement & Consulting	HR	human resources
		IDP	individual development plan
CE	customer experience		
CEO	chief executive officer	IM	instant messaging
CFO	chief financial officer	IoT	internet of things
CI	continuous improvement	IVR	interactive voice response
CIF	customer information file		
		KMS	knowledge management system
CIO	chief information officer		
CLV	customer lifetime value	NPS	net promoter score
CMO	chief marketing officer	POP	points of pain
CMS	content management system	RFID	radio-frequency identification
CRM	customer relationship management	ROI	return on investments
		SaaS	software as a service
CSI	customer satisfaction index	SCE	Southern California Edison
CSR	customer service representative	SEO	search engine optimization
CTI	computer telephony integration	SME	subject matter expert
		TARP	Technical Assistance Research Programs
DIRFT	do it right the first time		
DM	digital marketing	VOC	voice of the customer
ERP	Enterprise Resources Planning	WOM	word of mouth

ENDNOTES

Introduction

1. Melanie Ehrenkranz, "Amazon Confirms Alexa Heard a Couple's Background Conversation as a Command to Record Them," Gizmoto.com, May 25, 2018.
2. Scott M. Broetzmann, Marc Grainer, and John A. Goodman, *2017 National Customer Rage Study* (Alexandria, VA: Customer Care Measurement & Consulting, 2017).

Chapter 1

1. John A. Goodman and Marc Grainer, *Measuring the Grapevine Word of Mouth Study* (Atlanta: The Coca-Cola Company, 1978).
2. Scott M. Broetzmann, Marc Grainer, and John A. Goodman, *2017 National Customer Rage Study* (Alexandria, VA: Customer Care Measurement & Consulting, 2017).
3. John A. Goodman, interview with David Gordon, President, The Cheesecake Factory, October 15, 2013.
4. John A. Goodman, interview with Rick DuFresne, former National Manager Customer Care, Toyota Motor Sales Corporation, Torrance, CA, 2009.
5. Broetzmann, Grainer, and Goodman, 2017.
6. Joseph Juran and Joseph De Feo, *Juran's Quality Handbook,* Sixth Edition (New York: McGraw-Hill, 2010), p. 69.
7. Roland T. Rust, Valarie A. Zeithaml, and Katherine N. Lemon, *Driving Customer Equity: How Customer Lifetime Value is Reshaping Corporate Strategy* (New York: Simon & Schuster, 2000).
8. John A. Goodman and Ken Feldman, Ph.D., "Quality's New Frontier, Applying Continuous Improvement to Marketing and Sales," *Quality Progress* (June, 2016).

Chapter 2

1. Scott M. Broetzmann, Marc Grainer, and John A. Goodman, *2017 National Customer Rage Study* (Alexandria, VA: Customer Care Measurement & Consulting, 2017).
2. Broetzmann, Grainer, and Goodman, 2017.
3. Janelle Barlow and Claus Moller, *A Complaint Is a Gift* (San Francisco: Berrett-Koehler Publishers, 2008).

4. "Making Service a Potent Marketing Tool," *Business Week,* June 11, 1984, pp.164–70.
5. Broetzmann, Grainer, and Goodman, 2017.

Chapter 3

1. Scott M. Broetzmann, Marc Grainer, and John A. Goodman, *2017 National Customer Rage Study* (Alexandria, VA: Customer Care Measurement & Consulting, 2017).
2. Brad Cleveland, *Call Center Management on Fast Forward: Succeeding in the New Era of Customer Relationships* (Colorado Springs: International Customer Management Institute, 2012).
3. Chip R. Bell, *Kaleidoscope: Delivering Innovative Service That Sparkles* (Austin, TX: Greenleaf Book Group Press, 2017).
4. John A. Goodman, interview with Chip Horner, former Worldwide Director of Global Consumer Affairs, Colgate-Palmolive Company, New York, NY, 2009.
5. John A. Goodman, "Nice Doing Business with You," *SixSigma Forum Magazine,* Schofield Media, Chicago, January/February 2011, pp. 43–46.
6. Matthew Dixon, Karen Freeman, and Nicholas Toman, "Stop Trying to Delight Your Customers," *Harvard Business Review,* Cambridge, MA, July 2010.
7. Jeanne Bliss, *I Love You More Than My Dog* (New York: Penguin Group, 2009).

Chapter 4

1. Cynthia Grimm and Carla Barker, "Getting to the Next Level of Customer Engagement," *Customer Relationship Management Magazine,* SOCAP International, Arlington, VA, Spring 2017, p. 24.
2. Grimm and Barker, "Getting to the Next Level of Customer Engagement," p. 24.
3. Chip Bell, *Sprinkles: Creating Awesome Experiences Through Innovative Service* (Austin, TX: Greenleaf Books, 2015).
4. Jeff Toister, *Service Failure: The Real Reason Employees Struggle with Customer Service* (New York: AMACOM, 2013, p. 145).
5. Tom Peters, *The Excellence Dividend: Meeting the Tech Tide with Work That Wows and Jobs That Last* (New York: Vintage Books, 2018), pp. 131–32.
6. John A. Goodman and Crystal Collier, "Skills-Based Routing Versus Universal Rep, Which Is Best?," *Call Center Pipeline,* January 2013, p. 5.
7. Presentation by District Manager, PetSmart, Torrance, CA, November 2, 2017.
8. Toister, 2013, p. 139.
9. Jack Mitchell, *Hug Your Customer: The Proven Way to Personalize Sales and Achieve Astounding Results* (New York: Hyperion, 2003).
10. Chip Bell, 2015, p. 58.

11. Jeanne Bliss, *Would You Do That to Your Mother?: The "Make Mom Proud" Standard for How to Treat Your Customers* (New York: Penguin Random House, 2018).

12. Chip Bell, *Kaleidoscope: Delivering Innovative Service That Sparkles* (Austin, TX: Greenleaf Books, 2017), p. 43.

13. Tom Peters, 2018.

14. Darsana Vijay, "23 Ideas for Marketers Wondering What to Post on Instagram," Unmetric.com, https://unmetric.com/things-to-post-on-instagram, 2/28/18.

15. Kevin Freiberg and Jackie Freiberg, *Nuts!: Southwest Airlines' Crazy Recipe for Business and Personal Success* (New York: Broadway Books, 1996).

16. Tom Peters, 2018, pp. 208–9.

17. Amy Gallo, "A Refresher on A/B Testing," *Harvard Business Review,* June 28, 2017, https://hbr.org/2017/06/a-refresher-on-ab-testing, "A/B testing, at its most basic, is a way to compare two versions of something to figure out which performs better."

18. Ron Kohavi and Stefan Thomke, "The Surprising Power of Online Experiments," *Harvard Business Review,* Cambridge, MA, Sept/Oct 2017, p. 76.

19. Steve Curtin, *Delight Your Customers: 7 Simple Ways to Raise Your Customer Service from Ordinary to Extraordinary* (New York: AMACOM, 2013), p. 120.

20. Andrew M. Baker, Naveen Donthu, and V. Kumar, "Investigating How Word of Mouth Conversations About Brands Influence Purchase and Re-transmission Intentions," *Journal of Marketing Research,* April 2016, p. 225.

Chapter 5

1. Oral presentation by Lisa Salvi, Vice President for Business Consulting and Field Experience, Charles Schwab Advisor Services, San Francisco, November 3, 2017.

2. Oral presentation by District Store Manager, PetSmart, Torrance, CA, November 2, 2017.

3. Scott M. Broetzmann, Marc Grainer, and John A. Goodman, Results of the *2017 National Customer Rage Study* (Alexandria, VA: Customer Care Measurement and Consulting, 2017).

Chapter 6

1. CCMC aggregate baseline survey data from over fifty companies in the financial services, travel and leisure, medical device, insurance, auto, and telecom industries that compare customer satisfaction when a problem is resolved in one, two, or more contacts.

2. Phillip Schmitt, Bernd Skiera, and Christophe Van den Bulte, "Referral Programs and Customer Value," *Journal of Marketing,* January 2011, pp. 46–59.

3. John Rossman, *The Amazon Way* (Clyde Hill, WA: Clyde Hill Publishing, 2016), pp. 28–30.
4. CCMC aggregate baseline survey data questioning WOM impact in the electronic game, retail, e-commerce, medical device, and other industries.
5. Andrew M. Baker, Naveen Donthu, and V. Kumar, "Investigating How Word of Mouth Conversations About Brands Influence Purchase and Retransmission Intensions," *Journal of Marketing Research*, Chicago, April 2016, p. 235.
6. CCMC aggregate baseline WOM surveys for multiple clients.
7. John A. Goodman, "Examining the Myths and Costs of Agent Disengagement," White Paper, CustomerCaremc.com, Alexandria, VA, September 2016.

Chapter 7

1. John A. Goodman, Cindy Grimm, and Joshua Hearne, "Improving the Customer Experience," *Contact Center Pipeline* Pipeline Publishing Group, Inc., Annapolis, MD, January 2012, pp. 28-30.
2. John A. Goodman, interview with Ed O'Day, Senior Vice President of Member Communications, AARP, June 29, 2018.
3. IntelliResponse, "Consumer Use of Social Media for Customer Service," White Paper, Toronto, Canada, 2011.
4. Scott M. Broetzmann and Marc Grainer, *2011 National Customer Rage Study* (Alexandria, VA: Customer Care Measurement & Consulting, 2011).
5. Scott M. Broetzmann, Marc Grainer, and John A. Goodman, *2017 National Customer Rage Study* (Alexandria, VA: Customer Care Measurement & Consulting, 2017).
6. Eduardo Laveglia, *Complaint Behavior in Argentina* (Buenos Aires, Argentina: Proaxon, May, 2012).
7. Nobu Hatanaka and John A. Goodman, proprietary studies for two Japanese companies with 2,000+ responses each (Tokyo, Japan: LearningIt and Customer Care Measurement & Consulting, 2017).
8. John Rossman, *The Amazon Way* (Clyde Hill, WA: Clyde Hill Publishing, 2016).

Chapter 8

1. Scott M. Broetzmann, Marc Grainer, and John A. Goodman, *2017 National Customer Rage Study* (Alexandria, VA: Customer Care Measurement & Consulting, 2013).
2. Mark Suster, "73.6% Of All Statistics Are Made Up," *Business Insider*, February 17, 2010, www.businessinsider.com/736-of-all-statistics-are-made-up-2010-2.
3. Richard Mullins, "Two Months After J.D. Power Honor, Regulators Stepped In At WellCare!" *Tampa Bay Tribune*, March 20, 2009.

4. Andrew Carnegie, "The Gospel of Wealth," *The North American Review*, June/Dec. 1889.
5. "Watch Your Thoughts, They Become Words; Watch Your Words, They Become Actions," Quote.investigator.com, January 10, 2013.

Chapter 9

1. John A. Goodman, Crystal Collier, "Point/Counterpoint: Universal Rep vs. Skills-Based Routing to Specialized Splits," *Contact Center Pipeline*, January 2013.
2. Carla Marshall, "Cat Videos on YouTube: 2 Million Uploads, 25 Billion Views," Tublarinsights.com, October 29, 2014.
3. John A. Goodman, interview with Jennifer Hall, Chief Customer Officer, Intuit, 2016.
4. John A. Goodman, interview with Jim Albert, CEO of Neptune Flood, Inc., June 29, 2018.
5. Brian Naylor, "Facial Scanning Now Arriving at U.S. Airports," National Public Radio, March 16, 2018.
6. John A. Goodman, interview with Ben Cotton, Executive Director for Retention and Customer Experience at the *New York Times*, June 17, 2018.
7. John A. Goodman, interview with Dan Wakeman, Vice President of Technology, Educational Testing Service, Inc., June 2018.
8. Nathan Gehman and Jamon Horton, "Lean AGILE and Voice of the Customer: Aligned for Success!," presentation at American Quality Institute, Lean Six Sigma World Conference, Las Vegas, April 2018.

Chapter 10

1. Amy Elisa Jackson, "7 Types of Companies You Should Never Work For," Glassdoor.com blog, October 12, 2016.
2. John A. Goodman, "Examining the Myths and Costs of Agent Disengagement," Customer Care Measurement & Consulting, White Paper, CustomerCaremc.com, Alexandria, VA, September 2016.
3. Paul J. Zak, "The Neuroscience of Trust, Management Behaviors That Foster Employee Engagement," *Harvard Business Review*, Cambridge, MA, January–February 2017, pp. 85–90.
4. Paul J. Zak, *Trust Factor* (New York: AMACOM, 2017), p. 66.
5. Roger Connors and Tom Smith, *Change the Culture, Change the Game* (New York: Portfolio/Penguin, 2011), p. 33.
6. Matthew Dixon, Lara Ponomareff, Scott Turner, and Rick DeLisi, "Kick-Ass Customer Service," *Harvard Business Review*, Cambridge, MA, January–Feb 2017.
7. Steve Curtin, *Delight Your Customers* (New York, NY: AMACOM, 2013), pp. 9–10.

8. Steve Curtin, *Delight Your Customers*, pp. 9–10.

9. Dixon, Ponomareff, Turner, and DeLisi, 2017.

10. Zak, *Trust Factor*, 2017, p. 143.

11. James Harter, Amy Adkins, "What Great Managers Do To Engage Employees," *Harvard Business Review*, Cambridge, MA, April 2015.

12. Zak, *Trust Factor*, 2017, p. 149.

13. John A. Goodman, interview with Lisa Dandeneau, COO of Navigant Credit Union, June 5, 2018.

14. Patricia Sellers, "How Yahoo CEO Mayer Fixed 1000 Problems," *Fortune*, October 22, 2013.

INDEX